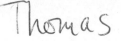

W9-CDY-312

Ada®

AN ADVANCED INTRODUCTION

PRENTICE-HALL SOFTWARE SERIES
Brian W. Kernighan, advisor

Ada®
AN ADVANCED INTRODUCTION

NARAIN GEHANI

Bell Laboratories
Murray Hill, New Jersey

PRENTICE-HALL, INC.
Englewood Cliffs, New Jersey 07632

Library of Congress Cataloging in Publication Data

Gehani, Narain (date)
  Ada, an advanced introduction.

  (Prentice-Hall software series)
  Bibliography: p.
  Includes index.
  1. Ada (Computer program language)   I. Title.
II. Series.
QA76.73.A35G43   1983   001.64'24   82-15125
ISBN 0-13-003962-4

Editorial/production supervision: Nancy Milnamow
Cover design: Ray Lundgren
Manufacturing buyer: Gordon Osbourne

Ada is a registered trademark of the U. S. Government, Ada Joint Program Office

Printed in the United States of America

10   9   8   7   6   5   4   3   2

ISBN 0-13-003962-4

Prentice-Hall International, Inc., *London*
Prentice-Hall of Australia Pty. Limited, *Sydney*
Editora Prentice-Hall do Brazil, Ltda., *Rio de Janeiro*
Prentice-Hall of Canada Inc., *Toronto*
Prentice-Hall of India Private Limited, *New Delhi*
Prentice-Hall of Japan, Inc., *Tokyo*
Prentice-Hall of Southeast Asia Pte. Ltd., *Singapore*
Whitehall Books Limited, Wellington, *New Zealand*

To
my wife,
our parents
and
my grandparents

Contents

Foreword		ix
Preface		xi
Acknowledgements		xvii
Chapter 1	Introduction	1
Chapter 2	More About Types	75
Chapter 3	Packages	97
Chapter 4	Concurrency	133
Chapter 5	Exceptions	201
Chapter 6	Generic Facilities	227
Chapter 7	Program Structure and Separate Compilation	255
Chapter 8	Representation Clauses and Implementation Dependent Features	271
Appendix	Stepwise Refinement	289
Annotated Bibliography		293
Index		309

Foreword

Ada Byron, Countess Lovelace, was the child of an unfortunate marriage. She cost her mother unexpected sums of money throughout her life and died at an early age. At the same time, she provided the needed connection between the machinery of computation and its potential application to the solution of human problems, stimulating and guiding the builder as well as the user.

Which, if any, of these attributes will apply to the life story of the Ada programming language, the subject of the present volume, is not as yet clear. This Ada has many supporters as well as some thoughtful critics. Its formidable list of advantages hardly needs reenumeration. Its restrictions are designed to enforce a programming discipline that facilitates the development of reliable and modular programs. Still, protective barriers can usually only delay and discourage self-injury by the desperate and the foolhardy. Ada's strong typing can be breached by *representation viewing*, appropriately renamed *unchecked conversion*; *goto*s are discouraged, but not altogether eliminated, because their use is necessary in rare cases; and so on. Ada's discipline is an aid to, but not a guarantee of, good programming practice. The familiar "Don't tell me your troubles, just get your job done" will still be a good recipe for bad programs, although the defects may now be buried a little deeper.

The long-term impact of the effort to create yet another programming language will ultimately depend upon the quality of programs written in it. Clearly, Ada does not have to become universal in order to be a useful aid in making large-scale programming a more productive enterprise. Truly modular programs appear to offer something for everyone. Write your module and deliver it early to avoid the last-minute rush at project deadline time. Test each module as it arrives, knowing that the system will work as long as each part checks out separately. Maintain the system by replacing bulky or obsolete parts. Too good to be true? We don't have all that long to wait to find out.

This book introduces problem solving in Ada by means of a set of well-chosen examples. The solutions to the problems are developed in the framework of stepwise refinement, thus providing the reader the added benefit of some practical instruction in top-down structured programming. At the same time, the reader ought to keep in mind that one of the big selling points of Ada is its modularity. Indeed, the extensive program libraries we can look forward to, and expect to make use of, might almost seem to argue for a *bottom-up* approach based on program components.

In practice, however, this dilemma is more apparent than real. The top-down approach of stepwise refinement is an iterative process. Each iteration aims at dividing the problem into tractable pieces, aiming toward pieces whose solutions are readily programmable or, better yet, fit an existing program module. At the same time, component-based programming involves purposeful browsing through the program library, looking for matches to pieces of the problem at hand; this implies that the problem must have somehow been decomposed into components at the beginning of this approach also.

In comparing the two approaches, the major issue is how well the decomposition will be carried out. Although we may not be able to rid ourselves of our bad habits entirely, we ought to recognize the value of the emphasis the author places on top-down programming. It offers us, among other things, the great advantage of understandability inherent in logically structured programs. Other programmers—and, after a short while, the original programmer—generally need to understand programs and need whatever help they can get in doing so.

Ideally, one would like to write programs which explain themselves. The examples in this book owe their clarity to the accessibility of their abstract solutions, hence their underlying structure. The refinements are gradual and understandable; they serve as examples of style as well as method. They illustrate the method's capabilities as a means of communication, from the programmer to the machine, as well as to readers of the program.

I think it is fair to say that this volume will itself help provide a "needed connection between the machinery of computation and its potential applications to the solution of human problems."

Murray Hill, N. J.   Arno A. Penzias
March 1982

Preface

1. The Development of Ada

The high level programming language Ada is named in honor of Augusta Ada Byron, the Countess of Lovelace and the daughter of the English poet Lord Byron. She was the assistant, associate and supporter of Charles Babbage, the mathematician and inventor of a calculating machine called the Analytical Engine. With the help of Babbage she wrote a nearly complete program for the Analytical Engine to compute the Bernoulli numbers circa 1830 [HUS80]. Because of this effort, the Countess may be said to have been the world's first computer programmer.

To dispel exaggerated ideas about the powers of the Analytical Engine, e.g., that the Analytical Engine could think and feel, Ada wrote the following assessment of its capabilities [MOO77]:

> The Analytical Engine has no pretensions whatever to *originate*
> anything. It can do whatever *we know how to order it to perform*. It
> can *follow* analyses; but it has no power of anticipating any analytical
> relations or truths. Its province is to assist us in making *available*
> what we are already acquainted with.

This assessment applies also to today's computers, even though they are far more sophisticated than the Analytical Engine! Indeed the Countess' statement is still quoted in modern debates on the nature and scope of artificial intelligence [MCC79].

Ada, the language which bears the Countess' name, was designed at the initiative and under the auspices of the United States Department of Defense (DoD). DoD studies in the early and middle 1970s indicated that enormous savings in software costs (about $24 billion between 1983 and 1999) might be achieved if the DoD used one common programming language for all its applications instead of the over 450 programming languages and incompatible dialects used by its programmers.

As a result of these studies requirements were drawn up for a new programming language that would replace most of the programming languages being used by the DoD. Starting with Strawman (a jocular name), these requirements were progressively refined by means of wide and public consultation, both domestic and international. The United States armed services, foreign military organizations, industrial organizations and universities were involved in this process. The refined requirements were successively called Woodenman, Tinman, Ironman [FIS78] and finally Steelman [WAS80].

Although the motive for the new programming language was initially economic, it was propelled by the desire to have a good programming language that addressed important and recognized problems in software development. Requirements for the new language addressed technical issues such as language simplicity and completeness, program reliability, correctness, maintainability and portability, the development of large programs, real-time programming and error handling. In response to the trend toward multicomputers and away from large computers,[1] the requirements also demanded concurrent programming, i.e., the ability to write a program whose components could be executed in parallel on different computers or on the same computer via interleaved execution.

An international competition was held to design a language based on the above requirements. Seventeen companies submitted proposals out of which four were selected as semifinalists. Interestingly, all the semifinalists chose to base their languages on Pascal [JEN74]. The competition was won by a language designed by a team of computer scientists lead by Jean Ichbiah of CII Honeywell Bull. After some modifications, this language was named Ada [DOD80b]. In the process of getting Ada adopted as an ANSI standard, further revisions were made to Ada in an effort to simplify it and remove inconsistencies. Ada was adopted as an ANSI standard in February 1983 [DOD83].

Another step in DoD's efforts to standardize its software has been to initiate an Ada Compiler Validation project [GOO80]. The goal of this validation effort is to develop a set of standard tests that an Ada compiler must pass before it can be certified as implementing the standard Ada. In parallel with this effort, the process of developing requirements for the environment of Ada programs and the Ada user interface has been initiated [DOD80a].

Ada is a modern programming language with facilities found in Pascal-like languages such as the ability to define types, the common control structures and subprograms. Moreover, Ada incorporates many of the advances made in programming language design in the 1970s. It supports logical modularity by which data, types and subprograms can all be packaged. Physical modularity

---

1. A multicomputer is a computer architecture that consists of several different computers that do not share any memory. Processes on the different computers communicate with each other by sending messages. With the advent of one-chip computers and their rapidly decreasing price, multicomputers are fast becoming an attractive means of providing large amounts of computing power at low cost.

is made possible by separate compilation. Ada supports real-time programming by providing mechanisms for concurrency and exception handling. Systems programming is facilitated by providing access to system-dependent parameters and by precise control over representation of data.

Ada enforces a strict programming discipline with the intention of making programs more readable, reliable, portable, modular, maintainable, efficient and so on—all qualities of a good program. For example, the programmer must declare all objects, use objects in a manner consistent with their types, and access objects only according to Ada's visibility rules. At first, a programmer used to programming in a language that imposes little or no discipline may not like or appreciate Ada's strictness. After having written a few nontrivial programs, however, the programmer will readily appreciate this strictness, realizing that the intent of Ada's restrictions and strict checking is to detect more errors early and automatically, and to help the programmer to write good programs—not to inhibit creativeness and ingenuity.

2. About the Book

This book is written especially for readers who have a good knowledge of at least one procedural programming language such as Pascal, C, PL/I, Algol 60, Simula 67, Algol 68 or FORTRAN. The book focuses primarily on the novel aspects of Ada, which are illustrated by many fairly difficult and concrete examples written out in full. Interesting differences between Ada and other programming languages are commented upon.

The many example programs are developed using stepwise refinement [WIR71, GEH81] to assist the reader in understanding their design and development. Solution of a problem by stepwise refinement consists of solving the problem by decomposing or *refining* it into smaller subproblems and then solving the subproblems. This refinement is accomplished by giving an abstract version of the algorithm and the data structures that will be used in solving the problem. The abstract solution contains abstract instructions which are the subproblems. Such an approach is an important aid for mastering the complexity involved in the design of complex or large programs, since only a part of the problem is solved in any one refinement. Stepwise refinement also facilitates the understanding and explanation of programs and their design. The usefulness of this approach is clearly demonstrated by the design of large or complex programs such as the elevator algorithm given in the chapter on concurrency. The Appendix contains some remarks on the requirements for a good programming methodology and suggestions on how to develop programs via stepwise refinement.

The first chapter is an introduction to the features of Ada that are rather common—such as those found in programming languages like Pascal, C, PL/I or FORTRAN. Elaborate details about each feature are not provided. The remaining chapters focus on the novel aspects of Ada:

- Treatment of Types
- Packages—Encapsulation/Data Abstraction
- Concurrency or Tasking
- Exception Handling
- Generic Facilities
- Program Structure and Separate Compilation
- Representation Clauses and Implementation Dependent Features

A chapter is devoted to each topic. Throughout the book, the syntax is presented informally and by means of examples. The formal syntax of Ada can be found in the Ada Reference Manual [DOD83].

Each chapter begins with an introduction to the concepts that it will discuss. The facilities provided in Ada for implementing these concepts are introduced and illustrated with the aid of small examples. Finally, several complete examples are given to illustrate how these facilities are used in conjunction with the rest of Ada in solving problems. Care has been taken to ensure that the examples are realistic and nontrivial.

Because stepwise refinement is used to solve the problems, abstract versions of the problem solution appear prior to the final version of the solution in Ada. Reading these abstract versions of the problem solution should facilitate understanding the final solution in Ada. The final version can be skipped by the reader who is not interested in the details of the solution.

Throughout the book, pointers to the appropriate section of the Ada Reference Manual [DOD83] are provided (numbers in brackets, e.g. [5.2]) as an aid in looking up additional details. These pointers appear in chapter and section headings, and in the text.

An annotated bibliography of articles and books on Ada, influences on the design of Ada, stepwise refinement and other relevant topics is given at the end of the book. Following most of the items in the bibliography are brief comments that highlight their main and/or interesting points. The reader is urged to look through the bibliography, especially because it lists many interesting and classic articles and books, not all of which have been cited in the text.

3. Preparation of the Book

This book was written using the extensive document preparation tools available on the UNIX™ operating system. Some of the tools used were

- TROFF (formatter)

- MM (collection of TROFF macros for page layout)

- EQN (preprocessor for formatting equations)

- TBL (preprocessor for making tables)

- PIC (preprocessor for drawing figures)

The availability of these and other software tools, and the typesetting facilities available at Bell Laboratories, made writing the book less tedious.

4. Testing of the Example Programs

The program fragments and example programs given in the book have been tested using the Ada compiler being developed by New York University.[2] Since the programs are in machine readable form, it was fairly easy to extract them from the text, strip off the formatting commands and execute them.

The NYU Ada compiler is a prototype and is not yet complete. It implements a large subset of Ada, is written in SETL, requires an enormous amount of memory to run and at the same time is very slow. Consequently, some of the programs had to be modified slightly so that they used only the subset implemented by the NYU Ada compiler and they finished execution within a reasonable amount of time. Moreover, extensive program testing was not feasible because of the substantial resources required by the Ada compiler.

Murray Hill, N. J.   Narain Gehani

---

2. The NYU Ada compiler used for testing the example programs implemented the pre-ANSI version of Ada [DOD80b]. Modifications to Ada, resulting from the process of getting it adopted as an ANSI standard, had only a minimal impact on the examples in the book, e.g., call to parameterless functions had to be modified to eliminate the parentheses following the function name.

Acknowledgements

I am very grateful to the many friends and colleagues who have helped me in writing this book. The support and feedback I got from them was instrumental in shaping the form and content of the book.

First of all, my management at Bell Labs, J. O. Limb, H. G. Alles, R. W. Lucky and A. A. Penzias, enthusiastically supported and encouraged my writing the book. Without their support, this book would probably not have been written.

Perusing a manuscript for technical errors and poor explanations, and suggesting changes is a very time consuming task. I was fortunate, since several friends and colleagues took time out of their busy schedules, to give extensive comments, both technical and stylistic, on the manuscript. They are R. B. Allen, A. R. Feuer, D. Gay, D. Gries, B. W. Kernighan, J. P. Linderman, M. O'Donnell, and C. Wetherell. Brian Kernighan and Charlie Wetherell gave detailed comments on two versions of the manuscript. I am also indebted to Charlie for the discussions clarifying several fine points in Ada.

I am grateful to A. A. Penzias and David Gries for their exhaustive stylistic and editorial comments on the manuscript. Arno Penzias and Charlie Wetherell stressed the importance of an easy and informal writing style—a style which I have tried to follow.

I am also thankful for the helpful comments I got from H. G. Alles, C. D. Blewett, T. A. Cargill, J. DeTreville, R. A. Finkel, C. N. Fischer, D. D. Hill, J. O. Limb, R. A. Maddux, R. H. McCullough, J. Misra, M. E. Quinn, and J. E. Weythman.

G. Fisher and D. Shields gave me a copy of the New York University Ada Compiler, using which I was able to test the example programs. I would have been very uncomfortable had the programs in the book not been tested. I am particularly grateful to Gerry Fisher who was very helpful in providing me with revisions to Ada and answering questions about the compiler.

I appreciate the help of N. E. Bock, F. L. Dalrymple, R. L. Drechsler and Brian Kernighan in overcoming typesetting problems of one form or another.

Finally, I must thank J. Wait and J. Fegen of Prentice-Hall for their constant and encouraging support of this book.

Ada®

AN ADVANCED INTRODUCTION

Chapter 1: **Introduction** [1-6, 8]

As a modern programming language Ada incorporates many of the advances made in programming language research in the 1970s. This chapter focuses on the conventional part of Ada while the remaining chapters are devoted to the novel concepts in Ada not found in the commonly used high level programming languages. The unconventional part of Ada includes concepts such as data encapsulation, exception handling, concurrency and generic subprograms.[3] The conventional part of Ada includes concepts present in existing high level languages such as Pascal, C, PL/I and, to quite an extent, in FORTRAN. Like Pascal, but unlike C, PL/I and FORTRAN, Ada is strict in its treatment of types. It is even stricter than Pascal, from which its type philosophy has been derived.

The flavor of Ada programs is illustrated by a small program, CALCULATOR, which simulates a simple calculator that can add, subtract, multiply and divide. The data appears as a list of operations in the format

A operator B

where *operator* is one of the symbols $+$, $-$, $*$ or $/$, and the operands A and B are real values.

The reader familiar with high level languages ought to be able to understand the program CALCULATOR and most of the conventional part of Ada without much difficulty:

---

3. PL/I [IBM70] supports exception handling (albeit not very well) and provides limited facilities for supporting concurrency and generic subprograms.

```
--comments begin with two dashes and continue until the end of the line
with TEXT_IO; use TEXT_IO; --make input/output available
procedure CALCULATOR is
    type REAL is digits 10;
        --precision of real values is specified to be at least 10 digits
    package IO_REAL is new FLOAT_IO(REAL); use IO_REAL;
                        --input/output for REAL values is now available

    A, B: REAL;    --A and B are declared to be real variables
    OPR: CHARACTER;
    RESULT: REAL;
begin
    while not END_OF_FILE(STANDARD_INPUT) loop
            --function STANDARD_INPUT returns the default
            --input file
        GET(A); GET(OPR); GET(B);    --read the input
        case OPR is    --case statement
            when '+' => RESULT := A+B;
            when '-' => RESULT := A-B;
            when '*' => RESULT := A*B;
            when '/' => RESULT := A/B;
            when others => PUT("ERROR***BAD OPERATOR");
                    exit; --exit from the loop on bad input
        end case;
        PUT(RESULT); NEW_LINE;
    end loop;
end CALCULATOR;
```

CALCULATOR is an Ada main program. Any Ada subprogram can be executed as a main program provided all the *contextual information* needed by the subprogram has been specified. The contextual information

```
with TEXT_IO; use TEXT_IO;
```

makes CALCULATOR complete, i.e., CALCULATOR can be compiled and executed. The *with* clause specifies that CALCULATOR needs to use the predefined package TEXT_IO containing the text input and output facilities. The *use* clause allows subprograms in TEXT_IO to be referenced in CALCULATOR without explicitly stating that they belong to TEXT_IO. Package TEXT_IO provides subprograms to do input and output for some predefined types (e.g., CHARACTER), while for other types it provides templates of subprograms. Using the template FLOAT_IO for floating point input and output, given in TEXT_IO, the declaration

```
package IO_REAL is new FLOAT_IO(REAL);
```

creates a package containing input and output subprograms for values of floating point type REAL.

The rest of this chapter contains details and discussion of the facilities in the conventional part of Ada. The first section is a discussion of the basic elements of Ada. Then follow sections on types, expressions, statements, subprograms, visibility of entities, input and output, main programs and compilation units, pragmas and, finally, a set of complete examples.

1. Basics [2]

The *basic character set* of Ada consists of the upper case letters, the digits, the special characters

$$" \# \& ' ( ) * + , - . / : ; < = > \_ \mid$$

and the space character. The *expanded character set*, which may not be supported by all the Ada implementations, consists of the 95 character ASCII graphics character set. In addition to the basic character set, the expanded character set includes the lower case letters and the additional special characters

$$! \$ \% ? @ [\backslash] \char`^ ` \{ \} \tilde{}$$

Any Ada program can be written using just the basic character set. Every Ada program can be converted to an equivalent Ada program that uses only the basic character set. Any lower case letter is equivalent to the corresponding upper case letter except within string and character literals.

Identifiers start with a letter and may be followed by any number of letters, digits and isolated underscore characters. Identifiers differing only in the upper and lower case letters, in corresponding positions, are considered identical.

Numeric literals are of two kinds—integers and reals. Some examples are

$$12 \qquad 12.0 \qquad 1.2E1 \text{ (or 1.2e1)}$$

Isolated underscores may be inserted between adjacent digits to facilitate ease of reading, as in

$$12\_000\_000$$

Literals can be written in a base other than decimal. For example 61.0 decimal can be written in base 8 as

$$8\#75.0\# \qquad \text{or} \qquad 8\#7.5\#E1$$

where 1 is the exponent in the second example. Both the base and exponent are written in decimal notation. For bases above 10, the letters A through F are used for the extended digits.[4]

A *character literal* is formed by enclosing a character within single quotes. For example, the literals A, *, ′ and the space character are denoted as

′A′   ′*′   ′′′   ′ ′

Strings are formed by enclosing a sequence of zero or more printable characters within double quotes. The double quote character " must be written twice to be included once in a string. Catenation, denoted by &, is used to represent strings longer than one line and strings containing control characters. Examples of strings are

    " "   ""   "A"   """""

    "A normal string"

    "This is a very very very very very very very very very very " &
    "long string"

    "This string contains" & ASCII.CR & ASCII.LF & "control characters"

Note how the carriage return and line feed control characters (ASCII.CR and ASCII.LF) are specified. There is no direct denotation for them in Ada. They are *imported* from the ASCII *package* by qualification with the identifier that represents them, as will be explained later.

Comments start with two adjacent hyphens anywhere on a line and are terminated by the end of the line:

```
    --all of Ada's statements must be terminated by a semicolon
    if MONTH = DECEMBER and DAY = 31 then
            --end of the year
        YEAR := YEAR + 1;
    end if;
```

Ada has some identifiers, designated as *reserved words* [2.9], which have a special meaning in the language. Reserved words may not be used as names of program entities. Reserved words will be printed in boldface in the text to distinguish them from other identifiers.

A character not in the basic character set may be *transliterated* into the basic character set by using the identifier that represents it in the ASCII package (Appendix C of the Reference Manual [DOD83]). For example, ′$′ is represented by DOLLAR in the ASCII package and the alternative denotation

---

4. The maximum base is thus limited to 16.

using the basic character set is ASCII.DOLLAR. This alternative denotation must be used if an Ada implementation supports only the basic character set. In such a situation, for example, the string

"$AMOUNT"

would be written as

ASCII.DOLLAR & "AMOUNT"

The following *replacements* are allowed for unavailable characters:

| may be replaced by a !

\#   may be replaced by : throughout any based number

"   may be replaced by % as a string terminator,
provided the string does not contain "".
Any % character in the string must now be written
twice. A string containing " is represented by using
catenation and the alternative denotation from
the ASCII package, i.e., ASCII.QUOTATION

2. Types, Constants and Variables [3]

A *type* is a set of values plus a set of operations that can be performed upon these values [MOR73]. An *object* is an entity with which a type is associated; a value of this type can also be associated with the object.

An object is created and its type specified by means of a *declaration*. All objects must be explicitly declared in Ada.[5] An initial value may be given to the object in the declaration (which will override a default initial value associated with the object type). There are two kind of objects—*constants* and *variables*. The value given to a constant cannot be changed, while that given to a variable can be changed.

2.1 Object Declarations

Object declarations have the form[6]

---

5. Loop variables are an exception to this rule. They are implicitly declared by their presence in the loop heading.

6. Extended BNF notation, as used in the Ada Reference Manual, is used in defining the syntax:

- **[** a **]**   specifies the optional occurrence of item a
- **{** a **}**   specifies 0 or more occurrences of item a
- a **|** b   specifies either item a or item b

Bold and bigger characters will be used for the BNF meta symbols **[ ] { }** and **|** to distinguish them from the Ada characters [ ] { } and |.

identifier_list: [constant] T [:= expression];
identifier_list: constant := N;

where T is a type or a *subtype* name with an optional *constraint*, or a constrained array type definition, *expression* is the initial value being given to the objects, and N is a *static* expression (i.e., an expression that can be evaluated at compile time). A constraint is a restriction on the set of possible values of the type it is associated with. (A *subtype* represents a type but with constraints on the associated set of values; every type is trivially a subtype of itself.)

2.1.1 *Examples of Constant Declarations [3.2.1]:*

PI: constant FLOAT := 3.1416;
                       ——a floating point real constant

NO_LINES, NO_WORDS: constant INTEGER := 1000;
                       ——integer constants

NO_BYTES: constant INTEGER := NO_WORDS * 4;
                       ——initialized to an expression; although this
                       ——expression is static, the initial expression
                       ——does not have to be static

GREET_1: constant STRING := "Welcome";
                       ——STRING is predefined type;
                       ——the string size is determined from the initial value.

GREET_2: constant STRING := GREET_1 & ASCII.CR & ASCII.LF
                       & "This is the display editor";
                       ——note how the constant is defined on two lines and
                       ——that the two parts of the greeting will appear on
                       ——two lines, because of the carriage return and line
                       ——feed characters

WEEK: constant array(1..7) of DAY
                       := (SUN, MON, TUE, WED, THU, FRI, SAT);
                       ——array of a user-defined type DAY whose elements are
                       ——initialized to appropriate days which are values of
                       ——type DAY. Positional notation has been used in the
                       ——initialization, i.e., WEEK(1) = SUN, etc.

A: **constant array**(1..10) **of** BOOLEAN := (1..10 => FALSE);
         −−all the elements of this boolean array constant are
         −−initialized to FALSE. Named notation has been
         −−used for initialization, i.e., element indices have
         −−been explicitly specified in the initial value

2.1.2 Number Declarations [3.2.2]: The type identifier may be left out in constants that are synonyms of numbers:

PI: **constant** := 3.1416;

2.1.3 Examples of Variable Declarations [3.2.1]:

PRESENT: BOOLEAN := FALSE;
HIGH, LOW: INTEGER;
         −−HIGH and LOW are not initialized
HOUR: INTEGER **range** 0..24;
         −−HOUR is an INTEGER variable whose values
         −−have been restricted to lie between 0 and 24
         −−by the range constraint *range 0..24*
COLOR_TABLE: **array**(1..N) **of** COLOR;
         −−upper bound is a variable
X, Y: STRING(1..80);
GRID: **array**(1..100, 1..100) **of** FLOAT;
         −−two-dimensional array
PAGE: **array**(1..60) **of** LINE;
         −−an array of arrays where LINE
         −−is some user-defined array type

All variables must be given a value before they are used in an expression; otherwise, an error occurs.

2.1.4 Type Definitions Allowed in Object Declarations: Only array type definitions, for example,

array(1..100) **of** INTEGER;

can be given directly in object declarations. In case of other type definitions, such as a record type definition, a type name representing the type definition must be declared and then used in the object declaration.[7]

---

7. Suppose that constant BOUNDS is to be declared having two values—a low limit and a high limit. BOUNDS can be declared as an array or a record constant. The following declaration of BOUNDS using an array definition is legal:

     BOUNDS: **constant** array(1..2) **of** INTEGER := (1, 100);

However, the alternative declaration of BOUNDS as a record constant

2.2 Type Declarations [3.3]

A *type declaration* associates a *name* with a *type definition.* Type declarations have the form

> **type** name **is** type_definition;

where *name* is an identifier.

Type declarations are used to collect the common properties of objects, in one place in a program, and give them a name. This *type name* can then be used in subsequent declarations of these objects. Type declarations enhance program maintainability, since a change in the properties of the objects requires a change in only one place in the program [DOD79b].

Types that can be defined are enumeration, integer, real, array, record and access types. A type definition always defines a *distinct* (different from any other) type even if two type definitions are textually identical.

Except for array type definitions, a type identifier must always be used when declaring an object. For example, the declaration of S as an enumeration type variable with values ON and OFF

> S: (ON, OFF);

is illegal, since the enumeration type definition

> (ON, OFF)

cannot be used directly in an object declaration. However, using the enumeration type SWITCH declared as

> **type** SWITCH **is** (ON, OFF);

variable S can be declared as

> S: SWITCH;

> BOUNDS: **constant record** LOW, HIGH: INTEGER; **end record** := (1, 100);

is illegal, since a record type definition has been used. Record type definitions are not allowed in the declaration of objects. An appropriate record type, say LIMITS, must be declared and then used to declare BOUNDS as a constant of a record type:

> BOUNDS: **constant** LIMITS := (1, 100);

Allowing only array type definitions but not definitions of other types, e.g., record or access types, in object declarations is not uniform and therefore undesirable.

2.3 Scalar Types [3.5]

Scalar types, viz., the *discrete* and *real* types, are types with simple values (the values have no components). *Enumeration* types and *integers* are the discrete scalar types. Integer and real types are called the *numeric* types. Each scalar type T has the attributes T'FIRST and T'LAST.

> T'FIRST   Smallest value of type T

> T'LAST   Largest value of type T

2.3.1 Enumeration Types [3.5.1]: The set of values of an enumeration type is defined by explicitly listing the values. Enumeration type declarations have the form

> **type** ENUM **is** $(a_1, a_2, ..., a_n)$

where the enumeration literals a_i can be identifiers or character literals. The position of the values a_i determines their ordering, that is, $a_1 < a_2 < a_3$ and so on. Some examples of enumeration type definitions are

> **type** DAY **is** (MON, TUE, WED, THU, FRI, SAT, SUN);

> **type** COLOR **is** (YELLOW, BLUE, RED);

> **type** TRAFFIC_LIGHT **is** (RED, YELLOW, GREEN);
>   --The literal value YELLOW belongs to two
>   --enumeration types. YELLOW is said to be
>   --overloaded. If the type of a literal cannot be
>   --determined from the context then the type must be
>   --explicitly supplied using a *qualified* expression,
>   --for example, TRAFFIC_LIGHT'(YELLOW)

> **type** HEXADECIMAL **is**
>   ('0', '1', '2', '3', '4', '5', '6', '7', '8', '9',
>   'A', 'B', 'C', 'D', 'E', 'F');

> **type** MIXED **is** ('A','B','C','*','?','%', NONE);

type CHESS_PIECES **is**
     (WHITE_PAWN, WHITE_ROOK, WHITE_KNIGHT,
     WHITE_BISHOP, WHITE_QUEEN, WHITE_KING,
     BLACK_PAWN, BLACK_ROOK, BLACK_KNIGHT,
     BLACK_BISHOP, BLACK_QUEEN, BLACK_KING,
     BLANK);
     --a chess board may be represented as squares
     --associated with values of type CHESS_PIECE only;
     --inclusion of piece BLANK allows indication of
     --an empty square.

2.3.2 Character and Boolean Types [3.5.2, 3.5.3]: Ada provides two predefined enumeration types—CHARACTER and BOOLEAN. They are declared as

type CHARACTER **is** (*the ASCII character set*);
     --see Appendix C of the Ada Reference Manual for
     --a detailed listing of values of type CHARACTER

type BOOLEAN **is** (FALSE, TRUE);
     --predefined boolean type

2.3.3 Integers [3.5.4]: Ada provides the predefined type INTEGER. An Ada implementation may also provide other predefined types such as SHORT_INTEGER and LONG_INTEGER. The smallest and largest integers supported by an implementation are given by the constants SYSTEM.MIN_INT and SYSTEM.MAX_INT. The predefined subtypes NATURAL and POSITIVE represent subsets of INTEGER values greater than or equal to zero ($\geqslant 0$) and greater than zero (> 0), respectively.

2.3.4 Attributes of Discrete (i.e., Enumeration and Integer) Types [3.5.5]: In addition to FIRST and LAST, some other attributes defined for every discrete type T are

    T'POS(X)   The position number of X in its definition. For example

                         COLOR'POS(BLUE) = 2
                         POSITIVE'POS(3) = 3

    T'SUCC(X)   The successor element of X in type T. For example

                          COLOR'SUCC(BLUE) = RED
                         NATURAL'SUCC(3) = 4

            T'SUCC(X) with X = T'LAST raises the error exception CONSTRAINT_ERROR.

T′PRED(X) The predecessor element of X. The error exception CONSTRAINT_ERROR is raised if X = T′FIRST.

T′VAL(N) The element of T with position number N. For example

$$COLOR′VAL(2) = BLUE$$
$$POSITIVE′VAL(2) = 2$$

The error exception CONSTRAINT_ERROR is raised if N < T′POS(T′FIRST) or N > T′POS(T′LAST).

2.3.5 Reals [3.5.6-3.5.10]: Ada provides elaborate facilities for reals [WIC81]. Values of type real are approximations to the mathematical reals. Reals come in two flavors—floating point and fixed point. Real values are represented differently in floating point and fixed point, and hence have different approximation errors.

Floating point reals are an approximation to the mathematical reals in which the error in representing a mathematical real is *relative* to its absolute value. On the other hand, the representation error in case of the fixed point reals is *independent* of its value. Consequently, small fixed point real values may have a correspondingly large relative error. The size of the error bounds for both types of reals depends upon the desired accuracy, called the *accuracy constraint*, which is specified by the user.

The error bound for floating point reals is specified by giving the minimum number of decimal digits that should be stored for the mantissa. The error bound for fixed point reals is specified as an absolute value called the *delta* of the fixed point real.

Associated with every real type definition is a set of numbers called the *model numbers*. The semantics of real arithmetic in Ada is defined in terms of these model numbers [BRO81]. Error bounds for the predefined real operations are also defined in terms of these numbers. Any implementation of a real type must include exact representations of these numbers. This requirement provides a basis for guaranteeing the consistency of real arithmetic computation across different implementations.

An implementation may provide a superset of the model numbers called the *safe numbers*. Safe numbers allow the programmer to exploit the extra precision provided by an implementation.

The characteristics of model and safe numbers, associated with a real type, can be determined using appropriate attributes which are provided for all real types.

2.3.5.1 Floating Point Reals [3.5.7]: Ada provides the user with the predefined floating point real type FLOAT. Additionally, an implementation may provide other predefined reals, such as SHORT_FLOAT and LONG_FLOAT.

2.3.5.2 Floating Point Attributes [3.5.8]: Some attributes defined for every floating point type F are

F'DIGITS	Precision in decimal digits
F'FIRST	The algebraically smallest value of type F
F'LAST	The algebraically largest value of type F
F'SMALL	Smallest positive model number associated with type F
F'LARGE	Largest positive model number associated with type F
F'EPSILON	Difference between model number 1.0 and the next greater model number

The values F'FIRST and F'LAST need not be model numbers.

2.3.5.3 Fixed Point Reals [3.5.9]: Fixed point real types are declared as

   type NEW_FIXED **is** *fixed_point_constraint*;

where *fixed_point_constraint*, the accuracy constraint for fixed point types, has the form

   delta DEL **range** L..R;

where DEL, L and R are static expressions of some real type. The delta value DEL, which must be positive, specifies the maximum absolute error that should occur in representing values of the fixed point type being specified. Elements of this fixed point type are consecutive multiples of DEL.

The range constraint *range L..R* must be specified in the definition of a fixed point type. A value satisfies a fixed point constraint if it satisfies any included range constraint.

Some examples of fixed point types are

   type CURRENCY **is delta** 0.01 **range** 0.0 .. 1_000_000_000_000.0;
   type HIGH_PRECISION **is delta** 0.0001 **range** 0.0 .. 500.0;

2.3.5.4 Fixed Point Attributes [3.5.10]: Some attributes defined for every fixed point type F are

F'DELTA	The delta value specified in the declaration of F

F'SMALL	The smallest positive model number associated with type F
F'LARGE	The largest positive model number associated with type F
F'FIRST	The smallest value of type F
F'LAST	The largest value of type F

2.4 Arrays [3.6, 4.3, 4.7]

An array is a composite object consisting of component objects (called elements) all of which have the same type (actually, the same subtype).[8] Array types come in two varieties—constrained and unconstrained. In case of a *constrained* array type, the bounds of the array are specified at the time the array type is defined or when an array object is declared. Constrained arrays are similar to Pascal arrays. In case of an *unconstrained* array type, the array bounds are not specified in its declaration. These bounds are supplied later, in type definitions using the unconstrained array type, in object declarations or during parameter passage. The unconstrained array type can be used only in type definitions and parameter declarations. It can be used for object declarations only if the constraints are supplied. It is the unconstrained array type that allows procedures and functions to accept actual parameter arrays of different sizes.[9]

2.4.1 Constrained Arrays: The constrained array type has the form

> **array** index_constraint **of** C

where subtype C is the type of the array components. C can be any type including an array (or a task) type. The *index_constraint* specifies the type of the array indices and is of the form

---

8. Requiring all elements of an array to be of the same subtype, instead of the same type, eliminates the possibility of *ragged* arrays. An array is ragged if its components have different sizes, e.g., a one-dimensional array whose components are one-dimensional arrays of different sizes. Arrays with different number of elements can be of the same *unconstrained* array type, i.e., an array type in which the array size is not specified. On the other hand, all arrays of the same array subtype have the same number of elements, since the size of the array is specified in the subtype.

9. The lack of unconstrained arrays (or a facility similar to it) is one of Pascal's major drawbacks, since a subprogram cannot be called with actual parameter arrays of different sizes (corresponding to the same formal parameter). It is possible to pass arrays of different sizes as parameters in many programming languages, e.g., PL/I, Algol 68, and C. The ISO Pascal Standard [ISO81] eliminates this drawback by providing *conformant arrays*.

(discrete_range {, discrete_range})

where *discrete_range* is a range of the form *L..U*, or is a type or subtype name followed, possibly, by a range constraint of the form *range L..U*. The expressions L and U defining the bounds of the discrete ranges can be dynamic, that is, they can depend upon computed results. An array whose bounds are not static is called a *dynamic array*. Some examples illustrating constrained array types are

> **type** SALES **is array**(MONTHS) **of** FLOAT;
>   —–MONTHS is a user-defined enumeration type
> **type** CHESS_BOARD **is array**(1..8, 1..8) **of** CHESS_PIECES;
> **type** CARD **is array**(INTEGER **range** 1..80) **of** CHARACTER;
>   —–objects of type CARD must be indexed by objects of
>   —–type INTEGER or subtypes of INTEGER, with values
>   —–between 1 and 80

Some examples of array object declarations are

> SET: **array**(1..SET_SIZE) **of** BOOLEAN;   —–dynamic array
> WEEKLY_SALES: **array**(DAY **range** MON..SAT) **of** FLOAT;

An array is a *null array* if at least one of its indices defines a *null range*. A range L..U is null if L > U. A null array has no components.

2.4.2 Unconstrained Arrays: Unconstrained array types definitions have the form

> **array**(index {, index}) **of** C

where subtype C is the array component type and *index* is of the form

> T **range** < >

T is a type or subtype name. < > is called the *box* and stands for an undefined range whose bounds are to be supplied later.

When declaring unconstrained array type objects, the *index_constraint* must be supplied. Different objects of the same unconstrained array type can have different bounds. For example, consider the unconstrained array type declarations

> **type** VECTOR **is array**(INTEGER **range** < >) **of** FLOAT;
> **type** MATRIX **is array**
>   (INTEGER **range** < >, INTEGER **range** < >) **of** FLOAT;

Some examples of arrays objects declared using these types and appropriate index constraints are

```
X: VECTOR(1..10);   ――1..10 is the index constraint
Y: VECTOR(−200..0);
              ――X and Y are of the same type VECTOR but they
              ――have different bounds
```

```
M: MATRIX(1..25, 1..40);
```

The use of an unconstrained type in parameter declarations is illustrated by the definition of procedure SORT:

procedure SORT(V: **in out** VECTOR);

Procedure SORT can be called with any array of type VECTOR, such as X, regardless of the size of the array. The bounds of the formal parameter array V are obtained from the corresponding actual parameter and are given by the attributes V'FIRST and V'LAST.

2.4.3 Strings [3.6.3]: Ada provides the predefined string type

type STRING **is array**(POSITIVE **range** <>) **of** CHARACTER;

Strings are one-dimensional arrays of characters. Some examples of the use of the STRING type are

```
type LINE is new STRING(1..80);
              ――defines a new type LINE whose values are strings
              ――of length 80. Type LINE is different from
              ――STRING(1..80); see derived types in Chapter 2 on
              ――More About Types
NAME: STRING(1..20);
L: LINE;
```

The relational operators =, /=, <, <=, >= and >, and the catenation operator & are predefined for strings.

As an example illustrating the use of strings, consider the subprogram REVERSE_STRING, which reverses strings of type STRING regardless of their length:

procedure REVERSE_STRING(S: **in out** STRING) **is**
  −−reverse string S; the bounds of S will be those
  −−of the corresponding actual parameter

  L: **constant** INTEGER := S'FIRST;
  U: **constant** INTEGER := S'LAST;
    −−the bounds of S are determined using the array attributes
    −−FIRST and LAST
  C: CHARACTER;

begin
  for I **in** L..(L+U)/2 **loop**
    C := S(I);
    S(I) := S(U−I+1);
    S(U−I+1) := C;
  end loop;
end REVERSE_STRING;

2.4.4 Array Elements, Slices and Aggregates [4.1.1, 4.1.2, 4.3, 4.3.2]: The element of an n-dimensional array A with subscripts i_1, i_2, ..., i_n is referenced using the notation

  $A(i_1, i_2, ..., i_n)$

Portions of one-dimensional arrays, called *slices*, can be referenced by using the notation

  A(discrete_range)

For example, the slice X(1..5) refers to the first 5 elements of X. Slicing does not produce copies of the elements of the array being sliced; changing an element of a slice is equivalent to changing the corresponding element of the array being sliced and vice versa. For example, the assignment

  X(1..5)(2) := X(1..5)(2) + 1.0;

is equivalent to the assignment

  X(2) := X(2) + 1.0;

Array values, called *array aggregates*, can be constructed directly from component values. Array aggregates can be used for assignment to array objects or in expressions. Array aggregates can be formed using a *positional* notation, a *named* notation or a combination of these two notations. An aggregate must be *complete*; that is, a value must be given for every component of the composite value.

The type of an array aggregate is determined from the context unless its type is explicitly stated. The type of an array aggregate may be explicitly stated by qualifying it with a type or subtype name:

T'aggregate

where T is a type or a subtype. This qualification is required when the type of the aggregate cannot be unambiguously determined from the context. The aggregate type must be the same as the base type of the explicitly specified type or subtype.

Some examples of array aggregates and slices are given below:

(1, 2, 3, 4, 5)	is a one-dimensional array value with 5 elements specified using positional notation; the ith element has value i.
(1..10 => 5.5)	is a one-dimensional array value with 10 elements, each having the value 5.5; named notation has been used to construct the aggregate.
CARD'(1 | 45 => '*', others => '_')	is an array value of type CARD (type of the aggregate is explicitly stated) with components 1 and 45 having the value '*'. All other elements have the value '_'. The index range is determined from type CARD. The choice **others** must be the last choice.
('T', 'e', 's', 't')	is a one-dimensional array of characters.
"Test"	same as above; "..." is an alternative notation for writing one-dimensional CHARACTER array aggregates.
M := (1..25 => (1..25 => 0.0));	the right hand side specifies a two-dimensional array aggregate value. It is depicted as an array of 25 one-dimensional arrays, each of whose elements has the value 0.0. Named notation has been used to specify the elements.
X(1..5) : = (2 => 5.0, 1 | 3..5 => 0.0);	assigns to the slice of the array X an aggregate with 5 elements; the second element of the aggregate has the value 5.0 while elements 1, 3, 4 and 5 have the value 0.0.

The bounds of a positional aggregate or any aggregate containing the choice **others** are determined from the context [4.3.2]. An N-dimensional array aggregate is written as a one-dimensional array aggregate consisting of (N−1)-dimensional array values.

2.4.5 Array Attributes [3.6.2]: The following attributes are defined for each array object or constrained array subtype A:

A′FIRST	Lower bound of the first index; same as A′FIRST(1)
A′FIRST(N)	Lower bound of the Nth index
A′LAST	Upper bound of the first index; same as A′LAST(1)
A′LAST(N)	Upper bound of the Nth index
A′LENGTH	Size of the first index (if the indices are integers, then A′LENGTH = A′LAST − A′ FIRST + 1); same as A′LENGTH(1)
A′LENGTH(N)	Size of the Nth index (if the indices are integers, then A′LENGTH(N) = A′LAST(N) − A′ FIRST(N) + 1)
A′RANGE[10]	The subtype A′FIRST..A′LAST corresponding to the legal values for the first index; same as A′RANGE(1)
A′RANGE(N)	The subtype A′FIRST(N)..A′LAST(N) corresponding to the legal values for the Nth index.

2.5 Records [3.7]

A record is a composite object consisting of named components that may be of different types (components of a record are *heterogeneous* whereas the components of an array are *homogeneous*). Record types are defined as

---

10. RANGE is a misnomer! DOMAIN would have been more appropriate. The domain of an array is the set of legal subscripts for it, while the range of an array is the set of values of its elements.

```
record
    component_declarations | null
end record
```

A component declaration declares one or more components to be of a specified type using a type or subtype name followed, optionally, by a constraint. If there are no components in a record, then the record type definition must contain the reserved word **null**; such a record is called a *null record*.

A component C of a record object R is referenced using the *selected component* notation:

R.C

Some examples of record types are

```
type POSITION is
   record
      X, Y: FLOAT;
   end record;

type SEQUENCE is
   record
      SEQ: STRING(1..MAX_SIZE);
      L: POSITIVE range 1..MAX_SIZE;
   end record;

type DATE is
   record
      YEAR: INTEGER range 1901..2099;
      MONTH: INTEGER range 1..12;
      DAY: INTEGER range 1..31;
   end record;
```

Objects of a record type can be given default initial values by specifying the values for the record components in the record type definition.[11] A default initial value can be overridden by an explicitly supplied initial value. For example, all objects of type POSITION can be given the default initial value of (0.0, 0.0) by declaring POSITION alternatively as

---

11. Default values for objects of a type T can be specified only if T is a record type!

```
type POSITION is
   record
      X, Y: FLOAT := 0.0;
   end record;
```

As a result of the declarations

```
P1: POSITION;                    --default initialization
P2: POSITION := (1.0, 1.0);      --explicit initialization
```

P1.X and P1.Y have the value 0.0 while P2.X and P2.Y have the value 1.0.

The use of records is illustrated by the function subprogram DISTANCE that computes the distance between two positions, (x_1, y_1) and (x_2, y_2), which is given by the expression

$$\sqrt{(x_1 - x_2)^2 + (y_1 - y_2)^2}$$

Function DISTANCE is declared as

```
function DISTANCE(P1, P2: POSITION) return FLOAT is
begin
   return SQRT((P1.X − P2.X) ** 2 + (P1.Y − P2.Y) ** 2);
end;
```

where SQRT is a user-defined function that computes the square root.

2.5.1 Record Aggregates [4.3.1]: Record values, called *record aggregates*, can be constructed directly from component values. Record aggregates can be used in assignments to record objects. A value must be provided for each component regardless of whether or not a default initial value exists for the component. Like array aggregates, record aggregates can be specified using either the positional or the named notation.

The following record aggregate examples use the type POSITION, declared earlier, and the type COMPLEX declared as

```
type COMPLEX is
   record
      R, I: FLOAT;
   end record;
```

Some record aggregate examples are

(5.0, 6.0)
The positional notation is fine as long as the type can be determined from the context; otherwise the aggregate must be qualified with the type as shown in the following examples.

>   POSITION′(5.0, 6.0)   The aggregate type is specified explicitly.
>   COMPLEX′(5.0, 6.0)

2.6 Access Types [3.8, 4.1.3]

Static objects are created by specifying them in a declaration. *Dynamic* objects, on the other hand, are created dynamically and explicitly during program execution. The storage *allocator*, which is called *new*, is used to create dynamic objects. The number of dynamic objects, unlike the number of static objects, is not fixed by the program text—they can be created or destroyed as desired during program execution. Dynamic objects, unlike static objects, do not have any explicit name and must be referred to using *access type* objects that point to them.[12]

The allocator *new* returns a value of an access type when a dynamic object is created. It is this value that is used to refer to the dynamic object. This access type value may be assigned to more than one object of the same access type. Thus, a dynamic object may be referred to using one or more objects of an access type; an object that can be referred to via two or more access type objects is said to have *aliases*.

Access types are defined by

>   **access** T [constraint]

where T is a type or subtype name and the *constraint* is a discriminant or index constraint. Objects of this access type are used to refer to objects of type T.

The access value **null** is associated with all access types. All objects of an access type are given the **null** value as the default initial value. The value **null** indicates that no object is being referred to by the access type object. Using this value to refer to a dynamic object is an error and raises an exception.

Some examples of access type declarations are

---

12. Access types are really pointers! Ada uses a different terminology to avoid the connotation of unsafeness usually associated with pointers. Also Ada's access types have more restrictions than those, if any, on pointers in most programming languages.

The lack of restrictions on pointers, as in PL/I, allows a pointer to refer to any type of object. This freedom defeats type checking, because the compiler cannot determine the type of the object being accessed. Pointers can be used to access portions of memory, which were used by the objects pointed to by them but which have since been deallocated. Pointer arithmetic is allowed in some languages, and if proper checking is not done, illegal access to other parts of storage is possible.

```
type TITLE is access STRING(1..40);
                       --refers to strings of length 40
type LOCATION is access POSITION;
type FIGURE is access GEOMETRIC_FIGURE;
```

Dynamic objects are created during program execution by a call to the allocator, which is of the form

new T [´(expression) | ´aggregate | discriminant or index constraint]

where T is a type or subtype name. An initial value for the dynamic object may be explicitly supplied at creation time. If T is an unconstrained type, then a constraint or an initial value must be supplied when creating dynamic objects of type T.

Using access type objects declared as

```
T1, T2: TITLE;
A, B: LOCATION;
F: FIGURE;
```

some examples of dynamic objects created using the allocator are

```
T1 := new STRING(1..40);              --index constraint supplied
T2 := new STRING´(1..40 => ´ ´);   --initial value supplied
A := new POSITION´(Y => 5.0, X => 10.0);
B := new POSITION;
F := new GEOMETRIC_FIGURE(CIRCLE);   --constraint supplied
```

The access value represented by an access type object P is referred to simply as P. The notation for referring to dynamic objects is P.**all**, where P is an access type object or a function call returning a value of an access type. If P refers to an object of a record type, then component C of that record object is referred to as P.C. For example, using variables A and B as declared above, the assignment

```
B.all := A.all;
```

copies the value of the object referred to by A into the object referred to by B. This assignment is equivalent to the assignments of the components of A to the components of B

```
B.X := A.X;
B.Y := A.Y;
```

On the other hand, the assignment

```
B := A;
```

just copies the value of A into B, with the result that B also refers to the object pointed to by A. The object, if any, referred to by B prior to the assignment becomes inaccessible unless another access type object refers to it.

2.6.1 Lifetime of a Dynamic Object: A dynamic object remains in existence as long as the object can be accessed. Conceptually, dynamic objects can be accessed only as long as the declaration of the corresponding access type is available. The storage allocated for the dynamic objects may be reclaimed when they are no longer accessible or have been deallocated. Inaccessible objects will be automatically deallocated if the implementation provides a *garbage collector*. Otherwise, these objects must be deallocated explicitly if the space occupied by them has to be used for other purposes. Explicit deallocation is done using *instantiations* of the generic procedure UNCHECKED_DEALLOCATION. Care must be taken to avoid errors resulting from the *dangling pointer* problem [PRA75], i.e., referencing objects that have been explicitly deallocated.

The total amount of storage set aside for objects of a particular access type can be specified by means of a length specification (see Chapter 8 on Representation Clauses and Implementation Dependent Features).

3. Expressions [4.4]

Expressions are formed using operators and operands. In evaluating an expression, operators with a higher precedence are applied first. Operators having the same precedence are applied in textual order from left to right. Parentheses may be used to change the order of evaluation imposed by the precedence of the operators.

A *static expression* [4.9] is an expression whose operands have values that can be determined without program execution. Static expressions can therefore be evaluated at compile time (without executing the program).

Static expressions consist of literals, literal expressions, constants initialized to static expressions, aggregates composed of static expressions, predefined operators, static attributes, function attributes with static expressions as actual parameters and so on.

Operator precedence and semantics are given in the following sections and tables:

3.1 Operator Precedence [4.5]

The operators are listed in order of increasing precedence:

logical	**and** | **or** | **xor** | **and then** | **or else**
relational/membership	**=** | **/=** | **<** | **<=** | **>** | **>=** | **in** | **not in**
adding (binary)	**+** | **−** | **&**
adding (unary)	**+** | **−**
multiplying	***** | **/** | **mod** | **rem**
highest precedence	****** | **abs** | **not**

3.2 Operator Semantics

3.2.1 Logical Operators [4.5.1]:

Operator	Operation	Operand Types	Result Type
and	conjunction	boolean boolean array	same boolean same boolean array
or	inclusive disjunction	boolean boolean array	same boolean same boolean array
xor	exclusive disjunction	boolean boolean array	same boolean same boolean array
and then	short circuit *and*	boolean	same boolean
or else	short circuit *or*	boolean	same boolean

A *boolean* type refers to either the predefined type BOOLEAN or any type derived from a boolean type (derived types are discussed in Chapter 2 on More About Types).

The result of an expression formed using the logical operators **and, or** or **xor** is determined by evaluating both operands. In case of the short circuit logical operators (**and then** and **or else**), the second operand is evaluated only if the result of the expression cannot be determined from evaluating the first operand. The phrase *optimization of boolean expressions*[13] has been used to mean that when generating code for boolean expressions, the normal logical operators (**and, or**) will be treated as if they were really short circuit logical operators [GRI71]. As long as the boolean expressions do not contain side effects this

---

13. Optimization is a misnomer! The phrase *code improvement* should be used instead, since the code produced after the so called optimization is usually not the most efficient code.

optimization poses no problems.

Programs relying on the knowledge that the boolean expressions are optimized in a particular implementation may become implementation dependent, because they may not produce correct results on an implementation that does not optimize boolean expressions. For example, evaluating the expression

$$I \; /= 0 \textbf{ and } A(I)$$

in which the lower bound of array A is 1 will cause no problems when I is equal to 0, if optimized code is produced, but will result in a *subscript out of range* error otherwise.

By separating the logical operators into the regular and short circuit forms, Ada provides the programmer with the option to specify exactly what is wanted. The use of short circuit operators can lead to elegant code [DIJ76]. For example, without the short circuit operator **and then**, the Ada program segment

```
I := 1;
while I <= N and then X(I) /= KEY loop
   I := I + 1;
end loop;
--if I <= N then I is the subscript of KEY in X
```

that searches the array slice X(1..N) for a value KEY may be written (inelegantly) using an additional BOOLEAN variable PRESENT as

```
I := 0;
PRESENT := FALSE;
while I < N and not PRESENT loop
   I := I + 1;
   PRESENT := X(I) = KEY;
end loop;
--if PRESENT is TRUE then I is the subscript of KEY in X
```

The additional variable must be used to avoid a subscript error in case KEY is not present in the array.[14] The **and then** operator allows evaluation of its second operand

---

14. Just writing the first program segment using simply **and** instead of **and then** as in

```
while I <= N and X(I) /= KEY loop I := I + 1; end loop;
```

causes a subscript error when I > N.

$$X(I) \mathrel{/=} KEY$$

only if its first operand

$$I \mathrel{<=} N$$

is true, so that $X(I)$ is a valid element of X.

3.2.2 Relational and Membership Operators [4.5.2]:

Operator	Operation	Operand Types	Result Type
= /=	equality inequality	any type	BOOLEAN
< <= > >=	test for ordering	any scalar type discrete array type	BOOLEAN BOOLEAN

Operator	Operation	Left Operand Type	Right Operand Type	Result Type
in **not in**	membership test to determine if a value belongs to a range, type or subtype	value of the right operand type	range, type or subtype name	BOOLEAN

3.2.3 Binary Adding Operators [4.5.3]:

Operator	Operation	Left Operand Type	Right Operand Type	Result Type
+	addition	numeric	same numeric	same numeric
−	minus	numeric	same numeric	same numeric
&	catenation	array type element type array type element type	same as left array type element type element type	same as left same array type same array type any array type

The catenation operator & can be used to catenate two arrays, extend an array at either end by one element and to form an array of two elements.

3.2.4 Unary Adding Operators [4.5.4]:

Operator	Operation	Operand Type	Result Type
+	identity	numeric	same numeric type
−	negation	numeric	same numeric type

3.2.5 Multiplying Operators [4.5.5]:

The first table in this section shows the multiplying operators for integer and floating point real values; the second table shows the multiplying operators for fixed point reals:

Operator	Operation	Operand Types	Result Type
*	multiplication	integer floating	same integer type same floating type
/	integer division floating division	integer floating	same integer type same floating type
mod	modulus	integer	same integer type
rem	remainder	integer	same integer type

The remainder operator **rem** and the modulus operator **mod** applied to operands with the same absolute value produce the same result only when both operands are of the same sign. Operation (A **rem** B) is defined by the relation

$$A = (A/B)*B + (A \text{ rem } B)$$

where A and B are integers, / represents integer division, and (A **rem** B) has the sign of A and an absolute value less than the absolute value of B. On the other hand, (A **mod** B) has the sign of B and an absolute value less than the absolute value of B. Subject to these restrictions, (A **mod** B) is defined by the relationship

$$A = B*N + (A \text{ mod } B)$$

where N is some integer.

Operator	Operation	Left Operand Type	Right Operand Type	Result Type
*	multiplication	fixed integer fixed	integer fixed fixed	same as left operand same as right operand *universal fixed*
/	division	fixed fixed	integer fixed	same as left operand *universal fixed*

The *universal fixed* point type, a type with arbitrarily fine precision, is not available to the user. Values of this type must be explicitly converted to some fixed point type before they can be used.

3.2.6 Highest Precedence Operators [4.5.6]:

Operator	Operation	Operand Type	Result Type
abs	absolute value	numeric	same numeric
not	logical negation	boolean boolean array	same boolean same array type

Operator	Operation	Left Operand Type	Right Operand Type	Result Type
**	exponentiation	integer floating	positive integer integer	left operand type left operand type

4. Statements [5]

In this section, Ada statements that are conventional in nature (such as those found in Pascal) are discussed. Statements such as those pertaining to concurrency, raising exceptions and the insertion of machine code are left for later chapters.

4.1 Null Statement [5.1]

Ada has a statement that does nothing. This statement is

> **null**;

The *null* statement is used in situations where no action is to be performed, but where the Ada syntax requires the presence of at least one statement.

4.2 Assignment [5.2]

Assignment statements have the form

> V := E;

where V is a variable name and E is an expression. Executing the assignment statement causes the value of E to be assigned to the variable represented by V. The type of both V and E must be the same. Additionally, the value of E must satisfy constraints imposed by the type of V. Assignment is defined for all types. For example, whole arrays, slices or records can be assigned values directly.

4.3 If Statement [5.3]

The *if* statement has the form

> **if** boolean_expression **then**
>   sequence_of_statements
> {**elsif** boolean_expression **then**
>   sequence_of_statements}
> [**else**
>   sequence_of_statements]
> **end if;**

The sequence of statements corresponding to the first boolean expression that is true is executed. Otherwise, the sequence of statements corresponding to the *else* part, if any, is executed. The following program segment, illustrating the use of the *if* statement, is taken from the abstract version of the program to sort an array, using the quicksort technique, given at the end of the chapter:

> **if** One element **then**
>   **null;**
> **elsif** Two elements **then**
>   Order them
> **elsif** More than two elements **then**
>   Partition the array into two parts and sort each part
> **end if;**

4.4 Case Statement [5.4]

The *case* statement is used to select one alternative sequence of statements out of many. It has the form

> **case** expression **is**
>   **when** choice {| choice} => sequence_of_statements
>   {**when** choice {| choice} => sequence_of_statements}
> **end case;**

The expression in the *case* statement must be of a discrete type. The sequence of statements corresponding to a choice matching the value of the expression is executed. The choices must be static expressions of a discrete type or discrete ranges. A choice that is a discrete range is an abbreviation for a list of choices representing the values in the range. The choices must cover all possible values the expression in the *case* statement might have and must be mutually exclusive. The choice **others** may be given for the last alternative as a shorthand for the remaining possible values of the expression.

An example of a *case* statement is a program segment from a simple Polish notation interpreter.

```
case C is
   when '+' => ADD;
   when '-' => SUBTRACT;
   when '*' => MULTIPLY;
   when '/' => DIVIDE;
   when others => PUT_ON_STACK;
end case;
```

The *case* statement is clearer and more efficient to implement than the multiway branch using the *if* statement:

```
if C = '+' then ADD;
elsif C = '-' then SUBTRACT;
elsif C = '*' then MULTIPLY;
elsif C = '/' then DIVIDE;
else PUT_ON_STACK;
end if;
```

The *case* statement, unlike the *if* statement, can be used only when the choice depends upon the value of a discrete expression.

4.5 Loops [5.5]

The *loop* statement has three forms:

```
while boolean_expression loop
   sequence_of_statements
end loop;

for loop_parameter in [reverse] discrete_range loop
   sequence_of_statements
end loop;

loop
   sequence_of_statements
end loop;
```

The first loop, called the *while* loop, is executed repeatedly as long as the boolean_expression is TRUE. For example, the following loop is executed until the end of file P is reached. The statements inside the loop copy a value from file P to file R:

```
while not END_OF_FILE(P) loop
   READ(P, X);
   WRITE(R, X);
end loop;
```

In the second form, called the *for* loop, the loop is executed once for each value in the discrete range with the loop parameter being equal to that value. The values are assigned to the loop parameter in increasing order when the keyword **reverse** is absent and in decreasing order when **reverse** is present. The loop parameter is not declared explicitly. It is implicitly declared by its presence in the loop and has the type of the specified discrete range. The loop parameter is local to the loop and its value cannot be changed in the loop body. No value can be assigned to it, nor can it be passed to a procedure in a manner that could allow its value to be modified. The loop parameter acts like a constant within the loop body. In the following example, the loop is executed once for each subscript of A, except the last one, with the loop parameter I being assigned the subscripts in decreasing order:

```
--from the program to evaluate a polynomial using Horner's
--rule given at the end of the chapter

for I in reverse A'FIRST..A'LAST-1 loop
    --loop variable I is implicitly declared by its presence
    --in the loop  header

    SUM := SUM * V + A(I);
end loop;
```

A *for* loop is not executed if a *null range* is specified. For example, this loop is not executed at all if LAST is equal to 0:

```
for J in 1..LAST loop
        --search table ST for the record with
        --value X in its ID field
    if ST(J).ID = X then
        return TRUE;
    end if;
end loop;
```

The third form of the loop is used when neither the *for* loop nor the *while* loop can be conveniently used. In this form, the loop iterates until it is exited explicitly, e.g., by executing an *exit*, a *return* or a *goto* statement, or implicitly when an exception is raised. The third loop form is also used to express infinite cycles that occur in *tasks* (concurrent programs) that are designed never to stop. Examples of such programs are a clock that runs forever and an infinite process that reads characters from a buffer and outputs their upper case form. The second of these examples is illustrated by the following program segment:

```
loop
    BUFFER.READ(X);
    PUT(UPPER(X));
end loop;
```

Execution of the statement BUFFER.READ is suspended when the buffer is empty and is resumed after at least one character has been put into the buffer.

4.5.1 Naming Loops: A loop may be named by prefixing it with an identifier, for example,

>   L:

A named loop must be terminated by its name, for example,

>   **end loop** L;

Loop names are used in *exit* statements. Also, naming loops is helpful when loops are nested several levels deep and when the first and last lines of the loop are textually far apart.

4.6 Blocks [5.6]

A *block* statement is a sequence of statements preceded optionally by a set of local declarations and followed optionally by a sequence of exception handlers (exception handling is discussed in Chapter 5 on Exceptions). A block can be named just as a loop can be named.

```
[ declare
    declarative_part]
begin
    sequence_of_statements
[ exception
    exception handlers]
end;
```

Blocks are used to confine the scope of declarations and exception handlers to the statements with which they are logically associated. Without blocks, these declarations would be visible to all other statements and it would not be possible to locally handle exceptions raised in these statements. Storage for objects declared in the block is allocated upon entering the block and is reclaimed on exit.

As an example, suppose that a program segment to exchange the values of two strings A and B of type STRING(1..80) is to be written. Using blocks, the program segment can be written as

```
declare
    TEMP: STRING(1..80);
begin
    TEMP := A;
    A := B;
    B := TEMP;
end;
```

TEMP is local to the statements that need to use it and is not visible to any other statements in the rest of the program. Storage for TEMP is allocated on block entry and released on block exit.

4.7 Exit Statement [5.7]

An *exit* statement is used to exit from a loop, either unconditionally (when no boolean expression has been specified) or conditionally (when a boolean expression is present).

    exit [loop_name] [when boolean_expression];

Unless a loop name is specified, the innermost loop surrounding the *exit* statement is the one exited.

4.8 Return [5.8]

A *return* statement is used to return from a function, a procedure or an *accept* statement. In case of a function, the *return* statement is also used to return the value computed by the function. A *return* statement of the form

    return expression;

must be used to return from a function. The value returned by the function is the value of *expression*. To return from a procedure, the form

    return;

is used.

4.9 Goto [5.9]

Each statement can be prefixed by a label of the form

    << identifier >>

Labels identify the statements they are associated with and are used in *goto* statements. The *goto* statement is used for explicitly transferring control to a statement whose label has been specified. The *goto* statement has the form

    goto label;

The unrestricted use of the *goto* statement is considered to be harmful, because it hampers program understandability [DIJ68b, KNU74]. Consequently a very restricted version of the *goto* statement is provided in Ada. The *goto* statement cannot be used to transfer control out of a subprogram, package or task body, or an *accept* statement. It cannot be used to transfer control from outside into a compound statement, an *if* statement, a *case* statement or any other control structure.

5. Subprograms [6]

There are four forms of *program units* from which programs can be composed—subprograms, packages, tasks and generic units. Subprograms can be compiled *separately* and are called *compilation units*.[15] Subprograms in Ada come in two varieties—procedures and functions. A procedure is executed for its effect (e.g., changing the values of the **in out** parameters, supplying values to **out** parameters or updating global variables) and functions are used to return values.

Subprograms are invoked (executed) by means of subprogram calls. A procedure call is a statement, while a function call is an operand in an expression. Execution of a procedure terminates upon reaching the end of the procedure or by executing a *return* statement. Execution of a function must terminate by executing a *return* statement that returns the function result. Subprograms in Ada are recursive and reentrant.

A subprogram consists of two parts:

- a subprogram specification and

- a subprogram body.

A subprogram specification consists of the name of the subprogram, the names and types of its parameters, and, in case of a function, the type of the result. Subprogram specifications are of the form

> **procedure** name [(formal parameters)];

> **function** name [(formal parameters)] **return** T;

where *name* is an identifier (or alternatively, in case of a function, an operator symbol surrounded by double quotes) and T is a type or subtype name. Some examples of subprogram specifications are

---

15. A program is a collection of one or more compilation units submitted to the compiler together or separately. Subprogram and package declarations and bodies, generic declarations and instantiations, and subunits (bodies of subprograms, packages and tasks declared in other compilation units) are the compilation units of Ada.

procedure EXTEND(S: **in out** SEQUENCE);

function SQRT(X: **in** NON_NEGATIVE_REAL;
                    EPS: **in** POS_REAL := 0.001) **return** FLOAT;

function NULL_SEQ **return** SEQUENCE;

Subprogram bodies have the form[16]

procedure name [(formal parameters)] **is**
    declarations
begin
    sequence_of_statements
[**exception**
    exception handlers]
end name;

function name [(formal parameters)] **return** T **is**
    declarations
begin
    sequence_of_statements
[**exception**
    exception handlers]
end name;

As stated above, T is the type of the function result.

In the *declarations* part of a subprogram body, declarations of all objects, types, subtypes, representation specifications and exceptions must come before the bodies of subprograms, packages and tasks.

A subprogram specification can be omitted only if the subprogram will be called after its body has been given (assuming it has not been declared in the visible part of a package). In this case the body of the subprogram acts as its own specification.

---

16. Supplying the subprogram name at the end of its body, i.e., after the reserved word **end**, is optional in Ada. However, it is good programming style to end a subprogram body with its name, since it aids program readability. For this reason, the forms shown for subprogram bodies do not indicate that the subprogram name at the end of its body is optional. This style will also be used for package specification and body, task specification and body, etc.

5.1 Formal Parameters

Formal parameters of a subprogram are local to the subprogram. They can have one of three modes—**in, out** and **in out**:[17]

formal parameter mode	formal parameter behavior
in	The formal parameter acts like a constant in the subprogram with its value being supplied by the corresponding actual parameter. **in** is the default mode if no mode is explicitly specified. This mode should be used when a value is supplied by the actual parameter to the corresponding formal parameter and no value is expected back from the subprogram.
out	The formal parameter acts like a local variable. Its value is assigned to the corresponding actual parameter on normal termination of the subprogram. This mode should be used when the actual parameter is to be supplied a value from the corresponding formal parameter.
in out	The formal parameter behaves like an initialized local variable. Its initial value is that of the corresponding actual On normal termination of a subprogram, the value of a formal parameter is assigned to the corresponding actual parameter. This mode is used when the actual parameter supplies a value to the corresponding formal parameter and it in turn is supplied a value by the formal parameter on normal termination of the subprogram.

The formal parameters of a function must all have the mode **in**. (The intent of this restriction is to discourage the definition of functions with side effects; however, global variables can still be changed to produce side effects.)

---

17. These modes are known in the computer science literature [GRI71, PRA75] as *value*, *result* and *value result* respectively.

5.2 Examples of Subprograms

5.2.1 Swap: The following procedure subprogram swaps or interchanges the values of two floating point variables:

```
procedure SWAP(X, Y: in out FLOAT) is
    T: FLOAT;   ——temporary variable
begin
    T := X;
    X := Y;
    Y := T;
end SWAP;
```

5.2.2 Square Root by Newton's Method: Function SQRT calculates the positive square root of a floating point real using Newton's method. The $k+1^{th}$ approximation a_{k+1} to the square root of a value X is given by the iterative formula

$$a_{k+1} = 0.5 \ (a_k + \frac{X}{a_k})$$

The iteration is stopped when the absolute difference between two successive approximations of the square root is less than EPS, which is a very small positive number. SQRT uses subtypes NON_NEGATIVE_REAL and POS_REAL declared as

```
subtype NON_NEGATIVE_REAL
                is FLOAT range 0.0 .. FLOAT'LAST;
subtype POS_REAL
                is FLOAT range FLOAT'SMALL .. FLOAT'LAST;
```

NON_NEGATIVE_REAL values are values of type FLOAT $\geqslant 0.0$ while POS_REAL values are $\geqslant$ the smallest positive (non-zero) model number associated with FLOAT.

```
function SQRT(X: in NON_NEGATIVE_REAL;
              EPS: in POS_REAL := 0.001) return FLOAT is

        --only floating point numbers ≥ 0.0 are accepted,
        --the positive square root is returned with the specified
        --accuracy EPS, which has a default value of 0.001

    OLD_VALUE: FLOAT;
        --the kth approximation of the square root
    NEW_VALUE: FLOAT;
        --the k+1th approximation of the square root
begin
    OLD_VALUE := 0.0;     --just some value to go through the loop;
    NEW_VALUE := X/2.0; --the initial guess

    while abs (NEW_VALUE−OLD_VALUE) > EPS loop
        OLD_VALUE := NEW_VALUE;
        NEW_VALUE := 0.5 * (OLD_VALUE + X/OLD_VALUE);
    end loop;

    return NEW_VALUE;
end SQRT;
```

5.2.3 Matrix Addition: The operator +, which denotes integer and real addition, will now be extended so that it also represents matrix addition. This example illustrates the use of an unconstrained array type as the type of a formal parameter and *operator overloading*. The unconstrained array type allows arrays of different sizes to be passed as actual parameters to a subprogram. Operator overloading is the declaration of an operator with operand types other than the built-in ones.

Matrix addition will be declared for matrices of the unconstrained array type MATRIX, which was defined earlier as

```
type MATRIX is array
          (INTEGER range <>, INTEGER range <>) of FLOAT;
```

The overloaded + is declared as

```
function "+"(X, Y: MATRIX) return MATRIX is

    --Matrices X and Y can have any bounds but they must
    --be the same for matrix addition. This requirement could be
    --checked explicitly in the subprogram.
    --The mode of the formal parameters has not been specified and
    --is assumed to be in by default. This mode is the only
    --one allowed for formal parameters of a function.

    SUM: MATRIX(X'FIRST..X'LAST, X'FIRST(2)..X'LAST(2));
        --note how the bounds of SUM are supplied
begin
    for I in X'RANGE(1) loop
        for J in X'RANGE(2) loop
            --for loop variables are implicitly declared
            SUM(I, J) := X(I, J) + Y(I, J);
                    --the + used here is that for FLOAT
        end loop;
    end loop;
    return SUM;
end "+";
```

In overloading + for matrix addition, the type of the elements of MATRIX does not matter as long as the operator + used inside the body of the overloaded + is defined for the element type. For example, suppose that the declaration of MATRIX is modified so that the matrix elements are now of type INTEGER instead of type FLOAT. The overloaded declaration of + remains legal for the modified type MATRIX, since + is also defined for type INTEGER.

All operators, except the membership and the short circuit operators, can be overloaded.

The declaration of the formal parameters X and Y

    X, Y: MATRIX;

could alternatively have been written as

    X: MATRIX; Y: MATRIX;

It would have been nice had Ada differentiated between these two forms of declaring unconstrained type objects—the first form, unlike the second form, could require that the bounds of the corresponding actual parameters be identical. Explicit checks to ensure that the bounds of X and Y in the declaration of + would then not be needed.

5.3 Subprogram Calls, Actual Parameters and Parameter Matching [6.4]

Subprogram calls have the form

procedure_name [(actual parameter list)];

function_name (actual parameter list) | function_name

Actual parameters may be specified in positional or named notation. Actual parameters may be given default initial values by associating the default initial values with the corresponding formal parameters. Such actual parameters may be omitted, but the named notation must then be used for the rest of the actual parameters in the subprogram call.

A procedure call is a statement by itself, e.g.,

```
SWAP(P, Q);
PUT(UPPER(CHAR));
```

A function call, on the other hand, can be used only as part of an expression, since functions return values.

```
SQRT(5.0)
        ——default value is used for the second actual
        ——parameter, i.e., 0.001; see the declaration
        ——of SQRT in section 5.2.2

SQRT(Y, 0.05) > 3.0

SQRT(EPS => 0.05, X => Y)
        ——alternative version of the above using
        ——named notation for parameters

A := B + C + D;
        ——A, B, C and D are arrays of type MATRIX
        ——with the same bounds. The + operator used here
        ——is the one overloaded for arrays of type MATRIX
```

The types of the formal and actual parameters must match exactly. In the case of parameters of a scalar type the range constraints must be satisfied. Index and discriminant constraints must be satisfied for access types. For parameters of an array type, a record or a private type with discriminants, the constraints specified for the formal parameter type must be satisfied. The bounds of an unconstrained array type formal parameter are obtained from the corresponding actual parameter.

5.4 Subprogram Overloading [6.6]

Subprogram overloading is the use of the same subprogram name for *different* subprograms. For example, in most programming languages the same name + designates the various functions used for adding different types of integers and reals. Overloading is convenient, since the user has to remember only one name for the addition functions and since it corresponds to common mathematical notation. A programming language should also allow users to overload subprograms, particularly if a user is allowed to define new types. For example, it would be nice if the operator + could be overloaded to represent addition of user-defined types such as complex, rational and polynomial.

Ideally the same name should be used for subprograms that are similar in some important ways, e.g., they use the same abstract algorithm but differ in details such as the type and number of their parameters. It would be bad practice to use the same name for subprograms that implement significantly different ideas. For example, it would not be good style to use the name MAX both for a function that computes the maximum value of a real array and a function that determines a value occurring the maximum number of times in an array of strings. However, it makes sense to use the name MAX for functions that compute the maximum values of real, integer and character arrays, and so on.

Ada allows the user to overload subprogram names. Overloading a subprogram hides the subprogram being overloaded if it and the new subprogram have *identical* specifications. Two subprograms have identical specifications if both subprograms have the same

- name,
- number of parameters,
- types (actually *base* types) for the corresponding parameters and
- result type (in case of function subprograms only).

A call to an overloaded subprogram name is illegal if it is ambiguous, i.e., if it cannot be decided exactly to which one of the overloaded subprograms it refers. Such ambiguities can be resolved in several ways, such as prefixing the name of the subprogram by the name of the *package* it is contained in or by *renaming* it.

6. Visibility Rules [8]

The discussion of the visibility of entities in this section refers mainly to identifiers (variable names, subprogram names and so on) but also to literals, enumeration values and other entities.

A *declaration* associates an identifier with a program entity such as a variable, type definition, subprogram or formal parameter. An entity can be declared in several ways, such as in

- the declarative part of a subprogram, block or a package,
- a package specification,
- a record as one of its components,
- a subprogram formal parameter,
- in a loop implicitly as a loop parameter (simply by the occurrence of an identifier in the loop heading).

6.1 Scope of Entities [8.2]

The *scope* of an entity is the region of the program text where its declaration is in effect. The scope of

1. an entity declared in a block, subprogram or task extends from the declaration to the end of the block, subprogram or task.

2. an entity declared in the visible part of a package declaration extends to the scope of the package declaration, which includes the rest of the package specification and the package body. On the other hand, the scope of an entity declared in the *private part* of a package extends to the end of the package specification and the package body.

3. an entry in a task declaration extends from its declaration to the end of the scope of the task declaration. It includes the task body.

4. a record component extends from its declaration to the end of the scope of the record definition.

5. a loop parameter extends from its first occurrence to the end of the associated loop.

6. the scope of a parameter (including a generic parameter) extends from its declaration to the end of the scope it is declared in.

(Only the first item of this list is directly relevant to this chapter; the remaining items are included to make the discussion complete.)

6.2 Visibility of Entities

The scope of entities with the same identifier can overlap as a result of overloading of subprograms and enumeration literals, nesting and so on. Ada *program units* such as subprogram, tasks and packages along with statements and blocks can be nested. Ada's visibility rules for entities are similar to those of Algol 60. In addition, Ada provides the user with a mechanism to control visibility to some degree.

An entity is said to be *directly visible* if the entity can be referred to directly by using the identifier associated with it. If the entity is not directly visible, then context can sometimes be added to make it directly visible. For example, a component C of a package P can be made visible in the context in which the package P is visible by using the *selected component notation* P.C for it.

An identifier associated with an entity for which overloading is not possible (e.g., variables, constants, loop parameters and labels) is *hidden* in an inner construct if the inner construct contains an entity with the same identifier. Within the inner construct, the hidden outer entity is not directly visible. An entity that can be overloaded is said to be *hidden* in an inner construct when the inner construct contains a declaration for another entity with the same identifier and with identical specifications. For example, a subprogram, which can be overloaded, is hidden in an inner construct only when a subprogram with an identical specification is declared in the inner constructs.

Enumeration literals are treated like parameterless functions in determining the visibility of entities. Consequently, an enumeration literal may hide a parameterless function and vice versa.

The following program segment illustrates the difference between the visibility rules for entities that can be overloaded and those that cannot:

```
procedure P is
    A, B: FLOAT;
    procedure Y is ... end Y;
    procedure Q is
        A: INTEGER;
        function B return INTEGER is ... end B;
        procedure Y(X: FLOAT) is ... end Y;
    begin
        --variables A and B of the outer procedure P are
        --not directly visible here, because Q contains entities
        --with the same identifier; however, they can be referred to
        --using the selected component notation P.A and P.B;
        --procedure Y, declared outside Q, is visible, because the
        --procedure Y inside Q has a different specification
        .
        .
    end Q;
        .
        .
begin
        .
        .
end P;
```

6.3 Making Package Components Directly Visible

If a package is visible at a given point in a program, then its components are also visible at that point, using the selected component notation. The *use* clause can be used to make the components of such a package directly visible.

Use clauses do not result in an identifier being hidden, although they may cause overloading of an identifier. If an entity cannot be made visible by means of a *use* clause (because a similar entity is already directly visible), then the selected component notation must be used. In case of overloading, identifiers made visible are considered only if a valid interpretation of the program cannot be found without them.

6.4 Renaming Entities [8.5]

Ada provides a facility, the *renaming declaration*, for giving an alternative name to an entity. Both the original name and the new name can be used to refer to the renamed entity. Renaming can be used to resolve name conflicts (e.g., those caused by overloading) and for convenient abbreviations.

For example, a procedure or function can be given another name. The procedure TEXT_IO.PUT for writing character values to the standard output is renamed PUT for convenience in using the declaration

> **procedure** PUT(A: CHARACTER) **renames** TEXT_IO.PUT;
> --shorthand notation for PUT

The operator +, overloaded for matrix addition, can be renamed MATRIX_SUM by the declaration

> **function** MATRIX_SUM(X, Y: **in** MATRIX) **return** MATRIX
> **renames** "+";

The statement

> A := B + C + D;

where A, B, C and D are all arrays of type MATRIX having the same bounds can now also be written as

> A := MATRIX_SUM(D, MATRIX_SUM(B, C));

Operators can be renamed as functions and vice versa. A function corresponding to a unary operator must have exactly one formal parameter while a function corresponding to a binary operator must have exactly two formal parameters.

7. Input/Output [14]

General high level input and output facilities are provided by the predefined packages SEQUENTIAL_IO, DIRECT_IO and TEXT_IO. They define the file types, file *modes* and file operations. SEQUENTIAL_IO and DIRECT_IO, which are generic, are used to interface with files in binary format. TEXT_IO is used to read from or write to a text file, i.e., a file represented as a sequences of characters. (Text files, unlike binary files, are human readable.) A package, named LOW_LEVEL_IO, is also provided for controlling peripheral devices directly.

An *external* [14.1] file is anything external to a program that can produce or receive a value. It is identified by a *name*, which is a string. System dependent characteristics of a file, such as its *access rights* and its physical organization, are given by a second string, called the *form*. An external file cannot be operated upon directly. An *internal* file object (called simply a file unless there is an ambiguity) must first be created and then associated with an external file. It is this internal file which is used in performing file operations, such as reading from or writing to the associated external file. Files, both internal and external, are homogeneous objects, i.e., they contain only elements of the same type.

7.1 Direct and Sequential Files [14.2]

Two kinds of access to external files are supported—direct and sequential. A file that is used for direct access is called a *direct* file. (Of course, the associated external file must reside on a medium that supports direct access, e.g, a disk.) Such a file is viewed as a set of elements occupying consecutive positions in a linear order. Elements at arbitrary positions can be accessed and updated. The position of an element is given by its index. The index of the first element, if any, is one. The number of elements in a file is called is its *current size*. A direct access file can have one of three modes—read only (IN_FILE), write only (OUT_FILE) and read/write (INOUT_FILE).

An internal file object used for sequential access is called a *sequential* file. Elements in a sequential file cannot be accessed by position; they must be accessed sequentially. Unlike direct access files, sequential files can have only two modes—read only (IN_FILE) and write only (OUT_FILE).

7.1.1 Using Direct and Sequential Files: Files with elements of type T are declared and used in a subprogram (or a package) in the following manner:

1. Specify the appropriate generic input/output package that the subprogram (or package) is to be compiled with, by using a *with* statement, e.g.,

   with SEQUENTIAL_IO;

2. Instantiate the generic input/output package for elements of type T, e.g.,

package T_IO **is**
      new SEQUENTIAL_IO(ELEMENT_TYPE => T);

Package T_IO contains the declaration of type FILE_TYPE (which is used for declaring files with elements of type T), modes applicable to sequential files, (i.e., IN_FILE and OUT_FILE) and operations for sequential files with elements of type T.

3. Create internal files of type T_IO.FILE_TYPE. For example,

    A, B: T_IO.FILE_TYPE;

declares A and B to be internal files with elements of type T.

4. Establish the connection between the internal and external files by opening an existing external file or creating a new one; the mode of the internal file is specified at the same time, e.g.,

    T_IO.OPEN(A, IN_FILE, "student.grades");
      ––associates file A with an existing external file
      ––"student.grades" from which values can be read
      ––but not written to

    T_IO.CREATE(B, OUT_FILE, "student.statistics");
      ––associates file B with a newly created external file
      ––"student.statistics" and leaves it in an open state
      ––for writing; B is a write only file

5. Process the files, e.g., read values from A and write these or other values to B, using procedures T_IO.READ and T_IO.WRITE, e.g.,

    T_IO.READ(A, X);
      :
    T_IO.WRITE(B, Y);

where X is a variable and Y is an expression, both of type T.

6. When processing of the files is complete, connection between external and internal files is severed by closing the internal files using the operation T_IO.CLOSE, e.g.,

    T_IO.CLOSE(A);
    T_IO.CLOSE(B);

7. The need for explicitly prefixing entities provided by package T_IO can be avoided (except in case of ambiguity) by giving a *use* clause of the form

    use T_IO;

For example, operation

T_IO.CLOSE(A);

can now be written simply as

CLOSE(A);

7.2 Direct and Sequential File Operations

An instantiation of DIRECT_IO and SEQUENTIAL_IO makes the following file management operations available for the file type provided by the instantiation:

procedures	functions
CREATE	MODE
OPEN	NAME
CLOSE	FORM
DELETE	IS_OPEN
RESET	

7.2.1 Additional Sequential File Operations [14.2.2]: In addition to file management operations, an instantiation of SEQUENTIAL_IO also makes the following operations available:

procedures	functions
READ	END_OF_FILE
WRITE	

7.2.2 Additional Direct File Operations [14.2.4]: In addition to the file management operations, an instantiation of DIRECT_IO also makes the following operations available:

procedures	functions
READ	INDEX
WRITE	SIZE
SET_INDEX	END_OF_FILE

7.3 Text Files [14.3]

Package TEXT_IO provides file management operations (similar to those provided by DIRECT_IO and SEQUENTIAL_IO), operations for default input and output file manipulation, input and output operations, and layout control operations.

TEXT_IO provides procedures GET and PUT for reading and writing, instead of READ and WRITE as provided by DIRECT_IO and SEQUENTIAL_IO. GET and PUT do the necessary conversions between the internal representation of a value and its character representation on the text file. Only one item at a time, can be input or output by means of GET and PUT (READ and WRITE also operate on one item at a time). GET and PUT must be called an appropriate number of times, if more than one item is to be input or output.

Procedures GET and PUT are overloaded for types CHARACTER and STRING. To get versions of GET and PUT, for enumeration types, integers and reals, appropriate generic packages, provided in TEXT_IO, must be instantiated. GET and PUT are also overloaded, for numeric and enumeration types, so that an item can also be read from or written to a string (instead of a file). If a file name is not specified, when using GET or PUT, then by default, *standard input* and *standard output* files are used. These files are associated with the appropriate external files by an Ada implementation.

Logically, a text file may be viewed as a sequence of pages, a page as a sequence of lines, and a line as a sequence of characters. The ends of a file, page and line are marked by a *file terminator*, a *page terminator* and a *line terminator*, respectively. Terminators can be generated and recognized by appropriate subprograms, e.g., NEW_LINE and END_OF_FILE. Terminators are implementation dependent and their exact nature need concern only users interested in the input and output of control characters.

Facilities provided by TEXT_IO are now summarized:

1. File management operations

2. Function END_OF_FILE

3. Character input and output operations

4. String input and output operations (a string read using GET or written using PUT can span several lines; procedures GET_LINE and PUT_LINE read and write whole lines)

5. Generic package INTEGER_IO

6. Generic package FLOAT_IO

7. Generic package FIXED_IO

8. Generic package ENUMERATION_IO

9. Default input and output file manipulation operations

10. Layout control operations

11. Exceptions

Operations provided for default input and output file manipulation are

procedures	functions
SET_INPUT	STANDARD_INPUT
SET_OUTPUT	STANDARD_OUTPUT
	CURRENT_INPUT
	CURRENT_OUTPUT

Operations provided for layout control are

procedures	functions
SET_LINE_LENGTH	LINE_LENGTH
SET_PAGE_LENGTH	PAGE_LENGTH
NEW_LINE	END_OF_LINE
SKIP_LINE	END_OF_PAGE
NEW_PAGE	COL
SKIP_PAGE	LINE
SET_COL	PAGE
SET_LINE	

7.3.1 Using Text Files: The use and manipulation of text files is now summarized. TEXT_IO is made available to subprograms and packages compiled separately by prefixing them with

with TEXT_IO;

Text file operations and objects need not be qualified by TEXT_IO provided the following *use* clause has been given (assuming there is no ambiguity):

use TEXT_IO;

Text files are used in a manner similar to direct and sequential files. Package TEXT_IO, unlike DIRECT_IO and SEQUENTIAL_IO, is not generic and is therefore not instantiated. After declaring internal files, they are associated with external files by creating a new external file or opening an existing one. Text files are sequential files; consequently, only two modes are applicable to them—read only (IN_FILE) and write only (OUT_FILE).

TEXT_IO provides operations GET and PUT, instead of READ and WRITE. GET and PUT for character and string values are directly available, while for integers, reals and enumeration (including boolean) types, they are obtained by appropriately instantiating the generic packages INTEGER_IO, FLOAT_IO, FIXED_IO and ENUMERATION_IO.

Assuming the above *use* clause has been given, GET and PUT for INTEGER and COLOR types are made available by the declarations

package IO_INTEGER **is new** INTEGER_IO(INTEGER);
package IO_COLOR **is new** ENUMERATION_IO(COLOR);

The *use* clause

use IO_INTEGER, IO_COLOR;

obviates the need to prefix GET and PUT for types INTEGER and COLOR by IO_INTEGER and IO_COLOR.

7.4 Interactive Input

One problem area is interactive input in which Ada suffers from a problem similar to that in Pascal [FEU82]. For example, use of the paradigm

while not END_OF_FILE(STANDARD_INPUT) **loop**
    Request data from user
    Read data
    :
    :
end loop;

to read input interactively from a terminal causes trouble. Function END_OF_FILE cannot be evaluated when there is no data, since it cannot be determined whether the data has been exhausted or that the data has not been supplied as yet. Consequently, evaluation of END_OF_FILE will be delayed until the user supplies the data—but the user has no way of knowing that the program is waiting for the data because the prompt will not be printed.

This problem can be avoided by using the following paradigm [GEHA83a] that uses the exception END_ERROR which is raised when an attempt is made to read past the end of file:

begin
>   ——begin a block so that the end of file exception
>   ——END_ERROR can be handled locally
> **loop**
>   Request data from user
>   Read data
>   ——this requires that either the data or an
>   ——indication of end of the file be supplied; in case
>   ——of an end of file, the END_ERROR exception is
>   ——raised by the read operation and control transfers
>   ——to the exception handler following the loop
>   .
>   .
>   .
> **end loop;**
> **exception**
>   **when** END_ERROR **=> null;**
>   ——the exception handler does nothing. Execution
>   ——of the block terminates.
>   ——Note the use of a *null* statement—at least
>   ——one statement is required in an exception handler
>   ——by the Ada syntax.
> **end;**

This solution is inelegant since it requires the use of an exception and enclosure of the program segment reading the data in a *begin* block (so that the exception can be handled locally) and the use of a null exception handler.

A better solution [WET83] that avoids the above problems is

> **loop**
>   Request data from user
>   **exit when** END_OF_FILE(STANDARD_INPUT);
>   Read data
>   .
>   .
>   .
> **end loop;**

8. Main Programs and Compilation Units

Any complete subprogram can be a *main program* in Ada. This philosophy is different from that adopted by most languages, such as FORTRAN, Pascal or PL/I, but is similar to that adopted by LISP. The main program will be executed from the command line in the environment, provided by an operating system, to support the development and execution of Ada programs. The main program must of course be prefixed by all the contextual information, such as the names of *compilation units*, necessary for its execution.

A main program can be a procedure or a function subprogram. If it is a procedure, then the result of executing the main program will be the side effects of the procedure, such as the creation of output on external files. If the main program is a function then the result of executing the main program will be the function result. A main program can have formal parameters. The corresponding actual parameters must be supplied on the command line using the notation specified by the environment in which the Ada program is being executed.

A program in Ada is a collection of one or more compilation units. A compilation unit is a declaration or a body of a subprogram or a package prefixed by any necessary *contextual information.* The contextual information consists of *with* and *use* clauses. The *with* clauses specify the compilation units required for the successful compilation of the declaration or body of the subprogram or the package. These compilation units must have been compiled before (or be predefined) since the *with* clauses specify dependencies between compilation units. The *use* clauses make the entities inside the specified compilation units directly visible inside the declaration or body that is being compiled.

9. Pragmas [2.8]

Pragmas are instructions (suggestions in some cases) to the compiler. For example, an Ada compiler can be instructed to pack arrays or records as densely as possible. Pragmas may be used to tune the behavior of the compiler so that it best meets the needs of the programmer. Suppose subprogram SWAP is being called repeatedly from a program segment whose execution speed is critical:

```
loop
   .
   .
   SWAP(A, B);
   .
   .
end loop;
```

The overhead associated with calling and returning from SWAP can be eliminated if the programmer replaces the call to SWAP by its body. Obliterating logical modularity, as represented by subprogram SWAP, in favor of execution speed is not desirable, since it makes a program less readable, less understandable and less modifiable. Logical modularity can be retained without sacrificing execution speed by having the compiler, instead of the programmer, make the replacement. Pragma INLINE instructs the compiler to replace all calls of the specified subprogram by its body:

pragma INLINE(SWAP);   --replace calls to the subprogram
                                --SWAP by a copy of its body

A pragma can appear after a semicolon and wherever a statement, a declaration, a clause such as *use* and *with* clause, an *alternative*, a *variant* or an *exception handler* is allowed. There are some minor restrictions on this rule that apply to all pragmas. Further restrictions are associated with specific pragmas to ensure that they appear in places where they are meaningful. Pragmas may be language-defined (Appendix B of the Ada Reference Manual) or implementation-defined (Appendix F of the Ada Reference Manual). Some more examples of pragmas are

pragma OPTIMIZE(SPACE);
                --try to optimize for space
pragma LIST(OFF);
                --suspend printing of the program listing

10. Complete Examples

Several complete examples are given to illustrate the Ada concepts presented so far. The first example, taken from mechanical engineering, illustrates a numerical iteration method. The rest of the examples, from computer science, are on topics such as sorting, matrix multiplication and polynomial evaluation.

Stepwise refinement is used to illustrate the development of examples whenever necessary. Some desirable features of a good programming methodology and suggestions for stepwise refinement are given in the Appendix. The notation P_i is used to indicate the ith refinement of the program with P_0 being the initial refinement.

10.1 Steady State Temperature Distribution

This example is a heat transfer problem taken from mechanical engineering. The problem is to find the steady state temperature distribution across the walls of the air duct (or chimney) shown in the figure given below, the inside and outside temperatures being T_IN and T_OUT.

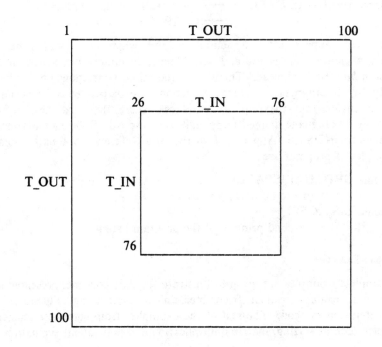

Cross Section of Duct

A heat transfer analysis of this problem reduces it to the simpler problem of solving the Laplace equation $\nabla^2 t = 0$ (t is the temperature) over the same cross section. The method used to solve the Laplace equation is Jacobi iteration (more on Jacobi method at the end of the example). It is defined as follows:

P_0:

Guess a temperature distribution for the cross section

loop

Let the temperature distribution computed in the
last iteration be the old temperature distribution
for this iteration;

Calculate the new temperature distribution from the
old one by letting the new temperature at each point
be the average of the old temperatures at the four
surrounding points

exit when the maximum absolute change in the
temperature at all the points is < EPS

end loop;

where 0.0 < EPS << 1.0 is the desired accuracy of the result.

In the Ada program, arrays of size 100×100 are used (i.e., indices will have
values between 1 and 100) to represent the duct; the array REGION is defined
as

REGION(I, J) has the value TRUE if the point I, J
is inside the duct boundaries and FALSE otherwise

Array REGION simplifies testing to determine whether or not a point is within
the duct boundaries. The boundary temperatures are constant and it is not
necessary to visit points on the boundaries. Exclusion of the outside boundary
points is achieved easily by simply looping between 2 and 99 inclusive.
Consequently, REGION will be defined only for points I and J between the
limits 2 and 99.

Instead of comparing the complete old and new temperature distributions to
compute the maximum absolute temperature change at any point, this change
will be computed on a continuing basis every time a new temperature at a point
is computed. The abstract instruction *Calculate the new temperature
distribution from the old* ... in the above algorithm is therefore refined as

```
    MAX_CHANGE := 0.0;
    for all points I, J in REGION loop
        New temperature at point I, J is the average of the
        old temperatures at the four surrounding points;

        Let the new value of MAX_CHANGE be the maximum of the
        old value of MAX_CHANGE and the absolute difference
        between the old and new temperatures at the point I, J
    end loop;
```

The instruction **exit when** *the maximum* ... can now be refined as

```
    exit when MAX_CHANGE < EPS;
```

The Ada main program based on the above algorithm and refinements is

```
with TEXT_IO;
        --the string I/O routines, the generic FLOAT, INTEGER
        --packages and other I/O routines become available

use TEXT_IO;      --the above routines no longer need to be
                  --qualified by TEXT_IO


procedure DUCT_TEMPERATURE is

    package IO_FLOAT is new FLOAT_IO(FLOAT);
            --instantiation of the generic FLOAT package
    package IO_INTEGER is new INTEGER_IO(INTEGER);
            --instantiation of the generic INTEGER package
    use IO_FLOAT, IO_INTEGER;
            --GET and PUT for FLOAT and INTEGER are now
            --directly visible



    subtype OUTSIDE is INTEGER range 1..100;
            --outside dimension of the duct
    type DUCT is array(OUTSIDE, OUTSIDE) of FLOAT;

    IN_TEMP, OUT_TEMP, EPS, MAX_CHANGE: FLOAT;
    OLD_TEMP, NEW_TEMP: DUCT;
                --contain the old and the new temperature
                --distributions in the duct
    REGION: constant array(2..99, 2..99) of BOOLEAN :=
            (2..25  => (2..99 => TRUE),
            26..75 => (26..75 => FALSE, 2..25 | 76..99 => TRUE),
            76..99 => (2..99 => TRUE));
```

     --note the elegant use of an array aggregate

     --the aggregate could not have been written as
     --(26..75 => (26..75 => FALSE), **others** => TRUE),
     --since (1) a two-dimensional array aggregate must be
     --written as a list of one-dimensional array values and
     --(2) the choice **others** can be used only in an
     --aggregate if its type has been explicitly supplied.

function MAX(A, B: **in** FLOAT) **return** FLOAT **is**
begin
  if A < B **then return** B; **else return** A; **end if**;

  --The above style has been used for the *if* statement
  --instead of the style usually used, as shown below, because
  --of its small size. Style should not be rigid; it should
  --be flexible to suit needs
  --
  -- **if** A < B **then**
  --   **return** B;
  -- **else**
  --   **return** A;
  -- **end if**;

end MAX;

begin

  --Read in the boundary temperatures and the result accuracy

  PUT("What is the inside temperature?"); NEW_LINE;
  GET(IN_TEMP);

  PUT("What is the outside temperature?"); NEW_LINE;
  GET(OUT_TEMP);

  PUT("What is the desired accuracy?"); NEW_LINE;
  GET(EPS);

  --initialize NEW_TEMP to the guessed temperature
  --the boundaries are initialized to the specified temperatures
  --and the inside region to the average of the two boundary
  --temperatures

```
for I in OUTSIDE loop
   for J in OUTSIDE loop
      if I = OUTSIDE'FIRST
           or I = OUTSIDE'LAST
           or J = OUTSIDE'FIRST
           or J = OUTSIDE'LAST then
         NEW_TEMP(I, J) := OUT_TEMP;
            --outside boundary points
      elsif REGION(I, J) then
         NEW_TEMP(I, J) := (IN_TEMP + OUT_TEMP) / 2.0;
                                 --inside region
      else
         NEW_TEMP(I, J) := IN_TEMP;
            --points on inside boundary and within it;
            --the array points enclosed by the inside boundary
            --will never be used
      end if;
   end loop;
end loop;

--compute the steady state temperature distribution

loop
   OLD_TEMP := NEW_TEMP;
                  --ready for next iteration
                  --note use of array assignment
   MAX_CHANGE := 0.0;
            --maximum change for any of the points
            --examined up to now
   for I in OUTSIDE'FIRST+1 .. OUTSIDE'LAST-1 loop
      for J in OUTSIDE'FIRST+1 .. OUTSIDE'LAST-1 loop
         if REGION(I, J) then
            NEW_TEMP(I, J) := (OLD_TEMP(I-1, J) +
                  OLD_TEMP(I+1, J) +
                  OLD_TEMP(I, J-1) +
                  OLD_TEMP(I, J+1)) /4.0;
            MAX_CHANGE := MAX(MAX_CHANGE,
                  abs (NEW_TEMP(I, J)-OLD_TEMP(I, J)));
         end if;
      end loop;
   end loop;

   exit when MAX_CHANGE < EPS;
end loop;
```

--Print the final version of the temperature distribution
--Identify each new row

```
for I in OUTSIDE loop
   PUT("ROW"); PUT(I);
   NEW_LINE;
            --default value of 1 is used for the actual
            --parameter in the call to NEW_LINE

   for J in OUTSIDE loop
      PUT(NEW_TEMP(I, J));
   end loop;

   NEW_LINE(2);
   end loop;
end DUCT_TEMPERATURE;
```

The initialization of the array NEW_TEMP to the guessed temperature could alternatively have been written using an aggregate:

```
NEW_TEMP :=
   (1 | 100 => (1..100 => OUT_TEMP),
            --top and bottom boundaries
   26..75 => (26..75 => IN_TEMP, 1 | 100 => OUT_TEMP,
               2..25 | 76..99 => (OUT_TEMP + IN_TEMP)/2.0),
            --rows that include the inside boundary and
            --points within it

   2..25 | 76..99 => (1 | 100 => OUT_TEMP,
                      2..99 => (OUT_TEMP + IN_TEMP)/2.0));
            --the rest of the points
```

This initialization will probably be implemented more efficiently than the previous one, because the control flow is not explicitly specified and this gives more freedom to the compiler in generating code. Moreover, this initialization does not contain any explicit tests. Deciding which initialization is more readable is left to the reader.

The Jacobi iteration method always converges. New values (temperatures in this example) at the points are not used until the next iteration. In a variation of this method, called the Gauss-Seidel method, new values are used as soon as they are computed. The Gauss-Seidel method converges twice as fast as the Jacobi method, but there are situations in which the Gauss-Seidel method will not converge [DAH74]. The Gauss-Seidel method requires less storage, since only one array of values is needed.

10.2 The Mode of a Sorted Array

The problem is to write a subprogram that determines the most frequently occurring value, called the *mode*, of a sorted integer array. The frequency of the mode is also to be computed. The elegant algorithm used to compute the mode is based on the following observation made by Griffiths (in [GRI75]).

Let A be a sorted one dimensional array with a lower bound L and an upper bound U. The frequency of the mode, MF, of the slice $A(L..I-1)$ will be different from the frequency of the mode of the slice $A(L..I)$, only if $A(I)=A(I-1)$ and all the elements of the slice $A(I-MF..I-1)$ are equal. These conditions imply that

$$A(I) = A(I-1) = ... = A(I-MF)$$

and this relationship is true if and only if $A(I)=A(I-MF)$, since A is sorted. Therefore the frequency of the mode of $A(L..I)$ is MF+1, since there are now MF+1 equal elements of A.

The mode of a sorted array is computed by the procedure MODE, which is declared as

```
procedure MODE(A: in INT_VECTOR; MF, MV: out INTEGER) is
              --Assuming that A has at least one element,
              --MV will contain the mode of A on return and
              --MF will contain the frequency of MV on return

    L: constant INTEGER := A'FIRST;
    U: constant INTEGER := A'LAST;
       --array bounds do not have to be passed, since
       --they can be determined using attributes
    I: INTEGER;
begin
   MV := A(L);
   MF := 1;
   I := L+1;
   while I <= U loop
      if A(I) = A(I-MF) then
         MF := MF + 1;
         MV := A(I);
      end if;
      I := I+1;
   end loop;
end MODE;
```

The type INT_VECTOR used in procedure MODE is an unconstrained array type:

> **type** INT_VECTOR **is array** (INTEGER **range** $<>$) **of** INTEGER;

This algorithm is linear, i.e., every element of the sorted array is examined exactly once in computing the mode.[18]

10.3 The Towers of Hanoi

There are three rods X, Y and Z and there are N disks, all of different sizes. These disks are stacked up in decreasing order of size, like a tower, on rod X.

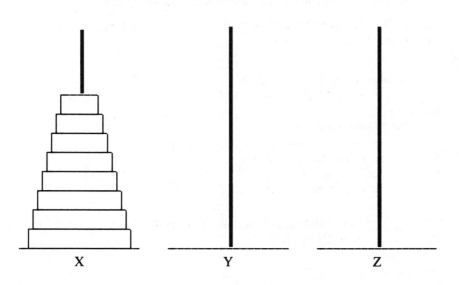

The Towers of Hanoi

The problem is to move these disks from rod X to rod Y so that they also end

18. The algorithm to compute the mode can be made sublinear on the average, i.e., not all elements of the array need be examined to compute the mode. The variable I is incremented by MF when $A(I) \neq A(I-MF)$ and then the array A is scanned backward from the element $A(I)$ to find the beginning of the sequence of elements equal to $A(I-MF)$. Computation of the new mode is resumed from this point. This improvement was suggested by John P. Linderman, a colleague at Bell Labs, and several others. Modifications, leading to improvements faster than the linear backward scan improvement, have also been suggested.

up in a decreasing size order on Y. Rod Z can be used as a temporary holding place. Only one disk can be moved at a time. Any disk may be placed on an empty rod but only a smaller disk can be placed on top of another disk. (The disks must never be placed on the ground.) The program is to read in the number of disks and print a series of move instructions.

The basic algorithm that generates the moves is

P_0

      move N$-$1 disks from X to Z using Y as temporary storage
      move the Nth disk from X to Y directly
      move N$-$1 disks from Z to Y using X as temporary storage

This algorithm is recursive and is further refined to include the termination condition and some more details.

P_1:

```
procedure Hanoi(N, X, Y, Z) is
      ——move N disks from X to Y using Z as temporary storage
begin
   if N /= 0 then
      ——move N−1 disks from X to Z using Y
        Hanoi(N−1, X, Z, Y)

      Move disk N from X to Y

      ——move N−1 disks from Z to Y using X
        Hanoi(N−1, Z, Y, X)
   end if;
end
```

The *Principle of Induction* is used to show that this algorithm works. To show that a proposition P is true for all values of $n \geqslant 0$, the The Principle of Induction states that it must be shown that

1.   P is true for n = 0.

2.   P is true for n = k by assuming P is true for n = k$-$1.

Using the Principle of Induction it is fairly easy to show that procedure Hanoi works for all positive values of N. Clearly it works for N = 0, because it does nothing. Assume that it moves k$-$1 disks correctly. To move k disks from X to Y Hanoi first moves k$-$1 disks from X to Z. Then it moves the k^{th} disk from X to Y. Finally, Hanoi moves the k$-$1 disks on Z to X. Thus the k disks are correctly moved from X to Y and by the Principle of Induction we conclude that Hanoi works correctly for all values of N that are positive.

The complete program (including a main program) is

```
with TEXT_IO; use TEXT_IO;
procedure TOWERS_OF_HANOI is

    package IO_INTEGER is new INTEGER_IO(INTEGER);
    use IO_INTEGER;

    NUMBER_OF_DISKS: NATURAL;
        --NATURAL is a subtype of INTEGER representing integer
        --values ⩾0

    procedure HANOI(N: NATURAL; X, Y, Z: CHARACTER) is
        --move N disks from X to Y using Z as temporary storage
    begin
      if N /= 0 then

            --move the top N−1 disks to Z using Y
            --as a temporary holder
              HANOI(N−1, X, Z, Y);

            --output the move instruction
              PUT("Move disk "); PUT(N);
              PUT(" from "); PUT(X); PUT(" to "); PUT(Y);
              NEW_LINE;

            --move the N−1 disks on Z to Y using X
            --as the temporary holder this time
              HANOI(N−1, Z, Y, X);
      end if;
    end HANOI;

    begin

      PUT("How many disks have to be moved?"); NEW_LINE;
      GET(NUMBER_OF_DISKS);
      HANOI(NUMBER_OF_DISKS, 'X', 'Y', 'Z');

    end TOWERS_OF_HANOI;
```

10.4 Insertion Sort

Using insertion sort,[19] write a procedure to sort nonnull arrays of type *vector* in nondecreasing order. Sorting an array A, with L and U being its lower and upper bounds (L $\leqslant$ U), results in $A_L \leqslant A_{L+1} \leqslant \cdots \leqslant A_{U-1} \leqslant A_U$ with the new values of the array A being a permutation of its old values.[20]

Type VECTOR is declared as the unconstrained array type

    type VECTOR **is array**(INTEGER **range** <>) **of** FLOAT;

The program is developed as follows:

P_0:   Sort array A

Pictorially, the state of array A at different stages of the insertion sorting process can be depicted as shown below:

Initially,

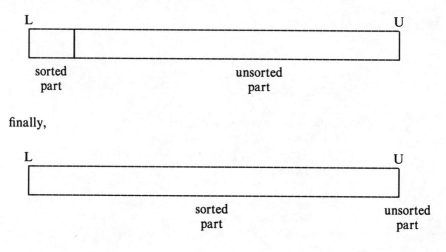

finally,

and at some intermediate stage

---

19. The third volume of D. E. Knuth's encyclopedic series titled *The Art of Computer Programming* [KNU73] contains an exhaustive discussion of various sorting algorithms and their performance.

20. Without the permutation requirement, changing the value of the array A such as assigning 0.0 to every element suffices, since the ordering condition $A_L \leqslant A_{L+1}...$ is then satisfied.

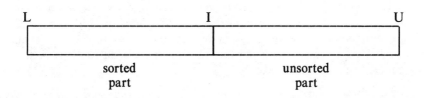

sorted
part

unsorted
part

The insertion sort algorithm can be stated abstractly as

P_1:

    I := L; --A(L..I) is (trivially) sorted so far
    while I /= U **loop**
       Extend sorted portion to include A(I+1)
       I := I+1;
    end loop;

A(L..I) is sorted represents the *loop invariant.*[21] It is true initially, since I is equal to L and the one element slice A(L..L) is trivially sorted. Upon termination of the loop I = U implying that A(L..U), i.e., the whole array, is sorted. It must be shown that the loop body leaves the loop invariant unchanged and for this the reader is referred to [DIJ76] and [CON73].

The abstract instruction *Extend sorted portion to include A(I+1)* of the refinement P_1 is refined as

    T := A(I+1);
    Shift all elements of A(L..I) > T one place to the right so that
       A(L..J−1) <= T and A(J+1..I+1) > T
    A(J) := T;

The second statement of the above refinement *Shift all elements ...* is refined as

    J := I+1;   --A(J+1..I+1) > T
    while A(J−1) > T **loop**
       Shift A(J−1) to the right
       J := J−1;
    end loop;

---

21. A loop invariant is a property that can be shown to be true before a loop is entered, true just before and after each time the loop body is executed, and true after the loop has terminated. Properly selected loop invariants can be used to demonstrate the correctness of programs containing loops. They also enhance program readability and understandability.

The condition A(J+1..I+1) > T is vacuously true prior to execution of the loop, since J = I+1 implies that the set of elements represented by A(J+1..I+1) is empty. On termination of the loop A(J+1..I+1) > T and A(J−1) <= T. This, along with the fact that at the start of the loop A(L..I) was sorted, leads to A(L..J−1) <= T.

The boolean expression in the above loop will lead to a *subscript out of range* error when J = L. When J = L we will have shifted all the elements one place to the right and the loop should terminate. So the boolean expression in the above loop is modified to use the short circuit operator **and then**, leading to

J /= L **and then** A(J−1) > T

The statement *Shift A(J−1) to the right* is refined as

A(J) := A(J−1);

Collecting all the refinements together and adding the appropriate procedure heading, and variable and constant declarations, we get the final version of INSERTION_SORT:

```
procedure INSERTION_SORT(A: in out VECTOR) is

    I, J: A'RANGE;
    T: FLOAT;
    L: constant INTEGER := A'FIRST;
    U: constant INTEGER := A'LAST;

begin
    I := L;
    while I /= U loop
        T := A(I+1);
        J := I+1;
        while J /= L and then A(J−1) > T loop
            A(J) := A(J−1);
            J := J−1;
        end loop;
        A(J) := T;
        I := I+1;
    end loop;
end INSERTION_SORT;
```

10.5 Quicksort

The problem is to sort an array as described in the example on insertion sort, but this time using the quicksort technique [HOA62]. Quicksort is on the average more efficient than insertion sort [KNU73].[22]

P₀: Quicksort(A, L, U)

P₁:
      if One element **then**
            null;
      elsif Two elements **then**
          Order them
      elsif More than two elements **then**
          Partition A such that

L		J	I		U
$\leqslant$ R			R	$\geqslant$ R	

(one element in the middle)

or

L		J	I		U
$\leqslant$ R				$\geqslant$ R	

(at least one element per partition in this case)[23]

where R is an arbitrary value
from the array A

---

22. The average running time of quicksort is of the order N log N, while that of insertion sort is N². In the worst case situations, both algorithms are of order N².

23. It is necessary for each partition to have at least one element to ensure that the recursion terminates.

−−I represents the scan from left to right
−−J represents the scan from right to left

Quicksort(A, L, J);
    −−the left partition which has elements <= R
Quicksort(A, I, U);
    −−the right partition which has elements >= R

  −−the values of elements, if any, with subscripts greater
  −−than J but less than I are all equal to R and these
  −−do not need to be sorted, since they are already in
  −−the right positions

end if;

Partitioning an array A into a left part that contains elements less than or equal to R (an arbitrary value from the array A) and a right part that contains elements greater than or equal to R is based on the following algorithm. Scan A from the left (to determine the left partition) until an element A(I) that is greater than or equal to R is found. Next scan A from the right (to determine the right partition) until an element A(J) that is less than or equal to R is found. Exchange A(I) and A(J) so that they belong to the correct partitions. The scans are then moved one step forward, i.e., I is increased by 1 and J decreased by 1. If the scans have not crossed, then the scanning is resumed.

Neither scan can go past the other, because the values contained in the partition represented by the first scan stop the second scan. Initially the right scan has no elements, but the left scan will still stop provided the value R is picked from the elements of the array A. Picking R from A and using weak inequalities (i.e. $\leqslant$ and $\geqslant$ instead of < and >, respectively) guarantees that *both* scans will halt, at R if not before.

At the end of the scan, if I is equal to J, then after the exchanging of the elements[24] and the updating of I and J, the state of the array A is represented by the first of the two partitions shown above. On the other hand, had I been equal to J−1 then we would arrive at the second partition (with each partition containing one element, since at least one exchange of elements would have been performed).

---

24. No real exchange takes place when I is equal to J, since A(I) and A(J) are aliases for the same array element.

The array partitioning algorithm was described *operationally*, i.e., by giving steps implementing it. An alternative way of describing an algorithm with a loop is to give an invariant for the loop and describe how the components of the invariant are changed by the loop to achieve the desired goal. An appropriate loop invariant for the partitioning algorithm is

$$A(L..I-1) \leqslant R \text{ and } A(J+1..U) \geqslant R$$

The invariant can be represented pictorially as

L	I	J	U
$\leqslant R$	?	$\geqslant R$	

The purpose of the loop will be to increase I and decrease J while keeping the invariant true. This description of partitioning is easier to understand than the operational description which is clouded by details describing the implementation of the algorithm. Moreover, a description using a loop invariant is more flexible than operational description, since the programmer is free to implement the algorithm in any way provided it conforms to the loop invariant.[25]

The algorithm given in refinement P_1 is refined further as follows:

P_2:   The boolean expressions *One element* and *Two elements*
              are refined as

$$U - L = 0$$

          and

$$U - L = 1$$

25. For more discussion on the use of invariants in program development and reasoning about loops see *The Science of Programming* by David Gries [GRI81].

The statement *Order them* is refined as

```
if A(U) <= A(L) then
       SWAP(A(L), A(U));
end if;
```

The boolean expression *More than two elements* is refined as

$$U - L > 1$$

The statement *Partition A such that* ... is refined as

```
R := A((U+L)/2);        --R is the middle element
I := L; J := U;
              --A(L..I-1) ≤ R and A(J+1..U) ≥ R
              --this is the loop invariant
while I <= J loop
       Extend left partition by increasing I
       Extend right partition by decreasing J
       Rearrange the elements so that the loop
       invariant is restored
end loop;
```

P₃: The statement *Extend left partition* ... is refined as

```
while A(I) < R loop
   I := I+1;
end loop;       --A(I) ≥ R
```

The statement *Extend right partition* ... is refined as

```
while A(J) > R loop
   J := J-1;
end loop;       --A(J) ≤ R
```

The statement *Rearrange the elements* ... is refined as

```
if I <= J then
   SWAP(A(I), A(J));
   I := I+1;
   J := J-1;
end if;
```

Procedure SWAP used here was defined earlier. Collecting all the refinements together, we get the final version of the quicksort program:

```
procedure QUICKSORT(A: in out VECTOR) is

   L: constant A'RANGE := A'FIRST;
   U: constant A'RANGE := A'LAST;
   I, J: A'RANGE;      --I and J can contain only values
                       --that are legal subscripts of A
   R : FLOAT;

begin

   if U-L = 0 then
      null;
   elsif U-L = 1 then
      if A(U) < A(L) then
         SWAP(A(L), A(U));
      end if;
   elsif U-L > 1 then
      R := A((U+L)/2);
      I := L;
      J := U;

      --Partition array with R as the dividing element
      while I <= J loop

         while A(I) < R loop
            I := I+1;
         end loop;

         while A(J) > R loop
            J := J-1;
         end loop;

         if I <= J then
            SWAP(A(I), A(J));
            I := I+1;
            J := J-1;
         end if;

      end loop;

   QUICKSORT(A(L..J));
```

```
                    --note use of slices. A new copy of the
                    --elements is not generated for the slice
             QUICKSORT(A(I..U));

        end if;
      end QUICKSORT;
```

The first two cases of the main *if* statement in procedure QUICKSORT can be coalesced into one case:

```
      if U-L <= 1 then
        if A(U) < A(L) then
           SWAP(A(L), A(U));
        end if;
      elsif ...
```

The amount of storage used by quicksort during recursion can be reduced by sorting first the smaller of the two slices, A(L..J) and A(I..U), and then the bigger slice.

10.6 Matrix Multiplication

Write a procedure MAT_MULT that multiplies two matrices A and B and puts the result in a third matrix C. Each matrix is of the unconstrained type

```
      type MATRIX is array
             (INTEGER range < >, INTEGER range < >) of FLOAT;
```

When multiplying two matrices, say A and B, the number of columns of A must be equal to the number of rows of B. The number of rows in the matrix that will be assigned the product should equal the number of rows of A and the number of columns in it should equal the number of columns in B. For programming simplicity, it is assumed that the corresponding index subtypes of the matrices of A and B, and the result matrix match.

The initial refinement for matrix multiplication is

P_0:

```
      Check that the bounds are correct for matrix multiplication
      for I in A'RANGE(1) loop
        for J in B'RANGE(2) loop
```

$$\text{Compute } C(I, J) = \sum_{K \in A'RANGE(2)} A(I, K) \times B(K, J);$$

```
        end loop;
      end loop;
```

P_0 is refined to give the following Ada procedure:

```
procedure MAT_MULT(A, B: in MATRIX; C: out MATRIX) is
begin

    if A'FIRST(1) /= C'FIRST(1)
            or A'LAST(1) /= C'LAST(1)
            or A'FIRST(2) /= B'FIRST(1)
            or A'LAST(2) /= B'LAST(1)
            or B'FIRST(2) /= C'FIRST(2)
            or B'LAST(2) /= C'LAST(2) then
        raise ERROR;      --raising exceptions will be discussed
                          --later in the chapter on exceptions
    end if;

    for I in A'RANGE(1) loop
      for J in B'RANGE(2) loop
        C(I, J) := 0.0;
        for K in A'RANGE(2) loop
          C(I, J) := C(I, J) + A(I, K) * B(K, J);
        end loop;
      end loop;
    end loop;


    end MAT_MULT;
```

When there is an error in the bounds of the matrices, the subprogram MAT_MULT raises the exception ERROR and terminates. This error condition must be handled by the caller of MAT_MULT.

Using MAT_MULT, the multiplication operator * can be easily overloaded for matrix multiplication:

```
function "*"(A, B: in MATRIX) return MATRIX is
    C: MATRIX(A'FIRST(1)..A'LAST(1), B'FIRST(2)..B'LAST(2));
begin
    MAT_MULT(A, B, C);
    return C;
end "*";
```

10.7 Horner's Rule

The straightforward evaluation of the polynomial

$$A(x) = a_n x^n + a_{n-1} x^{n-1} + \cdots + a_1 x + a_0$$

requires at least 2n multiplications whereas evaluation by Horner's rule requires only n multiplications [AHO75]. Horner's rule is given by the following evaluation scheme:

$$A(x) = (...((a_n x + a_{n-1})x + a_{n-2})x + \cdots + a_1)x + a_0$$

Evaluation of a polynomial by Horner's scheme is implemented by the function EVAL_POLY, where the type COEFF is declared as

    type COEFF **is array**(INTEGER **range** <>) **of** FLOAT;

The formal parameter array A expects the coefficients of the polynomial a_n, a_{n-1}, ..., a_1 to be in the elements $A(n)$, $A(n-1)$, ..., $A(0)$. V is the value at which the polynomial is to be evaluated:

```
function EVAL_POLY(A: in COEFF; V: in FLOAT) return FLOAT is
   SUM: FLOAT;
begin
   SUM := A(A'LAST);
   for I in reverse A'FIRST..A'LAST−1 loop     −−note use of reverse
      SUM := SUM * V + A(I);
   end loop;
   return SUM;
end EVAL_POLY;
```

Chapter 2: **More About Types** [3]

Ada requires that object types be explicitly specified in the interest of better program readability, error detection and code generation. Ada is also very strict in its treatment of types to enhance program reliability. Every object must be used consistently with respect to its type. Ada provides a wide variety of types and type definition mechanisms that allow a programmer to define types appropriate to the application. For example

- floating point types of any desired accuracy, subject to implementation restrictions, can be declared.

- records can be parameterized.

- the set of values associated with an existing type can be restricted so that erroneous use of values outside the restricted set can be detected automatically.

- a new type, with values and operations similar to an existing type, can be declared. This new type, however, is different from the existing type from which it was derived. Thus, a variable representing the age of a person cannot be inadvertently assigned to a variable representing the person's social security number.

1. Strong Typing

Ada is *strongly typed*. The concept of strong typing was first popularized by the programming language Pascal. Since the design of Pascal the trend has been toward strong typing in programming languages, e.g., Euclid, Modula, Clu, Mesa and now, Ada. Although the phrase *strongly typed programming language* has been used for about a decade, it has been used loosely and it is hard to find a definition for it. In the context of the discussion in this book the following definition will be used:

Definition: A language is *strongly typed* [Gehani and Wetherell in FEU82] if

1. every object in the language belongs to exactly one type,

2. type is a *syntactic property*, i.e., the type of an expression can be determined from the program syntax,[26] and

3. type conversion occurs by converting a *value* from one type to another; conversion *does not* occur by viewing the representation of a value as a different type. In FORTRAN, for example, viewing the representation of a value as a different type is possible by means of the *equivalence* statement.

Specification of the type of an object provides the compiler with information about the intended usage of the object. A strongly typed language requires that objects be used in a fashion that is consistent with their types. For example, the bit pattern representing an integer value cannot be interpreted as a real, a character cannot be interpreted as an integer or an array name cannot be interpreted as a pointer to the beginning of the storage allocated for the array. Consequently, program errors resulting from usage of an object that is inconsistent with its type can be detected at compile time.

Limited experiments have suggested that strongly typed languages lead to increased program clarity and reliability [GAN77]. Violation of strong typing by means of *representation viewing* also hampers program portability, since the representation of an object may be different on different implementations.

Ada is a strongly typed language. However, its typing mechanism can be breached (i.e., bypassed) by means of specific mechanisms provided in the language. Programs that use these mechanisms are designated as *unchecked programs*, since potential errors resulting from the breach can no longer be detected. Breaching of strong typing may be necessary in rare cases (usually in machine dependent system programming) and must be used with great caution.

2. Subtypes [3.3]

Suppose variable CUR_FLOOR is to be used to indicate the current floor number in a program to control the elevator in an eight-floor building. CUR_FLOOR can be declared to be of type INTEGER, but in this case erroneous assignments to CUR_FLOOR outside the range 1 to 8 will not be automatically detected. It would be desirable to restrict the values of CUR_FLOOR to lie between 1 and 8 so that attempts to assign values outside this range to CUR_FLOOR are automatically flagged as errors. The *subtype* mechanism is used to specify such a restriction.

The set of values of a type T can be restricted by associating a constraint with it. The set of operations, except for assignment, is not affected. The new set of values plus the old set of operations is said to constitute a *subtype*; T is its *base*

---

26. This property of a strongly typed language was pointed out by Professor David Gries.

type. Subtype declarations do not introduce a new type. Every type T is a subtype of itself. Subtypes are declared as

subtype identifier **is** subtype_indication;

where *subtype_indication* is a type or subtype name followed by an optional constraint. Constraints can be of four kinds—*range*, *index*, *accuracy*, and *discriminant*. For example, the range constraint *range 1..8* is used in the declaration of subtype STORIES

subtype STORIES **is** INTEGER **range** 1..8;

to restrict the legal values of all objects of the subtype STORIES to be the integers between 1 and 8.

Certain characteristics of types and subtypes, such as specific values and operations, are available to the user and are called *attributes* of the types and the subtypes. The base type of any subtype (or type) T is given by the attribute T′BASE. This attribute can be used only to form other attributes, e.g., T′BASE′FIRST, which denotes the smallest element of the base type of T. (A list of all the predefined attributes is given in Appendix A of the Ada Reference Manual.)

By declaring a subtype, a user provides additional information that enhances program readability and allows a compiler to ensure that all values assigned to variables of the subtype satisfy the constraints associated with it. An optimizing compiler can use the restrictions on the set of values specified by a subtype to optimize the amount of storage required for objects of the subtype (compared to the storage required for objects of the base type of the subtype).

2.1 Examples of Subtypes

subtype WEEKDAY **is** DAY **range** MON..FRI;
            ——type DAY is defined above
            ——note the range constraint

subtype WEEKEND **is** DAY **range** SAT..SUN;

subtype BUFFER_SIZE **is** INTEGER **range** 0..MAX;

subtype GRADES **is** VECTOR(1..50);
            ——VECTOR is an unconstrained array type; the index
            ——constraint 1..50 is supplied in the subtype declaration

subtype MALE **is** PERSON(SEX **=>** M);
                           ––PERSON is a record type with a discriminant;
                           ––the discriminant SEX is constrained to
                           ––have the value M (record types with discriminants
                           ––will be discussed later in this chapter)

3. Derived Types [3.4]

Suppose two variables P and S represent the price of fuel and the speed of a train. Both P and S can be declared to be of some real type, say FLOAT, but then inadvertent mistakes such as assigning P to S or vice versa cannot be detected automatically. It would be desirable to specify that P and S are of types CURRENCY and SPEED that have the same set of values and the same set of operations as FLOAT, but that are different from each other and from FLOAT. Mistaken use of variables of type CURRENCY for those of type SPEED or FLOAT, and so on, should be detected automatically. Such a facility is provided by the *derived types* in Ada.[27]

A derived type is a new and distinct type derived from an existing type, called the *parent* type. The values and operations of the derived type are copies of the values and operations of its parent type. Derived types are declared as

type NEW_TYPE **is new** OLD_TYPE [constraint];

The constraint specified in the declaration of the derived type NEW_TYPE must be compatible with any constraints imposed by the parent type OLD_TYPE. As with subtypes, constraints can be of four kinds—*range*, *index*, *accuracy*, and *discriminant*.

Conversion is possible between a derived type and its parent type. The derived type uses the same notation for the literals and aggregates as the parent type. Such literals and aggregates are termed *overloaded*, since they designate values for more than one type. The type of the literal or the aggregate must be determinable from the context; otherwise it must be supplied explicitly by the programmer.

---

27. This strategy does not provide for a general treatment of values with different *units of measure* or for automatic conversion between values having equivalent units of measure [GEH77, GEH82b, GEH82c].

3.1 Examples of Derived Types

> **type** PRIMARY_COLOR **is new** COLOR;
> $\qquad$ ——no new constraint is imposed
> **type** AGE **is new** INTEGER **range** 0..150;
> $\qquad$ ——range constraint imposed
> **type** CARD **is new** LINE(1..80);
> $\qquad$ ——index constraint imposed

4. Type Equivalence

Type equivalence has been classified into two broad classes—*name* and *structural* [WEL77]. When are two types equivalent in Ada? Ada uses the concept of name equivalence[28] to decide when two types are equivalent. Two objects have *equivalent types* if and only if they are declared using the same type identifier.

Each instance (or elaboration) of a type definition such as

> **array**(1..10) **of** INTEGER

creates a new type, called an *anonymous* type, which is different from all other types. For example, A and B declared separately in *single object declarations*

> A: **array**(1..10) **of** INTEGER;
> B: **array**(1..10) **of** INTEGER;

are not of the same type, because each declaration creates a new anonymous array type definition. Even if A and B had been declared together in one *multiple object declaration*

> A, B: **array**(1..10) **of** INTEGER;

they would be of different types, since a multiple object declaration is equivalent to a series of single object declarations [3.3.1].

As another example, consider the type identifier ARRAY10 declared as

> **type** ARRAY10 **is array**(1..10) **of** INTEGER;

As a result of the declarations

---

28. Name equivalence is conceptually simpler and much easier to implement than structural equivalence. Under structural type equivalence, two types are equivalent if and only if their components are of the same type regardless of the names of the components. There are several variations of this scheme.

E, F: ARRAY10;
G: ARRAY10;

E, F and G all have the same type, since they are all declared with the same type identifier.

5. Type Conversions [4.6]

An expression E may be converted to another type or subtype by qualifying it with the type or subtype name T; this is written as

T(E)

Type conversions are allowed only among

Numeric Types	E can be an expression of any numeric type. Conversion of reals to integers is by rounding to the nearest integer.
Derived Types	T and the type of E must be derivable from each other, directly or indirectly, or there must exist a third type from which they are derived directly or indirectly. This conversion may result in a change of representation [13.6].
Array Types	Both T and E must have the same dimensionality, the same index and component types. In case the index types are different they should be convertible to each other. If the component types are access or record types then they must both either be constrained or unconstrained. If T denotes a constrained type and E has exactly the number of elements required by T then the bounds of the result are those imposed by T. If T denotes an unconstrained type, then the bounds of the result are the same as those of E.

Whenever a type conversion is allowed, the reverse conversion is also allowed.

5.1 Implicit Conversions

Ada does not allow implicit conversions.[29] Some computer scientists believe that implicit conversions should rarely be permitted even if they make sense mathematically, because conversions make programs more difficult to understand [LIS76].

Going from a subtype to its base type or vice versa (provided the value is a legal value for the subtype) is not considered a type conversion, because a subtype declaration does not really introduce a new type. An object of a subtype S effectively has type T, the base type of S, but the values that can be assigned to the object have been restricted as specified in the declaration of S.

6. Qualifying Expressions with their Types

The type of an expression is determined from its operand types and the types of values returned by the operators. A *qualified expression* is used to state explicitly the type of an expression or an aggregate. Qualification of an expression or an aggregate with the type is necessary in situations where the type cannot be determined from the context. As an example, consider two literals A and B, which both belong to two different enumeration types E and F. Then the expression

$$A < B$$

is ambiguous, because it cannot be determined from the context whether A and B belong to E or F. The value of such an expression may be different depending upon the type of A and B. For example, A may precede B in E so that A < B is TRUE (for type E) while A may follow B in F so that A < B is FALSE (for type F). This ambiguity can be resolved by *qualifying* A and B with their types. If both A and B are to be of type E, then the above expression can be unambiguously written as

$$E'(A) < E'(B)$$

or even

$$E'(A) < B$$

A *qualified expression* has the form

T'(expression) | T'aggregate

where T is a type or subtype name. The expression or the aggregate must have the same type as the base type of T.

---

29. PL/I and Algol 68 take the opposite approach. In PL/I just about any type can be implicitly converted to any other type.

7. More Types

This section contains more details about scalar types (particularly integers and reals), record types and access types. The use of constraints in defining new integer and real types is illustrated along with facilities for parameterizing record types and defining recursive types.

7.1 Scalar Types

A range constraint specifies that only a subset of the values of a type will be used. A range constraint is said to be *compatible* with an earlier range constraint if the set of values specified by the later range constraint is a subset of the values specified by the earlier constraint. A new range constraint must be compatible with earlier ones. A value is said to *satisfy* a range constraint if it is in the set of values specified by the range constraint.

7.1.1 Boolean: A boolean type is either the predefined type BOOLEAN or a type derived from a boolean type. The predefined comparison and membership operators produce a value of type BOOLEAN.

7.1.2 Integers: Additional integer types can be declared as

> **type** NEW_INTEGER **is range** L..R;

where NEW_INTEGER is the name of the type being declared, and L and R specify the smallest and largest value of type NEW_INTEGER. This type declaration is equivalent to

> **type** *integer_type* **is new** *predefined_integer_type*;
> **subtype** NEW_INTEGER **is** *integer_type*
> > > **range** *integer_type*(L) .. *integer_type*(R);

where *predefined_integer_type* is selected by the Ada implementation to be one of the predefined integer types that includes the values in the range L to R. Some examples are

> **type** RANK **is range** 1..10;
> **type** ID **is range** 1..INTEGER'LAST;
> **type** PRIORITY **is new** INTEGER **range** 1..10;

    subtype NATURAL **is** INTEGER **range** 0..INTEGER'LAST;
        ——predefined subtype in Ada

    subtype POSITIVE **is** INTEGER **range** 1..INTEGER'LAST;
        ——predefined subtype in Ada

    subtype HIGH_PRIORITY **is** PRIORITY **range** H..10;
        ——the bounds on the values of types and subtypes
        ——can be static or dynamic expressions. H must
        ——be ≤ 10 at run time, otherwise a constraint error
        ——will occur (the exception CONSTRAINT_ERROR
        ——will be raised)

    type FILE_ID **is new** ID;   ——derived type

The types ID, FILE_ID and the subtype POSITIVE have the same set of values; however, they are all different.

7.2 Reals

Real types with any desired accuracy (subject to the limitations of the implementation) can be defined by specifying the *accuracy constraint*.

7.2.1 Floating Point Types: The accuracy constraint for floating points, called the *floating point constraint*, is of the form

    digits D [**range** L..R]

where D is a positive static expression of type integer, and L and R are static expressions of some real type. D is the precision of the real type being defined and indicates the minimum number of digits that should be stored for the mantissa. The optional range constraint specifies that the values will range between L and R.

A new floating point type NEW_FLOAT is declared as

    type NEW_FLOAT **is digits** D [**range** L..R];

This declaration is equivalent to

    type *float_type* **is new** *predefined_float_type*;
    subtype NEW_FLOAT **is** *float_type* **digits** D
                [**range** *float_type*(L) .. *float_type*(R)];

where *predefined_float_type* is chosen appropriately by the Ada implementation so that the specified floating point constraint is satisfied. A value satisfies a floating point constraint if it satisfies any included range constraint.

Some examples of floating point types are

    type WT_KG is digits 6;
    type TEMPERATURE is digits 8 range 0.00 .. 1000.00;

    subtype APPROX_TEMPERATURE is TEMPERATURE digits 6;

    type WT_LB is new WT_KG;
                --weights in the two different units of measure
                --will not be mixed inadvertently now
    type MASS is new REAL digits 7 range 0.0 .. 1.0E10;

For a subtype, a derived type or an object declaration, one can specify either
the floating point constraint or just the range constraint. In defining a new
floating point type or a floating point subtype F, the floating point constraint
must be compatible with any earlier floating point constraints on the base or
the parent type, i.e., the number of digits must not exceed those specified in the
earlier constraint. Also if both F and the base or the parent type have range
constraints, then the new range constraint must be compatible with the earlier
ones.

7.2.2 Portability of Programs with Floating Point Objects: Different Ada
implementations may implement predefined floating point types such as
FLOAT with different precisions. Portability of programs with floating point
objects can be achieved by using floating point types declared to have the
desired precision. For example, a user may declare a new floating point type
REAL as

    type REAL is digits 10;

and use it instead of FLOAT. When a program with such a type is moved
from one Ada implementation to another, it is the responsibility of the Ada
implementation to implement REAL with at least the precision specified (10
digits in this example).

This strategy is much better than that provided in other languages, say
FORTRAN. FORTRAN does not define the accuracy of its single precision
floating point; the accuracy varies on common systems from 24 to 48 bits.
Consequently, the user has to select between single precision and double
precision according to the implementation [DOD79b]. For example, in moving
FORTRAN programs from the 60 bit CDC 6600 to the 32 bit IBM 370, users
must change single precision variables to double precision to get approximately
the same degree of accuracy. This can be extremely inconvenient.

7.3 Fixed Point Types

As stated in Chapter 1, the accuracy constraint for fixed point types,
fixed_point_constraint, has the form

delta DEL **range** L..R;

where DEL is the maximum error permitted in implementing the fixed point type and, L and R are expressions specifying the range of values. When declaring fixed point subtypes or derived types, specification of the range constraint is optional.

A new fixed point type NEW_FIXED is declared as

type NEW_FIXED **is delta** DEL **range** L..R;

This declaration is equivalent to

> **type** *fixed_type* **is new** *predefined_fixed_type*;
> **subtype** NEW_FIXED **is** *fixed_type* **delta** DEL
> **range** *fixed_type*(L) .. *fixed_type*(R);

where *predefined_fixed_type* is chosen appropriately by the Ada implementation so that the specified fixed point constraint is satisfied.

Some examples of fixed point subtypes and derived types are

> **subtype** LOW_PRECISION **is** HIGH_PRECISION **delta** 0.1;
>   --HIGH_PRECISION was declared in Chapter 1 as
>   --a fixed point type with a delta of 0.00001
> **type** DOLLARS **is new** CURRENCY;
>   --CURRENCY is a floating point type
> **type** RUPEES **is new** CURRENCY;

A fixed point constraint must be compatible with any previous fixed point constraint. The delta of the later constraint must not be less than the earlier delta. If both have range constraints, then the later constraint must be compatible with the earlier ones.

7.4 Record Types

Objects of a record type need not have the same number and type of components. Record types can be parameterized to implement objects that are basically similar but that differ in some details, such as the size and the number of components.

7.4.1 Record Types with Discriminants [3.7.1]: Discriminants are used to parameterize record type definitions. They allows values of a record type to have alternative forms. Discriminants must be of a discrete type and are specified in the declaration of a record type. A discriminant is a named component of any object of such a record type. Within a record type definition a discriminant may be used only

1. as part of the default expression specifying the initial value of a record component,

2. as the discriminant of a variant part and

3. in a component subtype definition, either as an index bound or a discriminant value.

In the last case, the discriminant must be used by itself and not as the component of a larger expression. A discriminant does not have to be used within the record type definition.

Discriminants may be given default initial values. The default initial values can be overridden by explicitly giving initial values at object declaration time or while defining a subtype. When an object is being declared, an explicit initial value *must* be given for the discriminant if a default initial value has not been specified. The value of a discriminant in an object can be changed only by assigning the entire object a new value and not by assigning a value to just the discriminant.[30]

Examples of record types with discriminants are

```
type RECTANGLE(L, B: INTEGER := 10) is
        --the record type RECTANGLE is parameterized by the
        --discriminants L and B that represent the sides of the
        --rectangle. L and B are given a default initial value of 10,
        --which can be overridden by explicitly supplied initial values
    record
        R: MATRIX(1..L, 1..B);
            --MATRIX was declared in Chapter 1 as a
            --two-dimensional array with FLOAT elements
    end record;


type SQUARE(SIDE: POSITIVE) is
        --SIDE is the discriminant. It does not have a default
        --initial value; SIDE must be given a value when
        --an object of type SQUARE is declared
    record
        SQ: RECTANGLE(SIDE, SIDE);
    end record;
```

---

30. This restriction prevents a discriminant value from being changed without a corresponding change in the component values. In case of *variant records* (discussed in the next section), a change in the value of the discriminant may result in change in the type and number of record components. Without this restriction it would be possible to breach strong typing. The lack of this restriction is a major loophole in Pascal's typing mechanism.

```
type BUFFER(SIZE: BUFFER_SIZE := 128) is
        --BUFFER_SIZE was declared earlier as an integer
        --subtype with values in the range 0..MAX
record
   POS: BUFFER_SIZE;
   VALUE: STRING(1..SIZE);
end record;

type ITEM(NUMBER: POSITIVE) is
     --discriminant is not used inside the record definition
record
   CONTENT: INTEGER;
end record;
```

Objects of record types with discriminants are declared as

```
R1: RECTANGLE;            --has the default size of 10 by 10
R2: RECTANGLE(5, 50);
            --default initial values overridden. Initial
            --values supplied in positional notation
R3: RECTANGLE(L => 10, B => 50);
            -- named notation used to supply initial values
S: SQUARE(SIDE => 10);
            --discriminant must be given an explicit initial value
            --if a default initial value has not been specified
B1: BUFFER(SIZE => 64, POS => 0, VALUE => (1..64 => ' '));
            --initial values supplied for all the components
            --of the record including the discriminant
B2: BUFFER(64, 0, (1..64 => ' '));
            --this declaration, uses positional notation.It is
            --equivalent to the one for B1.
            --The discriminant comes before the other components.
```

Discriminants are like the other components of a record except that they cannot be directly assigned a value. Discriminants L and B, of variable R1, are modified by the assignment

```
R1 := (L => 15, B => 20, R => (1..15 => (1..20 => 75.0)));
```

However, the following set of assignments, apparently equivalent to the above assignment, causes an error, because direct assignment to discriminants is not allowed:

```
R1.L := 15;
R1.B := 20;
R1.R := (1..15 => (1..20 => 75.0));
```

7.4.2 Variant Records [3.7.3]: Programs often contain objects that are
conceptually very similar to each other, differing only in some minor details. It
would be nice to be able to specify them as being of the same type. For
example, all values representing information about motorized vehicles may be
specified to be of type VEHICLE. Different vehicles such as cars, buses and
trucks have common information such as the names of the owner and the
manufacturer, the model and the year of make of the vehicle. However, some
information is not applicable to all vehicles. For example, tonnage (capacity in
weight) is applicable only to trucks while the maximum seating capacity is
relevant for buses only. Another example is the representation of geometric
figures. Common information might include items such as area and perimeter.
However, applicable information about their dimensions is different and
depends upon their shape.

Variant records[31] are used to implement record types, such as VEHICLE, that
have basically similar values but which differ in some small details. Variant
records are a special case of records with discriminants. A record may have a
variant part that specifies alternative lists of components. A component list can
be empty in which case it must be specified as **null**. Each list is prefixed by a
set of *choices*. The component list selected is one that has a choice that is
equal to the value of the discriminant. Only components of the selected list can
be referenced; referencing components of the other lists in the variant will
result in an error.

The general form of a record definition is

> **record**
>   component_declarations [variant_part] | **null**
> **end record**

The variant part of a record has the form

> **case** discriminant_name **is**
>   **when** choice {| choice} => component_list
>   {**when** choice {| choice} => component_list}
> **end case**;

where a choice can be a static expression, a static discrete range or the
keyword **others**. The particular list of components selected corresponds to a
choice that has a value equal to the discriminant value. A choice that is a
discrete range is an abbreviation for a list of choices representing all values of
the range. The keyword **others** can appear only as the choice for the last

---

31. The concept of variant records was first introduced in Pascal.

alternative. It appears by itself and stands for all possible values the discriminant can assume that have not been covered by the choices prefixing the preceding alternatives.

The following two examples illustrate the use of variant records. The first record type, GEOMETRIC_FIGURE, uses type SHAPE, which is declared as

>   **type** SHAPE **is** (RECT, CIRCLE, POINT);

GEOMETRIC_FIGURE has three or four components depending upon the value of the discriminant S:

```
      type GEOMETRIC_FIGURE(S: SHAPE) is
        record
          PERIMETER: FLOAT;    --perimeter of a point is 0.0
          case S is
            when RECT => L, B: INTEGER range 0..INTEGER'LAST;
            when CIRCLE => RADIUS: FLOAT := 1.0;
            when POINT => P: POSITION;
          end case;
        end record;
```

The first component, the discriminant S, is used to indicate the type of the geometric figure, that is, whether it is a rectangle, a circle or a point. The second component is PERIMETER. If S is RECT then an object of type GEOMETRIC_FIGURE will have two more components L and B. Otherwise it has only one more component, RADIUS or P.

Examples of declarations of variables of type GEOMETRIC_FIGURE are

```
          C: GEOMETRIC_FIGURE(CIRCLE);
                    --C has components S, PERIMETER and RADIUS
          R: GEOMETRIC_FIGURE(RECT);
                    --R has components S, PERIMETER, L and B
```

The radius of circle C has the default initial value 1.0, whereas the dimensions of rectangle R have no default initial values.

The second example [DOD83] shows how record type PERIPHERAL is used to represent different types of peripheral devices. Two enumeration types DEVICE and STATE used in this example are declared as

```
          type DEVICE is (PRINTER, DISK, DRUM);
          type STATE is (OPEN, CLOSED);
```

Each peripheral device has a component STATUS indicating the availability of the device.

```
    type PERIPHERAL(UNIT: DEVICE := DISK) is
                    --UNIT has the default initial value DISK
  record
     STATUS: STATE;
     case UNIT is
       when PRINTER =>
         LINE_COUNT: INTEGER range 1..PAGE_SIZE;
       when others =>
         CYLINDER: CYLINDER_INDEX;
         TRACK: TRACK_NUMBER;
     end case;
  end record;
```

In this example the drum is treated as logically similar to a disk, except that it has one cylinder while a disk has many. Examples of subtypes of PERIPHERAL are

```
  subtype DRUM_UNIT is PERIPHERAL(DRUM);
  subtype DISK_UNIT is PERIPHERAL(DISK);
```

Examples of peripherals, which are constrained record objects of type PERIPHERAL, are

```
  BACKUP_DISK: PERIPHERAL;
  WRITER: PERIPHERAL(UNIT => PRINTER);
                --default initial value of UNIT overridden
  ARCHIVE: DISK_UNIT;
```

The discriminant should be treated like any other component; it precedes all other components of a record, as illustrated by the aggregate assignment

```
  ARCHIVE := (UNIT => DISK, STATUS => CLOSED,
              CYLINDER => 9, TRACK => 1)
```

7.5 Access Types—Recursive and Mutually Dependent

Direct recursion in record type definitions is not allowed. Indirect recursion is allowed and is accomplished by means of access types. *Incomplete type declarations* must be used to define *recursive* and *mutually dependent* access types.

Consider the declaration of record type EMPLOYEE which contains three components representing the name, the identification number and the manager of an employee—NAME, ID and MANAGER. Since the manager is also an employee, component MANAGER must also be declared to be of type EMPLOYEE, thus making the definition of EMPLOYEE recursive. Since direct recursion is not allowed in Ada, an intermediate access type, say MGR, is used.

Type EMPLOYEE is declared by first giving an incomplete declaration for it:

> **type** EMPLOYEE; ――incomplete type declaration

Type MGR is then declared as

> **type** MGR **is access** EMPLOYEE;

Finally, type EMPLOYEE is declared completely.

> **type** EMPLOYEE **is**
>   **record**
>   NAME: STRING(1..30);
>   ID: INTEGER;
>   MANAGER: MGR;
>   **end record**;

The incomplete type declaration is required, because in Ada every object and type must be declared (an incomplete declaration suffices) before use. Of course, the complete declaration must be supplied later.

Type EMPLOYEE could not have been declared as

> **type** EMPLOYEE **is**
>   **record**
>   NAME: STRING(1..30);
>   ID: INTEGER;
>   MANAGER: **access** EMPLOYEE; ――****ILLEGAL****
>   **end record**;

since Ada does not allow an access type definition to be used in an object declaration, as illustrated by the above declaration of component MANAGER in the record type EMPLOYEE.

8. Examples

The examples in this section focus on the additional capabilities of records and access types. In the first example, the area of a geometric figure represented by a variant record is computed. This example illustrates the suitability of using *case* statements for dealing with variant records. The second and third examples concern printing and searching a binary tree, each node of which is represented by a recursive record type. Recursive programming blends very well with accessing recursive types.

8.1 Using Variant Records

Function AREA computes the area of an object of type GEOMETRIC_FIGURE (declared earlier in the section on variant records):

```
function AREA(F: GEOMETRIC_FIGURE) return FLOAT is
   PI: constant := 3.1416;
begin
   case F.S is
      --The choice is based on the discriminant of F
         when RECT => return FLOAT(F.L * F.B);
                              --note explicit conversion to real
         when CIRCLE => return PI * F.RADIUS * F.RADIUS;
         when POINT => return 0.0;
   end case;
end AREA;
```

8.2 Printing a tree

The problem is to print the values at the nodes of a binary tree with root R. Each node is of the form

VALUE	
LEFT	RIGHT

where the component VALUE is the value (of type INTEGER), and the components LEFT and RIGHT designate the left and right subtrees. The presence of a **null** value in components LEFT or RIGHT indicates an empty subtree. The node type is given by the following declarations, which are part of package TREE:

```
type NODE;    --incomplete type declaration

type BRANCH is access NODE;

type NODE is
              --type declaration being completed
   record
     VALUE: INTEGER;
     LEFT, RIGHT: BRANCH;
   end record;
```

Note how recursive types are defined in Ada. As mentioned earlier, instead of specifying the recursion directly, an access type must be used. First an incomplete type declaration is given. Using this incomplete type declaration, an access type is declared. Finally, the incomplete type declaration is completed.

The name of an incomplete type can be used only in the declaration of an access type.[32] Consequently, the following alternative formulation is illegal:

type BRANCH;   ——incomplete type declaration

type NODE **is**
  record
    VALUE: INTEGER;
    LEFT, RIGHT: BRANCH;
        ——illegal use of the incomplete type BRANCH
  end record;

type BRANCH **is** access NODE;

The procedure to print the binary tree, PRINT, is based on the abstract algorithm

if the tree is not empty **then**
    print the left sub-tree
    print the root of the tree
    print the right sub-tree
end if;

that prints the nodes in *inorder*. Any printing order may be used, since no specific order was specified in the problem statement. Procedure PRINT is

---

32. Otherwise, it becomes harder to compile definitions that use the incomplete type.

```
with TEXT_IO, TREE;
      --include these packages in the compilation unit
use TEXT_IO, TREE;
      --make their components directly visible
procedure PRINT(R: in BRANCH) is

   package IO_INT is new INTEGER_IO(INTEGER);
   use IO_INT;

begin
   if R /= null then
         PRINT(R.LEFT);

         PUT(R.VALUE);
               --integer PUT from IO_INT
         NEW_LINE;

         PRINT(R.RIGHT);
   end if;
end PRINT;
```

8.3 Binary Tree Search

The problem is to write two equivalent functions, one recursive and the other iterative, that search an *ordered binary tree* with a root R (of type BRANCH that was defined earlier) for a value X. The two functions return TRUE if X is in the tree and FALSE otherwise.

Ordered binary trees are binary trees that are ordered according to some rule. One definition of an ordered binary tree is that it is a binary tree in which the left child of a node always has a value that is less than that of its parent and the right child always has a value greater than that of its parent.

```
      --recursive version of binary tree search
      function BIN_SRCH_REC(R: in BRANCH; X: in INTEGER)
                                        return BOOLEAN is
      begin
         if R = null then return FALSE;
         elsif X = R.VALUE then return TRUE;
         elsif X < R.VALUE then return BIN_SRCH_REC(R.LEFT, X);
         else return BIN_SRCH_REC(R.RIGHT, X);
         end if;
      end BIN_SRCH_REC;
```

```
--iterative version of binary tree search
function BIN_SRCH_ITER(R: in BRANCH; X: in INTEGER)
                                  return BOOLEAN is
    T: BRANCH;  --temporary variable for tree traversal
begin
    T := R;
    loop
        if T = null then return FALSE;
        elsif X = T.VALUE then return TRUE;
        elsif X < T.VALUE then T := T.LEFT;
        else T := T.RIGHT;
        end if;
    end loop;
end BIN_SRCH_ITER;
```

In this example, both the recursive and iterative versions are simple and easy to understand. However, some problems are best expressed recursively, e.g., the Towers of Hanoi problem and the quicksort algorithm given Chapter 1. Many programmers avoid recursion and treat it as a novelty [GRI75]. Languages such as FORTRAN and COBOL do not allow recursion, and this limitation has inhibited many programmers from thinking recursively. Also the examples of recursion, commonly given in the introductory texts, such as factorial and Fibonacci numbers, are often best expressed iteratively and are therefore not convincing examples of the appropriateness of recursion.

Chapter 3: **Packages** [7]

1. Introduction

Packages, subprograms, tasks and generic units constitute the four forms of program units from which Ada programs are composed. Packages, like subprograms, can be compiled separately, thus allowing partitioning of large programs into smaller and more manageable parts. Partitioning programs into smaller pieces helps in building, understanding and maintaining large systems [HOR79]. Packages are generally defined in two parts—the package specification and the package body. The specification specifies the facilities provided by the package. The body implements the facilities. Package specifications and package bodies can be compiled separately. However, the compilation of a package specification must precede the compilation of the corresponding package body.

Packages are an information hiding and data encapsulation mechanism. They can be used to group logically related entities such as constants, variables, types and subprograms. The user of a package can see only the package specification and not the implementation details supplied in the package body. Moreover, only the entities specified in the *visible* part of a package specification can be referred to by the package user.

As the implementation details of a package are hidden from the package user, the user cannot exploit this knowledge in a program; thus a program cannot be made dependent on the package implementation. Consequently, once the package specification has been agreed upon, the package implementor is free to implement the package in any way consistent with the package specification. The implementation of a package can be changed in any way provided it remains consistent with the package specifications.

2. Package Specifications [7.2]

The specification of a package has the form

        package identifier **is**
            basic declarative items
        [**private**
            basic declarative items]
        end identifier;

97

A *basic declarative item* is either a *basic declaration*, a *use* clause or a *representation* clause. A *basic declaration* is any declaration except the body of a subprogram, package or a task, or a *body stub* (body stubs are discussed in Chapter 7 on Program Structure and Separate Compilation).

The body of a subprogram, package (if there is one), task or a generic unit declared in a package specification must be given in the package body. Alternatively, a body stub or an INTERFACE pragma may be given.

Two sets of declarations can appear in a package specification. The first set constitutes the *visible* part of the package. Objects declared here can be accessed using the selected component notation (i.e., by prefixing the object with the name of the package and a period) or directly by means of the *use* clause.

The second set of declarations follows the keyword **private**; it is not visible outside the package. These declarations contain structural or implementation details of private types that were declared in the visible part of the package. These details, which do not concern the user of the package, are provided in the package specification only to help the compiler in implementing the visible part of the package (e.g., the representation of a private type declared in the visible part of the package must be given in the private part so that the compiler can determine how much storage is to be allocated for objects of this type).

Nothing declared in the body of the package is visible outside the body. This restriction on visibility along with the restriction provided by the private part of a package specification supports the information hiding provided by packages.

Some examples of package specifications are now given. The first example is the package PLOTTING_DATA, which consists only of a group of common variables and has no corresponding package body [DOD83].

```
package PLOTTING_DATA is
    PEN_UP: BOOLEAN;
    CONVERSION_FACTOR,
    X_OFFSET, Y_OFFSET,
    X_MIN, X_MAX,
    Y_MIN, Y_MAX: FLOAT;
    X_VALUE: array(1..500) of FLOAT;
    Y_VALUE: array(1..500) of FLOAT;
end PLOTTING_DATA;
```

These declarations can be used by more than one subprogram.[33]

The second example is a package ORDERED_SET that implements a set whose elements are ordered by the time value associated with them. The elements are of a discrete type ID and the time values of the predefined type DURATION. The elements represent job identification numbers and the time value represents job execution time in seconds. Type ID is declared as

> **type** ID **is range** 1..100;

and this declaration is directly visible in the context in which ORDERED_SET is being declared. The specification of ORDERED_SET is

```
package ORDERED_SET is
    procedure INSERT(JOB: in ID; T: in DURATION);
                --add JOB to the set; JOB is a job that requires
                --T seconds of execution time
    procedure SMALLEST(JOB: out ID);
                --Store in JOB, a job from the ordered set with the
                --smallest execution time; this job is deleted from the
                --set; SMALLEST should be called after ensuring
                --that the set is not empty.

                --SMALLEST is not implemented as a function, since it
                --has the side effect of deleting an element.
                --Functions should not have any side effects.
                --A function should always return the same value if it
                --is called with the same actual parameters.
                --This convention corresponds to the mathematical
                --notion of a function


    function EMPTY return BOOLEAN;
end ORDERED_SET;
```

Declarations given in a package specification are visible outside the package at points in a program only if the package name is visible at these points. Identifiers in the visible part of the package specification can be referred to using selected component notation—the name of the item prefixed with the name of the package and a period. For example,

> ORDERED_SET.EMPTY

---

33. The use of these data declarations by parallel processes, called *tasks*, will cause the *concurrent update* problem [BRI73] unless great care is taken.

The items can be made directly visible by means of the *use* clause. If the *use* clause

    use ORDERED_SET;

has appeared, then the function EMPTY can be referred to directly as

    EMPTY

provided no parameterless BOOLEAN function with the same name already exists, in which case EMPTY will refer to the existing function. Also, if two identical identifiers are made visible with the aid of *use* clauses then an ambiguity may result. To avoid the ambiguity, these identifiers must be qualified.

3. Package Bodies [7.3]

A package body has the form

    package body identifier **is**
       declarations
    [**begin**
       sequence_of_statements
    [**exception**
       exception handlers]]
    end identifier;

The body of a package constitutes the implementation of a package. It contains local declarations and the bodies of the subprograms, packages and tasks whose specifications were given in the package specification. All items declared in a package specification are visible in the corresponding package body. However, the implementations of these items, given in the package body, are not visible outside. Items declared locally in a package body are likewise not visible outside the package body.

A package body can also contain a sequence of statements that are executed when the package body is processed. These statements can be used to initialize the objects declared in the specification and body of the package. Exceptions raised by the execution of the statements are handled by the exception handlers given in the package body. If no handler is provided for an exception then, when this exception occurs, it is *propagated* to the part of the program containing the package body (this will be discussed in Chapter 5 on Exceptions).

As an example, the body of package ORDERED_SET, which implements the ordered set specified earlier, is declared. It uses a BOOLEAN array IN_SET to indicate the jobs that are present in the set along with an array RANK that contains their execution times. IN_SET(I) is TRUE if job I is present in the set and FALSE otherwise. RANK(I) contains the execution time associated with job I (when it is present in the set). The set is empty when all elements of IN_SET are FALSE.

When the set is not empty, then the job SMALL with the smallest execution time is determined and deleted from the set by means of the following algorithm:

> T := maximum possible execution time
> **for** all jobs I in the set **loop**
>   Let SMALL be the job I if its execution time RANK(I) is $\leqslant$ T;
>   in this case let T be equal to RANK(I).
> **end loop**
> Delete SMALL from the set

The elements present in the set cannot be directly generated as specified in the above loop heading. All elements that can possibly be in the set must be generated and those not actually present in the set screened out by means of an explicit test in the loop body. Consequently, the algorithm to find the smallest job is refined as

> **for** all jobs I that can be in the set **loop**
>   Let SMALL be the job I if it is in the set and if its execution time
>   RANK(I) is $\leqslant$ T; in this case let T be equal to RANK(I).
> **end loop**

The package ORDERED_SET is implemented as

```
--ID is available in this environment
package body ORDERED_SET is

   IN_SET: array(ID) of BOOLEAN := (ID => FALSE);
                   --initially the set is empty
   RANK: array(ID) of DURATION;

   procedure INSERT(JOB: in ID; T: in DURATION) is
         --if an element is present in the set, then inserting it
         --has no effect as is the case with mathematical sets
   begin
      IN_SET(JOB) := TRUE;
      RANK(JOB) := T;
   end INSERT;

   procedure SMALLEST(JOB: out ID) is
                   --SMALLEST should be called only if the
                   --set is not empty
      T: DURATION := DURATION'LAST;
      SMALL: ID;
   begin
      for I in ID loop    --searching for the smallest rank job
         if IN_SET(I) and then RANK(I) <= T then
            SMALL := I;
            T := RANK(I);
         end if;
      end loop;
      IN_SET(SMALL) := FALSE;    --delete the job from the set
      JOB := SMALL;
   end SMALLEST;

   function EMPTY return BOOLEAN is
   begin
      for I in ID loop
         if IN_SET(I) then
            return FALSE;
         end if;
      end loop;
      return TRUE;
   end EMPTY;

end ORDERED_SET;
```

As an exercise for the reader, the package body should be reimplemented using ordered lists to store the elements of the set.[34]

4. Private Types [7.4]

The implementation details of types declared in a package specification may be hidden from the user of the package by designating the types to be *private*. A type is designated as private by associating with it either the attribute **private** or the attribute **limited private**. A *limited private* type is also called a *limited* type. A private type is declared using a *private type declaration* given in the visible part of a package specification. For example,

> **type** SET **is private**;
> **type** ORD_SET **is limited private**;
> **type** QUEUE **is limited private**;

The full type declaration is given later in the private part of a package specification instead of the package body. The full type declaration is given in the package specification itself to ensure that the specification contains sufficient information to allow the compilation of a unit using the package.

Objects of private types can be declared, passed as parameters, compared for equality and inequality and assigned values of other objects of the same type. Limited private type objects, however, can be declared and passed only as parameters.

The private type declaration and the corresponding full type declarations offer two different views of a private type—one each for the outside and the inside worlds. Outside the package in which a private type is declared, objects of this private type can be manipulated and operated upon only in a restricted manner;

---

34. When the maximum cardinality of a set is much larger than its cardinality at any given time, it is more storage efficient to use a list representation for the set than a BOOLEAN array representation. The storage used in a list representation is proportional to the number of elements in the set and is allocated or deallocated when an element is added to or deleted from the set. In the BOOLEAN array representation, storage for all possible elements must be allocated regardless of whether or not the elements are present in the set.

Operations on the set such as addition, deletion and membership tests are faster when a BOOLEAN array representation is used and their speed is independent of the set cardinality. In a list representation the addition operation is fast and its speed is independent of the set cardinality, but the speeds of the deletion operation and the membership test are proportional to the set cardinality. The membership test can be speeded up by using an ordered list, but this slows the addition operation, making its speed proportional to the set cardinality. Speedup of the membership test is advantageous when the frequency of the membership tests is much greater than the frequency of adding elements to the set. More discussion on set representations can be found in *The Design and Analysis of Computer Algorithms* [AHO75].

inside this package, on the other hand, private type objects are like objects of any ordinary (i.e., non-private) types.

Constants of a private type can be declared in the visible part of a package, but their values must be given only in the private part using a complete redeclaration. Private types implemented as records can have discriminants.

The implementation of a private type is visible inside the corresponding package body, so that the implementor of a private type can define operations on objects of the private type. This implementation is hidden from the users of a private type; this forces them to manipulate private type objects using only the operations automatically provided with the private type and those provided by the implementor of the private type.

The use of private types is illustrated in the examples discussed below.

4.1 More on Ordered Sets

The implementation of an ordered set by the package ORDERED_SET, given earlier, is inflexible, because only one instance of a set is made available to the user. This can be remedied by defining, in the package specification, a type ORD_SET which is a record consisting of two components—the BOOLEAN array IN_SET and the array RANK of type DURATION (these were defined in the body of ORDERED_SET). These arrays will be used as before to represent the set. The operations will now be redefined to include a parameter of type ORD_SET. Users will declare ordered sets by declaring objects of type ORD_SET. A user can now have as many ordered sets as desired by declaring an appropriate number of objects of type ORD_SET. Operations on a specific ordered set are performed by passing that ordered set as a parameter to the operation in question.

The specification of ORDERED_SET2 (ORDERED_SET modified as discussed) is

```
package ORDERED_SET2 is

   type SET_ARRAY is array(ID) of BOOLEAN;
   type RANK_ARRAY is array(ID) of DURATION;
   type ORD_SET is
      record
         IN_SET: SET_ARRAY := (ID => FALSE);
         RANK: RANK_ARRAY;
      end record;

   procedure INSERT(S: in out ORD_SET;
                              JOB: in ID; T: in DURATION);
   procedure SMALLEST(S: in out ORD_SET; JOB: out ID);
   function EMPTY(S: in ORD_SET) return BOOLEAN;

end ORDERED_SET2;
```

Assuming that the proper *use* clause has been given, ordered sets are declared as

    A, B, C: ORD_SET;   ——three ordered sets

Although this modification has solved the problem of being able to provide more than one ordered set, another problem arises now. The user of the package can directly manipulate the implementation of the ordered sets. This manipulation is possible, because the implementation of type ORD_SET, i.e., a record consisting of two arrays IN_SET and RANK, is visible outside the package specification. Moreover, the types SET_ARRAY and RANK_ARRAY are unnecessarily visible to the user. Information hiding, as provided by the package ORDERED_SET, no longer exists.

In situations like this, private types are useful in hiding the implementation details. The implementation of ORD_SET can be hidden from the user by declaring it as a limited private type. The user cannot even make copies of ORD_SET objects or compare them, since ORD_SET is declared to be a *limited* private type. The specification of the modified ORDERED_SET2, modified to declare ORD_SET as a limited private type, is

```
package ORDERED_SET2 is

   type ORD_SET is limited private;

   procedure INSERT(S: in out ORD_SET;
                                    JOB: in ID; T: in DURATION);
   procedure SMALLEST(S: in out ORD_SET; JOB: out ID);
   function EMPTY(S: in ORD_SET) return BOOLEAN;

private
   type SET_ARRAY is array(ID) of BOOLEAN;
   type RANK_ARRAY is array(ID) of DURATION;
   type ORD_SET is
      record
         IN_SET: SET_ARRAY := (ID => FALSE);
         RANK: RANK_ARRAY;
      end record;

end ORDERED_SET2;
```

The body of ORDERED_SET2 will look like

```
package body ORDERED_SET2 is

   procedure INSERT(S: in out ORD_SET;
                                    JOB: in ID; T: in DURATION) is
                     --the ordered set being manipulated is
                     --supplied as a parameter
   begin
      S.IN_SET(JOB) := TRUE;
      S.RANK(JOB) := T;
   end INSERT;

   --body of procedure SMALLEST
            --similar to that given in ORDERED_SET except
            --that the ordered set being manipulated is
            --supplied as a parameter
   --body of function EMPTY
            --same comment as for SMALLEST
end ORDERED_SET2;
```

Note that it was possible to provide a default initial value for objects of type
ORD_SET only, because ORD_SET is a record type. It is not possible to
associate default values with types that are not records. One could, of course,
embed every type in a record type to get this initialization facility.

4.2 A Key Manager

Another example that illustrates the use of private types is a key manager [DOD83]. A different key is supplied every time a key is requested by the package user. All that a user can do with the keys is to assign them, compare them for equality and determine which key is smaller. The user cannot forge objects of type KEY:

package KEY_MANAGER **is**

    type KEY **is private**;
    NULL_KEY: **constant** KEY;
            --deferred constant because it is of a private type;
            --value has to be supplied in the private part

    procedure GET_KEY(K: **out** KEY);
            --GET_KEY is not defined as a function, because every
            --time it is called it returns a different value.

    function "<"(X, Y: **in** KEY) **return** BOOLEAN;

private
    type KEY **is new** NATURAL;
    NULL_KEY: **constant** KEY := 0;
            --a complete redeclaration of the deferred constant
            --is given to assign it a value

end KEY_MANAGER;

The only operations that can be performed on objects of type KEY outside the package KEY_MANAGER are assignment, comparison for equality and inequality, and the less than operation, <, defined in the package. The body of KEY_MANAGER is

```
package body KEY_MANAGER is

    LAST_KEY: KEY := 0;
            --LAST_KEY is global to the subprograms in the
            --package; this is how one gets the effect of
            --own or static variables in Ada

    procedure GET_KEY(K: out KEY) is
    begin
       LAST_KEY := LAST_KEY + 1;
       K := LAST_KEY;
    end GET_KEY;

    function "<"(X, Y: in KEY) return BOOLEAN is
    begin
       return INTEGER(X) < INTEGER(Y);
            --if the key values X and Y are not converted back
            --to the parent type INTEGER of KEY, then X < Y
            --would recursively invoke < defined for KEY.
            --KEY can be converted to INTEGER, because it is a
            --type derived from INTEGER
    end "<";

end KEY_MANAGER;
```

5. Abstract Data Types

Packages can be used to implement *abstract data types*. Abstract data types are user-defined types for which the user supplies not only the set of values but also the operations on the values. Abstract data types provide data abstraction in much the same way that subprograms provide control abstraction. Details of how an abstract data type is implemented are hidden from the user. Hiding the details prevents the user from

1. making programs dependent on the representation. The representation of an abstract data type can be changed without affecting the rest of the program. For example, the abstract data type *set* may be implemented as a boolean array initially, but this representation may be changed to an ordered list later on for reasons of storage efficiency.

2. accidentally or maliciously violating the integrity of an abstract data type object. Integrity of abstract data type objects is preserved by forcing the user to manipulate these objects using only the operations provided by the designer of the abstract data type.

Abstract data types objects are declared and manipulated in exactly the same way as the predefined data types in the language. A package is not a true abstract data type facility, since it only partially supports the definition of abstract data types [SCH80]. For example, it is not possible to declare an array of packages.

A package is basically an information hiding mechanism. One cannot directly define an abstract data type T and declare objects of type T. In Ada one defines an information hiding package, say FENCE_FOR_T, and inside it specifies a private type definition T and the operations for T:

> **package** FENCE_FOR_T **is**
>
>   **type** T **is private**;   −− or limited private
>
>   −−operations for objects of type T
>
> **private**
>
>   **type** T **is** ... ;
>
> **end** FENCE_FOR_T;
>
> **package body** FENCE_FOR_T **is**
>
> **end** FENCE_FOR_T;

Objects are then declared as being of type T from the package FENCE_FOR_T.

> X, Y, Z: FENCE_FOR_T.T;

The operations are semantically associated with the package FENCE_FOR_T instead of directly with the type T. They must be qualified by the package name. Of course, the need for the qualification may be eliminated by the *use* clause

> **use** FENCE_FOR_T;

However, the operations are still associated with package FENCE_FOR_T and not type T.

Type ORD_SET, declared in the previous section, is an example of an abstract data type declaration using the facilities provided by Ada. Its *fence* is represented by the package ORDERED_SET2.

6. Examples of Packages and Programming with Packages

Several examples are now given to illustrate further the use of packages. The first example, a symbol table manager, is an essential part of every compiler. The symbol table is implemented first using an array and then using an ordered binary tree. The specifications of the symbol table package do not change with the implementation. The second example is a package that implements a set of priority queues that may be used to schedule jobs with different priorities in an operating system. The last two examples, the *no equal subsequence* problem and the *eight queens* problem, illustrate the *trial and error* method of finding a solution to a problem. The trouble with this approach is that the number of possible candidates for a solution can be very large. Consequently, all candidates should not be generated and checked to see if they represent a solution [WIR71]. The set of possible candidates must be reduced considerably without eliminating a candidate that may represent a desired solution.

The reader is urged to try solving the problems before looking at the solutions given.

6.1 A Symbol Table Manager

The problem is to write a symbol table manager. Operations to perform the following actions are to be provided:

1. Insert an item and the information associated with it into the symbol table.

2. Retrieve the information associated with an item in the symbol table.

3. Determine whether or not the symbol table is full.

4. Check to see if an item is in the symbol table.

5. Reinitialize (reset) the symbol table.

Only unique items will be inserted into the symbol table. An insertion may not be made if the symbol table is full.

The items are strings of length 20 (padded with blanks if necessary) and the symbol table should be able to hold at least 200 items. The only information that is to be associated with an item is whether the item is a variable identifier, a function or procedure name, a keyword, or a label name. The example is a simplified version of a real symbol table, because block structure is not handled and the information associated with the items is straightforward.

The specification of the SYMBOL_TABLE_MANAGER package is

```
package SYMBOL_TABLE_MANAGER is

    N: constant := 200;   --size of the symbol table
    ITEM_SIZE: constant := 20;
        --it is good programming style to give constants
        --symbolic names. This enhances program readability
        --and makes it easy to change values of the constants.

    type ITEM is new STRING(1..ITEM_SIZE);
    type ITEM_TYPE is (VAR, FUN, PROC, KEYWD, LABEL);

    procedure ADD(X: in ITEM; I: in ITEM_TYPE);
    function IN_TABLE(X: in ITEM) return BOOLEAN;
    function GET(X: in ITEM) return ITEM_TYPE;
    function FULL return BOOLEAN;
    procedure CLEAR;   --empty table

end SYMBOL_TABLE_MANAGER;
```

The symbol table will be implemented as an array. Searches for the items will be done by searching the array sequentially.

```
package body SYMBOL_TABLE_MANAGER is

    type ITEM_INFO is
        record
            ID: ITEM;
            T: ITEM_TYPE;
        end record;

    ST: array(1..N) of ITEM_INFO;
                --the symbol table representation
    LAST: INTEGER range 0..N := 0;
                --symbol table entries are in ST(1..LAST)

    procedure ADD(X: in ITEM; I: in ITEM_TYPE) is
    begin
        LAST := LAST + 1;
                --assuming that an item is inserted only
                --when the symbol table is not full
                --and the item is not in the table
        ST(LAST).ID := X;
        ST(LAST).T := I;
    end ADD;
```

```
function IN_TABLE(X: in ITEM) return BOOLEAN is
begin
   for J in 1..LAST loop    --search the table; the loop
                            --is not executed if LAST is 0
      if ST(J).ID = X then
         return TRUE;
      end if;
   end loop;
   return FALSE;
end IN_TABLE;

function GET(X: in ITEM) return ITEM_TYPE is
            --GET should be called only after ensuring
            --that item X is in the symbol table
begin
   for J in 1..LAST loop
      if ST(J).ID = X then
         return ST(J).T;
      end if;
   end loop;
end GET;

function FULL return BOOLEAN is
begin
   return LAST = N;
end FULL;

procedure CLEAR is
begin
   LAST := 0;
end CLEAR;

end SYMBOL_TABLE_MANAGER;
```

This simple representation of the symbol table will not be efficient if the number of searches to be performed is large. A hashed table or an ordered binary tree representation will be better, because the average search time will be much less.

6.1.1 An Alternative Representation of the Symbol Table: The SYMBOL_TABLE_MANAGER will now be reimplemented using an ordered binary tree representation for the symbol table. As long as no changes are made to the specifications of the SYMBOL_TABLE_MANAGER or the semantics of the subprograms defined in it, the program units using the package SYMBOL_TABLE_MANAGER *will not have to be modified.* The binary tree representation of the symbol table also illustrates the use of access types and how dynamic objects are allocated and created via the allocator *new*.

The procedure INSERT for adding an element X and the information associated with it to a binary tree with root R is declared as

> **procedure** INSERT(X: **in** ITEM; I : **in** ITEM_TYPE;
> R: **in out** NEXT_ELEMENT);

which is described abstractly as

> **if** R = **null then**
> add the element X with the associated information I at R
> **elsif** X < R.ID **then**
> INSERT(X, I, R.LEFT);
> **else**
> INSERT(X, I, R.RIGHT);
> **end if**;

The other procedures are straightforward. For variety, iteration is used instead of recursion in functions IN_TABLE and GET:

> **package body** SYMBOL_TABLE_MANAGER **is**
>
> **type** ITEM_INFO;   ––an incomplete type declaration.
> **type** NEXT_ELEMENT **is access** ITEM_INFO;
> **type** ITEM_INFO **is**   ––the complete type declaration
>   **record**
>   ID: ITEM;
>   T: ITEM_TYPE;
>   LEFT, RIGHT: NEXT_ELEMENT;
>   **end record**;
>
> ROOT: NEXT_ELEMENT;
>   ––points to the root of the binary tree implementation
>   ––of the symbol table; it is used as a global variable.
>   ––R is initially **null**, which is the default
>   ––initial value
> NUM_ELEMENTS: INTEGER **range** 0..N := 0;

```
procedure ADD(X: in ITEM; I: in ITEM_TYPE) is
        --ADD uses INSERT to  implement the recursive
        --algorithm described above. Duplicate items must
        --not be inserted. Items should be inserted only
        --after ensuring that the table is not full

  procedure INSERT(X: in ITEM; I : in ITEM_TYPE;
                         R: in out NEXT_ELEMENT) is
  begin
    if R = null then
      R := new ITEM_INFO(X, I, null, null);
              --dynamic object explicitly initialized
              --at allocation time
    elsif X < R.ID then
       INSERT(X, I, R.LEFT);
    else
       INSERT(X, I, R.RIGHT);
    end if;
  end INSERT;

begin
  INSERT(X, I, ROOT);
  NUM_ELEMENTS := NUM_ELEMENTS + 1;
end ADD;

function IN_TABLE(X: in ITEM) return BOOLEAN is
  R: NEXT_ELEMENT := ROOT;
              --temporary variable used for tree traversal
begin
  while R /= null loop
    if X = R.ID then
       return TRUE;
    elsif X < R.ID then
       R := R.LEFT;
    else
       R := R.RIGHT;
    end if;
  end loop;
  return FALSE;
end IN_TABLE;
```

```
function GET(X: in ITEM) return ITEM_TYPE is
   R: NEXT_ELEMENT := ROOT;
              --temporary variable used for tree traversal
begin
   while R /= null loop
      if X = R.ID then
         return R.T;
      elsif X < R.ID then
         R := R.LEFT;
      else
         R := R.RIGHT;
      end if;
   end loop;
end GET;

function FULL return BOOLEAN is
begin
   return NUM_ELEMENTS = N;
end FULL;

procedure CLEAR is
begin
   ROOT := null;
   NUM_ELEMENTS := 0;
end CLEAR;

   end SYMBOL_TABLE_MANAGER;
```

The number of items that can be inserted into the symbol table has been restricted to 200 in the ordered binary tree implementation to conform to the specifications of the symbol table package. This restriction is not really necessary in the binary tree implementation, because storage for the items is allocated dynamically, as needed. Items can be inserted into the symbol table as long as storage is available.

The storage area for the binary tree is lost whenever operation CLEAR is executed. This storage will be reclaimed by a garbage collector if the Ada implementation provides one. If reclamation of the storage is important and the implementation does not provide a garbage collector then the user can use an instantiation of the generic procedure UNCHECKED_DEALLOCATION provided by Ada[35] to deallocate unused storage explicitly. As mentioned before, the user must be very careful when deallocating storage explicitly, since the effect of referring to an access value that points to a deallocated object is unpredictable.

6.2 Set of Priority Queues

This example illustrates the use of data refinement, i.e., the use of a simpler package to construct a more complicated one.

Consider an operating system in which jobs are to be scheduled according to their priority (10 being the highest priority and 1 the lowest). The next job that is to be executed is the one with the highest priority. If there is more than one job with the highest priority, then the one that has waited the longest is executed. Each queue associated with a priority should be able to hold 50 jobs. Jobs will be added to a queue only after checking to make sure that the queue is not full. A request for the next job to be executed will be made only after ensuring that there is at least one queue that is not empty.

The set of priority queues will be implemented as the package PRIORITY_QUEUES whose specifications are given below. Type JOB_ID is assumed to be available in the environment where the package PRIORITY_QUEUES is being declared:

package PRIORITY_QUEUES **is**

    type PRIORITY **is new** INTEGER **range** 1..10;

    procedure ADD(P: **in** PRIORITY; J: **in** JOB_ID);
    procedure NEXT(J: **out** JOB_ID);
    function FULL(P: **in** PRIORITY) **return** BOOLEAN;
    function ANY_JOB **return** BOOLEAN;
              ——returns TRUE if there is at least one job and
              ——FALSE otherwise

    end PRIORITY_QUEUES;

Package PRIORITY_QUEUES will be implemented using a package FIFO (first-in first-out) which defines the type QUEUE. The different priority queues can then be implemented as an array of QUEUEs. The operations on objects of type QUEUE are supplied by package FIFO. The specification of

---

35. A list of free elements can be kept in the package body. Freed elements will be added to this list. Storage from this list will be used as and when needed. The storage allocator *new* will be called only when the list is empty. This list will be initially empty.

FIFO is

```
package FIFO is

    MAX_SIZE: constant := 50;
    type QUEUE is limited private;

    procedure ADD(Q: in out QUEUE; J: in JOB_ID);
    procedure FIRST(Q: in out QUEUE; J: out JOB_ID);
                --return and delete the first job in the queue
    function FULL(Q: in QUEUE) return BOOLEAN;
    function EMPTY(Q: in QUEUE) return BOOLEAN;

private
    type JOBS is array(1..MAX_SIZE) of JOB_ID;
    type QUEUE is
      record
        X: JOBS;
        FIRST, LAST: INTEGER range 1..MAX_SIZE := 1;
        CUR_SIZE: INTEGER range 0..MAX_SIZE := 0;
      end record;
end FIFO;
```

The CUR_SIZE values in the queue will be, in the order inserted, in

X(FIRST), X(FIRST mod MAX_SIZE + 1), ...

The body of package FIFO is

```
package body FIFO is
    procedure ADD(Q: in out QUEUE; J: in JOB_ID) is
    begin
      if FULL(Q) then
        PUT("ERROR: Queue Full"); NEW_LINE; return;
            --a better alternative would be to raise an exception
            --indicating to the caller of ADD that the queue is
            --full and that corrective action should be taken;
            --robust programs, check error conditions even if their
            --specifications do not explicitly require the checking
      end if;
      Q.X(Q.LAST) := J;
      Q.LAST := Q.LAST mod MAX_SIZE + 1;
                --mod has a higher precedence than +
      Q.CUR_SIZE := Q.CUR_SIZE + 1;
    end ADD;
```

```
procedure FIRST(Q: in out QUEUE; J: out JOB_ID) is
begin
   if EMPTY(Q) then
      PUT("ERROR: Queue Empty");
               --see the comment given in subprogram ADD
      NEW_LINE;
      return;
   end if;

   J := Q.X(Q.FIRST);
   Q.FIRST := Q.FIRST mod MAX_SIZE + 1;
   Q.CUR_SIZE := Q.CUR_SIZE - 1;
end FIRST;

function FULL(Q: in QUEUE) return BOOLEAN is
begin
   return Q.CUR_SIZE = MAX_SIZE;
end FULL;

function EMPTY(Q: in QUEUE) return BOOLEAN is
begin
   return Q.CUR_SIZE = 0;
end EMPTY;
end FIFO;
```

Use of variable CUR_SIZE is not necessary, since its value can be easily computed from variables FIRST and LAST. However, CUR_SIZE enhances program understandability.

Using the specifications of the package FIFO (i.e., the items declared in it), the package body of PRIORITY_QUEUES is now declared:

```
package body PRIORITY_QUEUES is

P_Q: array(PRIORITY) of FIFO.QUEUE;
                --the 10 priority queues; one for each priority

procedure ADD(P: in PRIORITY; J: in JOB_ID) is
begin
   FIFO.ADD(P_Q(P), J);
end ADD;

procedure NEXT(J: out JOB_ID) is
begin
   for I in reverse PRIORITY loop
                --search higher priority queues first
      if not FIFO.EMPTY(P_Q(I)) then
         FIFO.FIRST(P_Q(I), J);
            return;
         end if;
      end loop;
      PUT("ERROR: No Jobs");
      NEW_LINE;
end NEXT;

function FULL(P: in PRIORITY) return BOOLEAN is
begin
   return FIFO.FULL(P_Q(P));
end FULL;

function ANY_JOB return BOOLEAN is
         --returns TRUE if there is a job of any priority
         --and FALSE otherwise
begin
   for I in PRIORITY loop
      if not FIFO.EMPTY(P_Q(I)) then
         return TRUE;
      end if;
   end loop;
   return FALSE;
end ANY_JOB;

end PRIORITY_QUEUES;
```

The subprogram using these packages may look something like

```
with TEXT_IO; use TEXT_IO;
procedure OPERATING_SYSTEM is
    ––declaration of type JOB_ID
    ––specification and body of package FIFO
    ––specification and body of package PRIORITY_QUEUES
    .
    .
    .
    .
begin
    .
    .
    .
end OPERATING_SYSTEM;
```

6.3 No Equal Subsequence Problem [WIR73, DEN75]

Construct a sequence of length N consisting of the character elements 1, 2 and 3 such that it contains no adjacent equal subsequences. Examples of such sequences are the null sequence, 1, 12, 121 and so on. Some sequences that are invalid or not acceptable are 11, 1211, 1212 and 122.

The solution used generates a series of sequences such that

1. every valid sequence (containing no adjacent equal subsequences) is generated.

2. it is easy (efficient) to check if a sequence is valid or not.

We will start with the null sequence and extend it until we get a valid sequence of length N. The intermediate sequences will be extended only after ensuring that they are valid since all subsequences of a valid sequence are valid. If an intermediate sequence is not valid then it will be transformed until another valid sequence is found. By using this strategy the generation (and therefore validation) of many invalid sequences is ruled out, thus speeding up the finding of a valid sequence of length N.

Two operations will be used to extend and transform the intermediate sequences:

1. EXTEND(S): Extend the sequence S by appending a 1 to it.

2. NEXT(S): Change S to the next sequence in lexicographic order. (If the last element of S is a 1 or 2, increment it to 2 or 3, respectively; if the last element is a 3, delete it and apply NEXT to the truncated sequence.)

The algorithm GENERATE that generates the desired sequence is abstractly defined as

> Start with a null sequence
> **while** Length of sequence is not N or it is not a valid sequence **loop**
>   **if** The sequence is valid **then**
>   EXTEND the sequence
>   **else**
>   Find the NEXT sequence. If there is none then set the
>   sequence to null and quit
> **end loop**

The obvious strategy of checking all subsequences for determining the validity of a sequence is very inefficient. An examination of the algorithm GENERATE shows that a new sequence is obtained in one of two ways:

1. by extending a valid sequence S with the character 1, that is, by operation EXTEND(S), or

2. by taking a sequence S, which without its last element is a valid sequence, and changing its last element, that is, by operation NEXT(S).

Consequently, to determine the validity of a new sequence, it suffices to check only those adjacent subsequences that include the new (i.e., the last) element for equality. Using this fact makes validity checking efficient.

The largest subsequence containing the last element that must be considered in the above validity test will have half the length of the sequence. This observation is based on the fact that, for larger subsequences, there does not exist an adjacent subsequence of equal length.

Function VALID that checks the validity of a string is abstractly defined by the algorithm

> Let S be the sequence to be tested for validity
> Let I be 0 (length of subsequence of S containing its last element)
> **while** I < half the length of S **loop**
>   Increase I by 1
>   **if** the subsequence of length I that contains the last element
>   of S is equal to its adjacent subsequence **then**
>   **return** FALSE
>   **end if**
> **end loop**
> **return** TRUE

The following package, VALID_SEQUENCE_PACKAGE, will be used in procedure GENERATE:

```
package VALID_SEQUENCE_PACKAGE is

   MAX_SIZE: constant := 100;
   type SEQUENCE is private;

   function LENGTH(S: in SEQUENCE) return INTEGER;
   function VALID(S: in SEQUENCE) return BOOLEAN;
   function NULL_SEQ return SEQUENCE;
   function IS_NULL(S: in SEQUENCE) return BOOLEAN;
   procedure EXTEND(S: in out SEQUENCE);
   procedure NEXT(S: in out SEQUENCE);
   procedure PRINT(S: in SEQUENCE);
             --PRINT uses the package TEXT_IO; the body of
             --this package must be compiled with TEXT_IO

private
   type SEQUENCE is
      record
         SEQ: STRING(1..MAX_SIZE);
         L: INTEGER range 0..MAX_SIZE;
      end record;

end VALID_SEQUENCE_PACKAGE;
```

Procedure GENERATE is defined as

```
use VALID_SEQUENCE_PACKAGE;
procedure GENERATE(N: in POSITIVE; S: out SEQUENCE) is
begin
   S := NULL_SEQ;
   while LENGTH(S) /= N or not VALID(S) loop
      if VALID(S) then
         EXTEND(S);
      else
         NEXT(S);
         if IS_NULL(S) then
            return;   --no valid sequence of the desired length
         end if;
      end if;
   end loop;
end GENERATE;
```

GENERATE returns a null sequence if a valid sequence of the desired length does not exist. The body of the package is now defined:

```
package body VALID_SEQUENCE_PACKAGE is

function LENGTH(S: in SEQUENCE) return INTEGER is
begin
    return S.L;
end LENGTH;

function VALID(S: in SEQUENCE) return BOOLEAN is
    I: INTEGER := 0;
                    --I represents the length of the adjacent
                    --subsequences being compared. The right
                    --subsequence includes the last element of S;
                    --it is the element by which S was extended
begin
    while I < S.L/2 loop
                    --max subsequence length for comparison
                    --is half the sequence length
        I := I + 1;
        if S.SEQ(S.L-2*I+1 .. S.L-I)
                        = S.SEQ(S.L-I+1 .. S.L) then
            --equality and inequality are defined for strings
        return FALSE;
        end if;
    end loop;
    return TRUE;
end VALID;

function NULL_SEQ return SEQUENCE is
    S: SEQUENCE;
begin
    S.SEQ := (1..MAX_SIZE => ' ');    --string of blanks
    S.L := 0;
    return S;
end NULL_SEQ;

function IS_NULL(S: in SEQUENCE) return BOOLEAN is
begin
    return S.L = 0;
end IS_NULL;

procedure EXTEND(S: in out SEQUENCE) is
begin
    S.L := S.L + 1;
    S.SEQ(S.L) := '1';
```

```
      end EXTEND;

      procedure NEXT(S: in out SEQUENCE) is
      begin
         while S.SEQ(S.L) = '3' loop
            S.L := S.L - 1;    --delete the character 3
            if S.L = 0 then
               return;    --a sequence of length N cannot be found
            end if;
         end loop;
         S.SEQ(S.L) := CHARACTER'SUCC(S.SEQ(S.L));
                                         --successor of 1 or 2
      end NEXT;

      procedure PRINT(S: in SEQUENCE) is
      begin
         TEXT_IO.PUT(S.SEQ);
         TEXT_IO.NEW_LINE;
      end PRINT;

   end VALID_SEQUENCE_PACKAGE;
```

package VALID_SEQUENCE_PACKAGE implements sequences as strings of 100 characters. This implementation is wasteful, since storage for strings of length 100 must be allocated even if the valid sequence desired is much shorter. It is also restrictive, since the package cannot be used to generate a valid string of length greater than 100.

These problems are eliminated by making the sequence size a discriminant, that is a parameter, of the private type SEQUENCE and letting the user supply the length when declaring sequences. Specification of package VALID_SEQUENCE_PACKAGE is modified to allow for sequences of any length:

```
package VALID_SEQUENCE_PACKAGE is

type SEQUENCE(SIZE: POSITIVE) is private;
        --example of a private type with a discriminant

--specifications of the operations as before

private
    type SEQUENCE(SIZE: POSITIVE) is
    record
        SEQ: STRING(1..SIZE);
        L: INTEGER range 0..SIZE;
    end record;

end VALID_SEQUENCE_PACKAGE;
```

The body of the VALID_SEQUENCE_PACKAGE remains the same. Sequences of the desired length can now be declared as

```
S1: SEQUENCE(10);
S2: SEQUENCE(50);
```

6.4 The Eight Queens Problem

The problem is to place eight queens on a chess board so that they do not attack each other, i.e., every row, column and diagonal of the chess board has at most one queen (in this case, exactly one queen will be on each row and each column, since there are exactly eight rows and eight columns on a chess board).

A placement of the eight queens on the board is called a *configuration*. A configuration is partial if all the eight queens have not been placed. A configuration is *safe* if none of the queens attack each other.

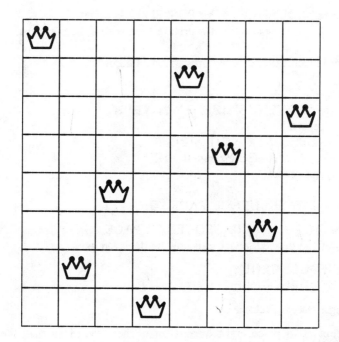

The Eight Queens
(safely placed)

This problem has been studied extensively in the computer science literature [WIR71, Dijkstra in DAH72, WIR76]. It is interesting, because of the trial and error nature of its solution and the choice of the data structure used to represent the chess board.

There are about 2^{32} ways ($\frac{64!}{56! \times 8!}$ combinations) in which the eight queens can be placed. Consequently, only a very poor strategy will attempt to generate all possible configurations in attempting to find a safe configuration. One good strategy is to start with an empty chess board and follow the rule that another queen will be placed only if the queens already on the board constitute a safe partial configuration. This strategy eliminates the consideration of a very large number of unsafe configurations [WIR71].

The solution is given by a recursive backtracking algorithm [WIR71, WIR76]. The procedure call

PLACE_QUEENS(I, SUCCESSFUL);

will place the queens numbered I to 8 on the chess board if it is possible to do it safely. It first places queen number I safely on some row in column I and then calls itself recursively to place the queens numbered I+1 to 8. If the recursive call fails then it tries another row and repeats the recursive call. If all rows have been tried without success then it returns with failure.

Procedure PLACE_QUEENS(I, SUCCESSFUL) returns with success (i.e., with the value TRUE for the variable SUCCESSFUL) when queens numbered I to 8 have been successfully placed. It is defined abstractly as

```
J := 0;  ––J+1 will be the next row in column I
              ––on which queen I will be placed
SUCCESSFUL := FALSE;    ––no success as yet
while not SUCCESSFUL and More rows to try loop
    J := J+1;  ––try next row J in column I
    if Square with column I and row J is safe then
        Put queen I on column I and row J
        if All eight queens have not been placed then
            ––try to place the remaining queens
                PLACE_QUEENS(I+1, SUCCESSFUL);
            if Not successful then
                Remove queen I from column I and row J
            end if;
        else SUCCESSFUL := TRUE;
        end if;
    end if;
end loop;
```

A package CHESS_BOARD with operations to

1.   put a queen on the chess board,

2.   remove a queen from the chess board,

3.   determine if a square is safe or not and

4.   print a configuration

is specified now:

package CHESS_BOARD **is**

> **procedure** PUT_QUEEN(ROW, COL: **in** INTEGER);
> **procedure** REMOVE_QUEEN(ROW, COL: **in** INTEGER);
> **function** SAFE(ROW, COL: **in** INTEGER) **return** BOOLEAN;
> **procedure** PRINT_POSITIONS;

> **end** CHESS_BOARD;

The chess board can be implemented directly as an 8 by 8 matrix of BOOLEAN elements. However, checking to see if a square is safe is not very efficient in this representation, because all the squares from which this square may be under attack may have to be examined. This operation will be executed very frequently and therefore it is important that the operation be implemented efficiently.

In the algorithm for placing the queens, only one queen is placed in each column—queen I is placed in column I. Consequently, a square for placing queen I in column I is safe if there is no queen on the row or the diagonals passing through it. With this in view, Wirth [WIR71] points out that a much better implementation of the chess board would be to use the following arrays:

ROW_POS(I)	is the row position of queen I (queen I is placed in column I) $1 \leqslant I \leqslant 8$
R(J)	is TRUE if there is no queen on row J, $1 \leqslant J \leqslant 8$ and FALSE otherwise
LD(K)	is TRUE if there is no queen on K^{th} diagonal pointing *left* and *down* (/), $2 \leqslant K \leqslant 16$; this kind of diagonal at the square ROW, COL is represented by the element COL+ROW of the array LD (the expression COL+ROW has the same value on all the squares of such diagonals).
RD(K)	is TRUE if there is no queen on K^{th} diagonal pointing *right* and *down* (\ ), $-7 \leqslant K \leqslant 7$; this kind of diagonal at the square ROW, COL is given by the element COL−ROW of the array RD (the expression COL−ROW has the same value on all the squares of such diagonals).

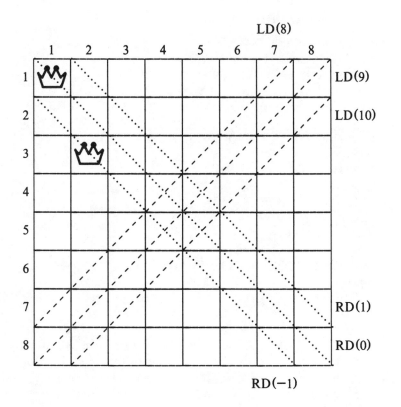

State of Board with 2 Queens

ROW_POS(1) = 1, ROW_POS(2) = 3
R(1) = FALSE, R(3) = FALSE, other elements of R are TRUE
LD(2) = FALSE, LD(5) = FALSE, other elements of LD are TRUE
RD(0) = FALSE, RD(−1) = FALSE, other elements of RD are TRUE

A square with row ROW and column COL can be determined to be safe simply by evaluating the BOOLEAN expression

R(ROW) **and** LD(COL+ROW) **and** RD(COL−ROW)

Assuming that there is no queen in the column COL, the square on row ROW is safe if this expression is TRUE, i.e., there is no queen attacking this square from the diagonals and the row going through it.

The body of the package CHESS_BOARD is

```
package body CHESS_BOARD is
   ROW_POS: array(1..8) of INTEGER;
   R: array(1..8) of BOOLEAN := (1..8 => TRUE);
   LD: array(2..16) of BOOLEAN := (2..16 => TRUE);
   RD: array(-7..7) of BOOLEAN := (-7..7 => TRUE);

   procedure PUT_QUEEN(ROW, COL: in INTEGER) is
   begin
      ROW_POS(COL) := ROW;
      R(ROW) := FALSE;
      LD(COL+ROW) := FALSE;
      RD(COL-ROW) := FALSE;
   end PUT_QUEEN;

   procedure REMOVE_QUEEN(ROW, COL: in INTEGER) is
   begin
      R(ROW) := TRUE;
      LD(COL+ROW) := TRUE;
      RD(COL-ROW) := TRUE;
      --ROW_POS(COL) could also be set to a value indicating
      --that there is no queen in the column COL, but this is not
      --necessary, since this element will be reset when another
      --queen is placed in column COL
   end REMOVE_QUEEN;

   function SAFE(ROW, COL: in INTEGER) return BOOLEAN is
   begin
      return R(ROW) and LD(COL+ROW) and RD(COL-ROW);
   end SAFE;

   procedure PRINT_POSITIONS is
   begin
      for I in 1..8 loop
         PUT("Queen number "); PUT(I);
         PUT(" is in column "); PUT(I);
         PUT(" and row "); PUT(ROW_POS(I));
         NEW_LINE;
      end loop;
   end PRINT_POSITIONS;
end CHESS_BOARD;
```

The procedure EIGHT_QUEENS that prints a safe configuration is

```
with TEXT_IO; use TEXT_IO;
procedure EIGHT_QUEENS is
   package IO_INTEGER is new INTEGER_IO(INTEGER);
   use IO_INTEGER;
   --insert specification and body of CHESS_BOARD here
   use CHESS_BOARD;

   procedure PLACE_QUEENS(I: in INTEGER;
                          SUCCESSFUL: out BOOLEAN) is
      J: INTEGER := 0;
            --J is the row number and I is the column number
   begin
      SUCCESSFUL := FALSE;
      while not SUCCESSFUL and J /= 8 loop
         J := J+1;
         if SAFE(J, I) then
            PUT_QUEEN(J, I);
            if I < 8 then
               PLACE_QUEENS(I+1, SUCCESSFUL);
               if not SUCCESSFUL then
                  REMOVE_QUEEN(J, I);
               end if;
            else
               SUCCESSFUL := TRUE;
            end if;
         end if;
      end loop;
   end PLACE_QUEENS;

   SUCCESSFUL: BOOLEAN;
begin     --body of main procedure EIGHT_QUEENS
   PLACE_QUEENS(1, SUCCESSFUL);   --place all 8 queens
   if SUCCESSFUL then
      PRINT_POSITIONS;
            --we do not really need to test for the
            --success of procedure PLACE_QUEENS as
            --safe configurations are known to exist.
   end if;
end EIGHT_QUEENS;
```

A variation of the eight queens problem, as an exercise for the reader, would be to print out all possible safe board positions the queens could be placed in. *Hint*: When all the queens have been placed safely, the board position is printed out and SUCCESSFUL set to FALSE to force PLACE_QUEENS to look for additional safe board positions. Another variation would be to generalize the problem to N queens and an N by N chess board.

Chapter 4: **Concurrency** [9]

1. Introduction

Ada provides high level facilities for expressing concurrent algorithms. An Ada implementation may provide true concurrency if the underlying computer is a multicomputer or a multiprocessor, or it may simulate concurrency by multiprogramming (i.e., interleaved execution). The ability to express concurrency in a programming language is desirable for two reasons. First, many algorithms are described naturally using concurrency. Second, programs with concurrency explicitly specified may be implemented more efficiently on multicomputers and multiprocessors than can sequential programs.

The model of concurrency in Ada is based on Hoare's Communicating Sequential Processes [HOA78] in which parallel processes synchronize and communicate by means of input and output statements. This model was strongly influenced by Brinch Hansen's Distributed Processes [BRI78]. The designers of Ada rejected control of concurrency by mechanisms such as semaphores, events and signals because of the low level nature of these mechanisms. Monitors were rejected, because they are not always easy to understand, and because their associated signals are low level in nature [DOD79b].

2. Tasks and Rendezvous [9.5]

Parallel processes in Ada are called *tasks*. Tasks, along with subprograms, packages and generic units, constitute the four kinds of program units from which programs are composed. Tasks may have *entries* in them, which may be called by other tasks. Synchronization between two tasks occurs when the task *issuing* an entry call and the task *accepting* an entry call establish a *rendezvous*. The two tasks communicate with each other during the rendezvous. Entries are also the primary means of communication between tasks.[36] Communication in both directions takes place via actual parameters in the entry call and the corresponding formal parameters in the *accept* statement accepting the entry call.

---

36. Tasks can also communicate via global variables.

The rendezvous concept is explained pictorially in Figure 4.1.

Rendezvous

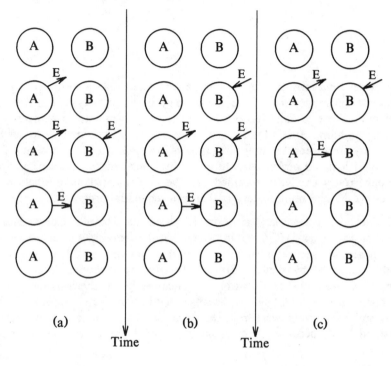

(a)   (b)   (c)

Time   Time

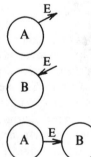

Task A has issued an entry call E to task B

Task B is ready to accept a call to entry E

Task A and B rendezvous at entry E

Figure 4.1

Three situations are illustrated. In the first case (a), task A issues the entry call E before task B is ready to accept it. Task A waits (its execution is suspended) until task B is ready to rendezvous. Having established the rendezvous, the two tasks interact (i.e., communicate). They both resume execution in parallel after completing the rendezvous.

In the second case (b), task B is ready to accept the entry call before A is ready to issue one. This time task B waits for task A to get ready for the rendezvous.

Finally (c), it is also possible for task A to issue the entry call at exactly the same moment that B gets ready to accept it.

The naming scheme used for the rendezvous is asymmetric; the caller (entry call issuer) is required to specify the name of the called task (entry call acceptor), while the called task does not specify the name of the caller. This asymmetry is present to allow the development of libraries containing *server* tasks.

Several tasks can rendezvous with each other, in groups of two or more, at any given instant. Generally, a task will complete a rendezvous with another task before engaging in a rendezvous with a third task.

However, there are situations where two tasks rendezvousing with each other need to interact with a third task before completing their rendezvous. Suppose task A calls task B for some information; task B can supply this information but only after interacting with task C. It is possible to write such interactions between tasks. The task accepting an entry call can, in the middle of a rendezvous, interact with other tasks. For example, suppose task A calls task B; task B can call task C in the middle of the rendezvous:

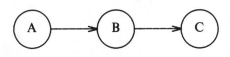

Task B in rendezvous with tasks A and C

In this situation task B must complete its rendezvous with task C before ending its rendezvous with task A. Alternatively, task B can accept an entry call from task T_1 in the middle of its rendezvous with task A. While communicating with T_1 it can accept another entry call from task T_2, and so on in a similar fashion with the additional tasks T_3, ..., T_{n-1}, T_n.

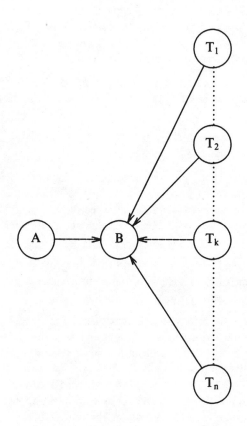

Task B in rendezvous with tasks
A, T_1, T_2,..., T_n.

Task B must complete its rendezvous with the tasks in the reverse of the order in which they were established, i.e., T_n, ..., T_1, A.

3. Task Specification and Body [9.1]

Tasks, subprograms, packages and generic units are the four program units in Ada from which programs are composed. Like a subprogram or a package, a task consists of two parts—a specification and a body.

A task specification has either the form

task identifier;

or the form

task identifier **is**
    entry declarations
    representation clauses
end identifier;

The first form is a task without entries, so it cannot be called by other tasks for a rendezvous. (The *representation clauses* in a task specification will be illustrated in the examples. Additional discussion can be found in Chapter 8 on Representation Clauses and Implementation Dependent Features.)

A task body has the form

task body identifier **is**
    declarations
begin
    sequence_of_statements
[**exception**
    exception handlers]
end identifier;

(*Exception handlers* will be discussed in Chapter 5 on Exceptions.)

As an example, consider a task PRODUCER that reads text from the standard input file and sends it to another task, CONSUMER (Figure. 4.2). CONSUMER converts all lower case characters to upper case and writes them on the standard output file.

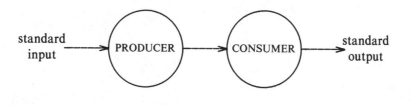

Figure 4.2

The specifications of the two tasks are

```
task PRODUCER;

task CONSUMER is
   entry RECEIVE(C: in CHARACTER);
            --C is a formal parameter, just as in a subprogram
end CONSUMER;
```

PRODUCER reads characters, one at a time, from the standard input and sends them to CONSUMER:

```
task body PRODUCER is
   C: CHARACTER;
begin
   while not END_OF_FILE(STANDARD_INPUT) loop
      GET(C);
      CONSUMER.RECEIVE(C);
   end loop;
end PRODUCER;
```

Entry calls are similar to procedure calls but, they must include the name of the task that contains the entries, e.g., CONSUMER.RECEIVE(C). (For the moment, entry calls may be thought of as being procedure calls that take effect when the two tasks rendezvous.) PRODUCER will terminate upon exhausting the data on the standard input.

CONSUMER accepts characters from PRODUCER and prints them on the standard output file:

```
task body CONSUMER is
   X: CHARACTER;
begin
   loop
      accept RECEIVE(C: in CHARACTER) do
               --the names of the calling tasks are not specified
            X := C;
               --X is needed to record the value of C for use
               --outside the accept statement, since C is local
               --to the accept statement
      end RECEIVE;
      PUT(UPPER(X));
               --output the upper case form. The PUT statement
               --has been placed outside the accept statement
               --so that the caller is not delayed while the
               --PUT statement is being executed.
   end loop;
end CONSUMER;
```

The two tasks rendezvous when PRODUCER has issued the entry call RECEIVE and CONSUMER is ready to accept it. They synchronize at the entry RECEIVE. PRODUCER is suspended until CONSUMER records the character sent to it (i.e., until CONSUMER reaches the end of the *accept* statement associated with entry RECEIVE).

As mentioned before, PRODUCER will terminate upon reaching the end of its body. However, CONSUMER will not terminate, because it never reaches the end of its body. It has an endless loop and will keep waiting at the *accept* statement, indicating its willingness to accept another call and rendezvous.

Only subprograms and packages are compilation units; only they can be compiled by themselves. Consequently, tasks must occur textually within a subprogram or a package. PRODUCER and CONSUMER, along with function UPPER, are put into procedure CONVERT_TO_UPPER_CASE to form a main program:

```
with TEXT_IO; use TEXT_IO;
    --package TEXT_IO contains the input and output
    --procedures GET and PUT and functions
    --END_OF_FILE and STANDARD_INPUT

procedure CONVERT_TO_UPPER_CASE is

    task PRODUCER;

    task CONSUMER is
        entry RECEIVE(C: in CHARACTER);
    end CONSUMER;

    --the characters a-z and A-Z appear sequentially in the Ada
    --character set (ASCII). The relative positions of the
    --corresponding upper and lower case letters are the same.
    --Translation from lower case to upper case is based on this
    --observation.
    function UPPER(C: in CHARACTER) return CHARACTER is
    begin
        if C >= 'a' and C <= 'z' then
            return CHARACTER'VAL(CHARACTER'POS(C)
                - CHARACTER'POS('a') + CHARACTER'POS('A'));

                --CHARACTER'POS(C) is the position of
                --character C in enumeration type CHARACTER.
                --CHARACTER'VAL(I) returns the character in
                --position I.

                --The test C in 'a'..'z' could
                --have alternatively been used in the if statement
        else
            return C;
        end if;
    end UPPER;

    task body PRODUCER is
        C: CHARACTER;
    begin
        while not END_OF_FILE(STANDARD_INPUT) loop
            GET(C);
            CONSUMER.RECEIVE(C);
        end loop;
    end PRODUCER;
```

```
            task body CONSUMER is
              X: CHARACTER;
            begin
              loop
                accept RECEIVE(C: in CHARACTER) do
                  X := C;
                end RECEIVE;
                PUT(UPPER(X));
              end loop;
            end CONSUMER;

            begin      ––PRODUCER and CONSUMER become active
              null;
                  ––according to the syntax, a subprogram body must
                  ––have at least one statement even if it is the
                  ––null statement
            end CONVERT_TO_UPPER_CASE;
```

The two tasks become active immediately before the executable part of the procedure CONVERT_TO_UPPER_CASE is entered (which is just the **null** statement).[37]

3.1 Queuing of Entry Calls [9.5]

Several tasks can issue calls to the same entry of another task. These entry calls are put in a queue associated with the entry and accepted in first-in first-out (FIFO) order. In Figure 4.3, tasks A and B are both interested in rendezvousing with task C at entry E. Tasks A and B issue entry calls before task C has indicated its readiness to accept an entry call. Task C rendezvous first with task B, because it issued the entry call before task A:

---

37. The loop in the body of PRODUCER could have been written simply as
```
    loop
      GET(C);
      CONSUMER.RECEIVE;
    end loop;
```
On reaching the end of the file, an execution of GET will raise an exception, which will cause termination of the task since no exception handler has been provided (see Chapter 5 on Exceptions).

Queuing of Entry Calls

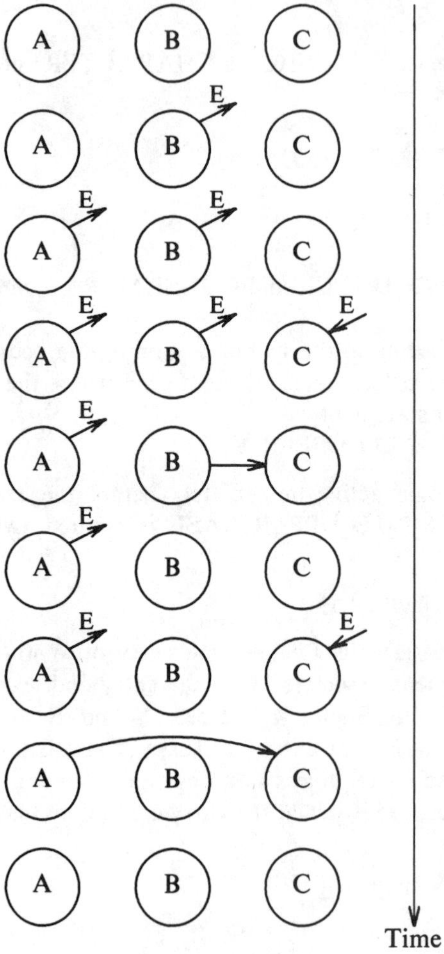

First B calls C and then A calls C
C services B first and then A

Figure 4.3

4. Entries and Accept Statements [9.5]

Entry declarations and calls are syntactically similar to procedure declarations and calls. An entry declaration can occur only in the specification of a task. The corresponding *accept* statements are given in the body of the task. More than one *accept* statement can be given for an entry declaration. Communication between two tasks takes place, when they rendezvous, through the actual parameters in the entry call and the formal parameters in the corresponding *accept* statement.

When a task issues an entry call and the task with the entry is not ready to accept the call (i.e., it is not ready to rendezvous) then the calling task is suspended and put on a queue associated with the entry. Tasks in an entry queue are removed from the queue, one by one, as their entry calls are accepted. The number of tasks waiting at an entry E of a task T is given by the attribute E′COUNT. At any given time a task can be in at most one entry queue.

The task accepting the entry call suspends execution of the calling task as long as necessary to exchange information. The duration of the suspension is equal to the time it takes to execute the statements associated with the *accept* statement. Unlike the called task, the calling task cannot suspend execution of the called task. This one-sided suspension of execution is another asymmetry in Ada's tasking mechanism. Tasks can also wait to accept entry calls from more than one task and issue calls for an immediate rendezvous or one within some specified time period.

If a task calls its own entry *deadlock* occurs, i.e., although the task has not completed or terminated, it will not be able to continue execution. Deadlock occurs because execution of the calling task, which is the same as the called task in this case, is suspended. Such calls are not prohibited in Ada although an implementation may not allow these calls or it may warn the user of their consequences.

As an example of the ability of the called task to suspend the calling task, consider a task A interacting with a task DATABASE that manages a database. When A establishes rendezvous with DATABASE to add information to the database, DATABASE delays A only as long as is necessary to get the information from A. Task A is then allowed to proceed while DATABASE does the conversion of information into the proper format and the actual insertion of the information into the database. On the other hand, when A establishes a rendezvous with DATABASE to retrieve information from the database, A is delayed until the computation and lookups necessary to find the requested information have been done and the information has been given to A.

An attempt to call an entry of a task that has completed, terminated or become *abnormal* results in an error (the exception TASKING_ERROR is raised).

Attribute T′CALLABLE (of type BOOLEAN) of a task T can be used to determine whether a task T has completed, terminated or become abnormal.

4.1 Syntax

The syntax of entry declarations, entry calls and *accept* statements is illustrated by means of examples. The following are some examples of entry declarations:

> **entry** SIGNAL;   −−no parameters
> **entry** SET(T: **in** DURATION);
> **entry** READ(C: **out** CHARACTER);
> **entry** WRITE(C: **in** CHARACTER);

A family of entries (i.e., an array of entries) can also be declared:

> **entry** REGISTER_REQUEST(ID)(D: **in out** DATA);
>   −−sign in for service
> **entry** D_WRITE(1..5)(B: **in** BLOCK);   −−for 5 disks

Some examples of entry calls are

> ALARM.SET(NEXT_MOVE_TIME);
> BUFFER.READ(C);
> DISKS.D_WRITE(J)(B);   −−write block B on disk J

Examples of *accept* statements are

> **accept** SIGNAL;
>
> **accept** SET(T : **in** DURATION) **do**
>   PERIOD := T;
>   −−calling task suspended while this assignment is executed
> **end** SET;
>
> **accept** READ(C: **out** CHARACTER) **do**
>   C := Q(INB **mod** N);
> **end** READ;
>
> −−*accept* statement corresponding to the Ith member
> −−of the entry family D_WRITE
> **accept** D_WRITE(I)(B: **in** BLOCK) **do**
>   −−sequence of statements
> **end** D_WRITE;

As mentioned before, the calling task is blocked while information exchange takes place. The duration of blocking is the amount of time it takes the called task to execute the statements contained within the **do** ... **end** part (if any) following the *accept* statement.

5. Delay Statement [9.6]

A task can temporarily suspend its execution by executing a *delay* statement. The statement

delay T;

causes suspension of the task executing the statement for at least T seconds. T is an arithmetic expression of the predefined fixed point type DURATION. If T is zero or negative, execution of the *delay* statement has no effect.

6. Activation, Completion, Dependence and Termination of Tasks [9.3. 9.4]

Tasks declared immediately within a declarative part (that is tasks that are not nested within a declaration) become active just prior to the execution of the first statement following the declarative part. (In case a package body does not have any statements then a *null* statement is assumed.) The tasks are activated in an arbitrary order; this prevents the user from relying upon the order of task activation and allows the implementation to activate the tasks in any order, such as the most efficient one.

A task, block or a subprogram is said to have *completed* execution when the statements associated with it have been executed, i.e., the end of its body has been reached.

Each task depends upon a *master*—a task, a currently executing block or subprogram, or a library package. A task created using the storage allocator (see section on *task types*) depends upon the master containing the associated access type definition. Other tasks depend upon the master whose execution created them.

A task terminates if it

1. has completed and it has no dependent tasks.

2. has completed and all dependent tasks have terminated.

3. is waiting at a *terminate* alternative and

   • it depends upon a master which has completed execution, and

   • all dependent tasks of this master have either already terminated or are waiting at a *terminate* alternative.

A block or a subprogram is left only if all dependent tasks have terminated.

7. Select Statement [9.7]

There are three kinds of *select* statements—the *selective wait*, the *conditional entry* call and the *timed entry* call. The *selective wait* statement allows a task to accept entry calls from more than one task in a non-deterministic fashion.

The conditional entry call, unlike the normal entry call, is a non-blocking entry call. The calling task does not wait if the called task is not ready but goes on to do other things. The timed entry call is similar to the conditional entry call except that the calling task waits a specified period for the called task to get ready to accept the entry call before giving up and going on to other work.

7.1 Selective Wait [9.7.1]

The *selective wait* statement has the form

```
select
    select_alternative
{or
    select_alternative}
[else
    sequence_of_statements]
end select;
```

where a *select_alternative* is of the form

```
[when condition =>]
             selective_wait_alternative
```

An alternative of the *select* statement is said to be *open* if there is no *when* clause before it or if the condition in the *when* clause is true. Otherwise it is said to be *closed*.

A *selective_wait_alternative* can be one of

```
    accept_statement [sequence_of_statements]
  | delay_statement [sequence_of_statements]
  | terminate;
```

A *selective wait* statement can have at most one *terminate* alternative. If a terminate alternative is present then the *selective wait* statement cannot contain the delay statement as an alternative. An *else* part is not allowed in a *selective wait* statement containing a terminate or a delay alternative.

The execution of a *selective wait* statement is defined as follows:

1. Determine all the open alternatives and start counting time for the *delay* statements (if any).

2. If there are open alternatives or there is an *else* part in the *selective wait* statement then the steps given below are followed in determining the next course of action:

    a. Select any one of the open alternatives that is an *accept* statement and for which a rendezvous can be established. Perform the rendezvous and execute the sequence of statments inside the *accept* statement and those following it.

b. Select an open alternative containing a *delay* statement with the shortest delay period, if no alternative has been selected yet. Execute the sequence of statements following the *delay* statement.

c. A *terminate* alternative may be selected if all dependent tasks of the master associated with the task containing the *terminate* alternative have terminated or are waiting at a *terminate* alternative. The selection of the *terminate* alternative is subject to the condition that there are no calls pending to any entry of the task containing the *terminate* alternative.

d. If no open alternative can be selected immediately or all the alternatives are closed then the *else* part is selected; if there is no *else* part then execution is suspended until an open alternative can be selected.

3. If all the alternatives are closed and there is no *else* part in the *selective wait* statement then raise the exception PROGRAM_ERROR.

The body of task CONSUMER, given earlier, is now modified so that it terminates instead of executing forever. The *accept* statement in CONSUMER is made part of a *select* statement that also has a terminate alternative. CONSUMER will now terminate by the selection of the terminate alternative after it determines that PRODUCER has terminated.

```
task body CONSUMER is
   X: CHARACTER;
begin
   loop
      select
            accept RECEIVE(C: in CHARACTER) do
               X := C;
            end RECEIVE;
            PUT(UPPER(X));
      or
            terminate;
      end select;
   end loop;
end CONSUMER;
```

The *terminate* alternative is selected in a task only after it is determined that all other tasks interacting with it have terminated.

7.2 Conditional Entry Call [9.7.2]

A conditional entry call is used to attempt an immediate rendezvous. If an immediate rendezvous is possible then the rendezvous takes place and the sequence of statements following the entry call is executed; otherwise the alternative sequence of statements specified in the *else* alternative is executed. A conditional entry call has the form

```
select
    entry_call [sequence_of_statements]
else
    sequence_of_statements
end select;
```

A conditional entry call can be used by a task to poll another task repeatedly to determine if it is ready to rendezvous. For example, a task X containing the following loop tries to read a card by calling entry READ of the card reader driver CARD. If CARD is not ready to rendezvous, task X does some local computations instead of wasting time waiting for CARD to be ready. This process is repeated indefinitely until a card can be read. Of course, it might be wiser to restrict the number of rendezvous attempts to a finite number:

```
loop
    select
        CARD.READ(C);
        process the card C
        exit;
    else
        do local computation
    end select;
end loop;
```

7.3 Timed Entry Call [9.7.3]

A timed entry call is an attempt to establish a rendezvous within some specified time period. If a rendezvous can be established within the specified period, then rendezvous takes place and the statements following the entry call are executed. Otherwise the statements following the specified delay period are executed. The timed entry call has the form

```
select
    entry_call [sequence_of_statements]
or
    delay_statement [sequence_of_statements]
end select;
```

The timed entry call can be used to monitor a critical device that must respond within a specified time period. If such a device does not respond within this period, then immediate corrective action must be taken. For example, in a nuclear reactor the task measuring the temperature of the walls of the vessel containing the fuel rods must supply a new temperature reading regularly within every 0.1 seconds. Otherwise an alarm, exception NO_TEMP_READING, is raised so that corrective action can be taken. This monitoring is implemented as

```
loop
  select
    accept NEW_TEMP(A: in TEMPERATURE) do
      T := A;
    end NEW_TEMP;
      .
      .
      .
    process latest temperature T
      .
      .
      .
  or
    delay 0.1;
            --wait one tenth of a second before raising an alarm
    raise NO_TEMP_READING;
            --alarm is raised; exceptions are discussed in
            --Chapter 5 on Exceptions
  end select;
end loop;
```

8. Mutual Exclusion

The rendezvous mechanism can be used to implement *mutual exclusion* of operations in time. Mutual exclusion is needed when several tasks update common data to ensure consistency of the data [BRI73]. Mutual exclusion is easily achieved in Ada by ensuring that only two tasks are involved in a particular rendezvous. One task can be assigned to monitor the region of shared data where mutual exclusion is desired. For example, task SHARED_DATA monitors shared data that is updated and read by several tasks:

```
task SHARED_DATA is
   entry UPDATE(formal parameters);
   entry READ(formal parameters);
end SHARED_DATA;

task body SHARED_DATA is
   .
   .
   declarations for the shared data
   .
   .
begin
   loop
       --accept, one at a time, calls to update or read the shared data
       select
           accept UPDATE(formal parameters) do
               Record the parameters
           end UPDATE;
           --let the task supplying the update resume execution
           --while the actual update is done
           Perform the update
       or
           accept READ(formal parameters) do
               Set the parameters to the appropriate values
           end READ;
       or
           --quit if all tasks interested in the shared data
           --have quit or are ready to quit
               terminate;
       end select;
   end loop;
end SHARED_DATA;
```

The common data is accessed by the entry calls

SHARED_DATA.UPDATE(actual parameters);

and

SHARED_DATA.READ(actual parameters);

This example shows that is very easy to achieve mutual exclusion in Ada.

It is often desirable to allow more than one task to read the shared data at the same time, since this results in a smaller average waiting time for the tasks. To allow this, a task must be designed that grants permissions to update or read the shared data but does not monitor the shared data itself, as is done by the task SHARED_DATA. The user tasks inform the permissions task when they are finished with the data so that the permissions task can keep track of the tasks accessing the shared data.

9. Task Types [9.1, 9.2]

Task types facilitate the declaration of similar tasks, since several tasks can be declared collectively in an array or individually. The declaration of a task type is syntactically similar to the declaration of a task, with the only difference being the presence of the keyword *type* in the task specification. For example a task type FORK is declared as

```
task type FORK is
    entry PICK_UP;
    entry PUT_DOWN;
end FORK;
```

The declaration

```
F1, F2: FORK;
```

declares two tasks F1 and F2. These tasks become active, as before, just prior to execution of the first statement of the subprogram or package in which they are declared. Arrays whose elements are tasks are declared just like arrays with other types of elements. For example, each element of array F declared as

```
F: array(ID) of FORK;
```

is a task.

Task types are like limited private types. Objects of task types are constants and cannot be assigned to or compared for equality. Tasks can be passed as parameters; the actual parameter and the corresponding formal parameter designate the same task for all parameter modes. If an application needs to create tasks dynamically or to store and exchange the identities of the tasks, then access types must be used. For example, consider access type ANOTHER_FORK declared as

```
type ANOTHER_FORK is access FORK;
```

and variable EXTRA_FORK declared as

```
EXTRA_FORK: ANOTHER_FORK;
```

A task can be created dynamically by calling the allocator as illustrated by the statement

```
EXTRA_FORK := new FORK;
```

Allocated tasks become active when allocated. All allocated tasks must have terminated or be ready to terminate when the scope of the block, subprogram or task in which the access type is declared is about to be left; otherwise, Ada prevents the scope from being left.

10. Abort Statement [9.10]

A task can be explicitly terminated by means of an *abort* statement. The statement

> **abort** T_1, T_2, ..., T_n;

causes all of the tasks T_1, T_2, ..., T_n, that have not already terminated, to become *abnormal* thus preventing any further rendezvous with these tasks. A task that depends upon an abnormal task also becomes abnormal.

A task that becomes abnormal terminates immediately if it is waiting at an entry call, an *accept* statement, a *select* statement, or a *delay* statement; otherwise, termination occurs as soon as the task reaches a synchronization point such as the start or the end of a *accept* statement, an exception handler and so on.

If the calling task becomes abnormal in the middle of a rendezvous, it is allowed to complete the rendezvous before being terminated; the called task is unaffected. If the task containing the *accept* statement becomes abnormal in the middle of a rendezvous, then the exception TASKING_ERROR is raised in the calling task at the point of entry call.

The exception TASKING_ERROR is raised, at the point of entry call, in all tasks waiting or attempting to rendezvous with an aborted task. The task attribute CALLABLE has the value FALSE if the task has become abnormal (or has completed or terminated).

A task in Ada can abort any task including itself. However, the tasks specified must be visible at the place in the program where they are aborted. Although this blanket ability to abort tasks can be misused, it may be required in applications, such as the control of nuclear reactors and missiles, where misbehaving tasks may have to be terminated in an effort to avoid a catastrophe. The *abort* statement should be used only in well understood situations.

11. Interrupts [13.5.1]

Hardware interrupts are handled elegantly in Ada. Queued interrupts are treated like ordinary entry calls, while interrupts that are lost if not processed immediately are treated like conditional entry calls. A task entry can be associated with a hardware interrupt by specifying that the entry should be located at the interrupt address. This specification is implementation dependent. An *accept* statement executed in response to an interrupt is accorded the highest priority (higher than any user task) so that efficient use can be made of devices and good response achieved in real-time control situations. (Further discussion on the association of entries with hardware interrupt addresses is given in Chapter 8 on Representation Clauses and Implementation Dependent Features.)

12. Task Priorities [9.8]

Each task may be assigned a priority that overrides the default priority assigned to a task by the implementation. Tasks can be assigned a priority by using the PRIORITY pragma which is of the form

pragma PRIORITY(P);

which is included in the specification of the task. P is a static expression of the implementation defined integer subtype PRIORITY. The higher the value of P, the higher the priority of the task.

The priority of a task is static and cannot be changed dynamically. A task with a higher priority is always given preference in the selection of a task for a rendezvous. For example, suppose that two tasks A and B, A having a higher priority than B, are ready to rendezvous with a third task C. If A and B have called different entries of C, then A will be selected, because of its higher priority. If A and B have called the same entry of C then the task selected will be the one that called C first; in this case the priorities do not make any difference. The order of scheduling tasks of equal priority is not specified and is left to the implementation. Priorities should be used to indicate the importance or the urgency of a task. They should not be used to control synchronization.

13. Task and Entry Attributes [9.9]

The following attributes are defined for tasks and task types:

T'CALLABLE	FALSE if task T has completed, terminated or become abnormal, and TRUE otherwise.
T'TERMINATED	TRUE if task T has terminated and FALSE otherwise.
E'COUNT	the number of tasks waiting to rendezvous at entry E

14. Examples

The power of Ada's tasking facilities is now demonstrated by several complete examples including one large example. The examples show how low level synchronization facilities such as signals and semaphores can be implemented, how tasks can communicate via a buffer and how tasks can be scheduled using a desired scheduling algorithm instead of the FIFO scheduling discipline provided by Ada. The *dining philosophers* problem was chosen, because it illustrates many of the problems encountered in concurrent programming. Real-time programming is illustrated by programs to control a traffic light and an elevator car. These examples also show how hardware interrupts are treated like entry calls. The program that controls the movement of an elevator car is quite large and illustrates most of the aspects of Ada discussed so far.

14.1 Implementing Signals via Ada Tasks

Signals are a low level facility used for synchronizing parallel processes (tasks in Ada terminology) in several programming languages (for example, PL/I [IBM70] and Modula-2 [WIR80]). When a signal is sent, one of the processes, if any, waiting for this signal is allowed to proceed further. If no process is waiting, then the signal is lost.

Signals can be implemented as tasks in Ada. For example, the signal SIGNAL is implemented as a task SIGNAL with entries WAIT and WAKEUP:

```
task SIGNAL is
   entry WAIT;
   entry WAKEUP;
end SIGNAL;
```

A call to the entry WAIT of the task SIGNAL makes the calling task wait until after SIGNAL accepts a WAKEUP entry call. Only one waiting task is released per rendezvous at the WAKEUP entry. Accepting a WAKEUP entry call has no effect if no tasks are waiting—this is the equivalent of a signal being lost. The task SIGNAL is implemented as

```
task body SIGNAL is
begin
  loop
     accept WAKEUP;
     ——release one waiting task (if any)
        if WAIT'COUNT > 0 then
           accept WAIT;
        end if;
     end loop;
  end SIGNAL;
```

The COUNT attribute of an entry should be used carefully to avoid subtle errors. For example, the above implementation of the task SIGNAL would be erroneous if tasks calling the entry WAIT withdraw the calls after some time period, i.e., timed entry calls. The error occurs when all the calls to WAIT are withdrawn after the task SIGNAL has determined that WAIT'COUNT is greater than 0 but before it has had a chance to accept an entry call.[38]

A separate task must be declared for every signal to be provided. If several signals have to be implemented then it will be more convenient to declare a task type to implement the signals. For example, instead of declaring SIGNAL a task type SIGNAL_TYPE is declared (SIGNAL_TYPE is identical to SIGNAL except for the keyword **type** in its specification). Several signals S1, S2, S3, S4 and S5 can now be easily declared as

     S1, S2, S3, S4, S5: SIGNAL_TYPE;

A task cannot exist by itself: it must be part of a subprogram or a package. A task that is to be made available to the users must be enclosed in a package. For example, the task SIGNAL might be enclosed in a package SIGNAL_PACKAGE, which is declared as

---

38. Suppose that timed entry calls were being used to call the entry WAIT in this example. Then the problem resulting from their use could be avoided by using the *selective wait* statement

     select
        accept WAIT;
     else
        null;
     end select;

is used instead of the *if* statement using the COUNT attribute of WAIT

     if WAIT'COUNT > 0 **then**
        accept WAIT;
     end if;

```
package SIGNAL_PACKAGE is
  procedure WAIT_SIGNAL;
  procedure WAKEUP_SIGNAL;
end SIGNAL_PACKAGE;

package body SIGNAL_PACKAGE is

  --specification of task SIGNAL

  --the specification of SIGNAL must be given before the following
  --subprograms, since they call entries of SIGNAL

  procedure WAIT_SIGNAL is
  begin
    SIGNAL.WAIT;
  end WAIT_SIGNAL;

  procedure WAKEUP_SIGNAL is
  begin
    SIGNAL.WAKEUP;
  end WAKEUP_SIGNAL;

  --body of task SIGNAL

end SIGNAL_PACKAGE;
```

Entries of task SIGNAL are called by using the appropriate procedure provided by SIGNAL_PACKAGE. In this example, the task specification and body are both declared in the body of the encapsulating package. Alternatively, specification of task SIGNAL could have been given in the specification of SIGNAL_PACKAGE and entries of task SIGNAL called directly, e.g.,

```
SIGNAL_PACKAGE.SIGNAL.WAIT;
```

Suppose that a user wants a different kind of signal—when a signal is received, all waiting processes, instead of one, are allowed to proceed. The above implementation of signals can be easily modified to allow this. Task SIGNAL_ALL is similar to task SIGNAL except that, after accepting a WAKEUP entry call, SIGNAL_ALL releases all waiting tasks:

```
task SIGNAL_ALL is
  entry WAIT;
  entry WAKEUP;
end SIGNAL_ALL;
```

```
task body SIGNAL_ALL is
begin
   loop
      accept WAKEUP;

         --all processes waiting at the time of evaluation
         --of the loop expression WAIT'COUNT (the number of
         --processes waiting at the entry WAIT) will be released
         --in FIFO order

      for I in 1 .. WAIT'COUNT loop
         accept WAIT;
      end loop;

   end loop;
end SIGNAL_ALL;
```

14.2 Semaphores

A *semaphore* is synchronization tool invented by E. W. Dijkstra [DIJ68]. A semaphore is a variable that is used to exchange timing signals between concurrent processes (tasks in Ada) by means of the operations P (wait) and V (signal)[39] [BRI73].

One use of semaphores is to implement mutual exclusion. A process executes the P operation before accessing the shared data and the V operation after its access is complete. The process executing the P operation is delayed if any other process is in the midst of accessing the shared data. It will be allowed to continue only after the process accessing the shared data has finished and executed its own V operation. In one version of the semaphore, processes executing the P operation are queued and released in FIFO order as a result of the V operations.

The following task type SEMAPHORE is used to implement semaphores:

```
task type SEMAPHORE is
   entry P;
   entry V;
end SEMAPHORE;
```

---

39. P and V are abbreviations for Dutch words.

```
task body SEMAPHORE is
begin
  loop
    accept P;
    accept V;
  end loop;
end SEMAPHORE;
```

Semaphores are declared by declaring tasks of type SEMAPHORE.

S1: SEMAPHORE;

To have exclusive access to the shared data, all the concurrent processes accessing the shared data must have code segments of the form

S1.P;
access the shared data
S1.V;

The semaphore is a low level synchronization tool and its usage is error prone [BRI73, DOD79b]. For example, synchronization calls can be inadvertently left out or the P operations mistakenly bypassed. It is to avoid such errors that Ada has selected the high level rendezvous for synchronization and mutual exclusion.

14.3 Task Communication via a Buffer Task

Communication between tasks in Ada is not automatically buffered. If buffering is needed then it must be explicitly provided by an intervening task.

The tasks PRODUCER and CONSUMER, in the procedure CONVERT_TO_UPPER_CASE given earlier, have to rendezvous once for each character transmitted. Variations in speed of the tasks PRODUCER and the CONSUMER are not possible, since there is no buffering of communication between them.

A modified version of the procedure described above, called CONVERT_TO_UPPER_CASE2, is now presented in which communication between PRODUCER and CONSUMER is buffered to allow variations in speed. Buffering is accomplished by introducing an intervening task called BUFFER with a maximum buffering capacity of 50 characters. Both the tasks PRODUCER and CONSUMER now call BUFFER to send and receive characters instead of interacting directly with each other. PRODUCER is forced to wait if it is producing characters much faster than CONSUMER can digest (i.e., when BUFFER contains 50 characters). On the other hand, CONSUMER is forced to wait if it consumes much faster than PRODUCER produces (i.e., when BUFFER is empty).

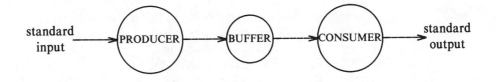

```
with TEXT_IO; use TEXT_IO;
procedure CONVERT_TO_UPPER_CASE2 is

    task PRODUCER;      --sends characters to the buffer
    task CONSUMER;      --reads characters from the buffer
    task BUFFER is      --buffers up to 50 characters
       entry WRITE(C: in CHARACTER);
       entry READ(C: out CHARACTER);
    end BUFFER;

    function UPPER(C: in CHARACTER) return CHARACTER is

       --as declared previously in
       --procedure CONVERT_TO_UPPER_CASE

    end UPPER;

    task body PRODUCER is
       C: CHARACTER;
    begin
       while not END_OF_FILE(STANDARD_INPUT) loop
          GET(C);
          BUFFER.WRITE(C);
       end loop;
    end PRODUCER;

    task body CONSUMER is
       X: CHARACTER;
    begin
       loop
          BUFFER.READ(X);
          PUT(UPPER(X));
       end loop;
    end CONSUMER;
```

```
task body BUFFER is
  N: constant INTEGER := 51;
  Q: array(1..N) of CHARACTER;
      --max number of elements in the buffer will be N-1,
  INB, OUTB: INTEGER range 1..N := 1;
      --INB mod  N: next free space in Q
      --OUTB mod N: first element in Q, if any
      --INB = OUTB: Q is empty; initially true
      --INB mod N + 1 = OUTB: Q is full; as a
      --consequence the buffer always has one unused
      --element in this implementation scheme
begin
  loop
    select
      when INB mod N + 1 /= OUTB =>    --Q not full
        --a character can be accepted
          accept WRITE(C: in CHARACTER) do
            Q(INB mod N) := C;
          end WRITE;
              --PRODUCER can resume execution
        INB := INB mod N + 1;
    or when INB /= OUTB =>          --Q not empty
        --a character can be read
          accept READ(C: out CHARACTER) do
            C := Q(OUTB mod N);
          end READ;
              --CONSUMER can resume execution
        OUTB := OUTB mod N + 1;
    or
        terminate;
    end select;
  end loop;
end BUFFER;

begin
    --PRODUCER, CONSUMER and BUFFER become active
  null;
end CONVERT_TO_UPPER_CASE2;
```

On reaching the end of standard input, task PRODUCER terminates. However, CONSUMER does not terminate after all the characters supplied by PRODUCER have been processed. BUFFER cannot terminate until both PRODUCER and CONSUMER have terminated or are willing to terminate.

CONSUMER cannot be modified easily as was possible in case of procedure CONVERT_TO_UPPER_CASE given earlier. Modification is not simple now, because a terminate alternative cannot be used in the task in CONSUMER as it does not accept entry calls (the terminate alternative can be used only in *selective wait* statements). However, this problem can be rectified in one of several ways. For example

1. modify PRODUCER to send an *end of transmission* character when it is done; modify CONSUMER to terminate when it gets this character from BUFFER. With this approach one character must be reserved to indicate termination.

2. add additional entries to BUFFER by which PRODUCER informs BUFFER that it will not be sending any more data and CONSUMER determines that no more data will be available. CONSUMER aborts when it determines that no more data is available.

3. Add an entry to BUFFER by which a task can determine if BUFFER has any characters. CONSUMER completes execution by exiting the loop when it determines that PRODUCER has completed or terminated (using the attribute CALLABLE), and BUFFER has no characters.

4. Restructure the program.

None of these alternatives is very satisfactory. The first one seems to be the best.

Tasks PRODUCER and CONSUMER are suspended by BUFFER as long as it is necessary for BUFFER to communicate with them, i.e, until the end of the *accept* statement corresponding to the entry called by them. It would be inefficient to hold up these tasks longer than necessary. For example, the *accept WRITE* statement in BUFFER could alternatively have been written as

```
accept WRITE(C: in CHARACTER) do
   Q(INB mod N) := C;
   INB := INB mod N + 1;
end WRITE;
```

This would be inefficient, since PRODUCER will be unnecessarily suspended while BUFFER is doing its internal bookkeeping (incrementing INB). Statements inside the **do** ... **end** of an *accept* statement should be kept to a minimum to avoid delaying the calling task unnecessarily.

14.4 Controlling Task Scheduling

Entry calls are accepted in first-in first-out order. In some situations, a different scheduling discipline is desired. For example, disk access requests may be accepted in an order that minimizes head movement and an operating system may schedule jobs with the smallest execution times first to minimize the average waiting time.

One strategy that can be used to implement a different scheduling scheme is to use a family of entries. Suppose requests for service are classified into three categories declared as

> **type** REQUEST_LEVEL **is** (URGENT, NORMAL, LOW);

Urgent requests are accepted before any other kind of requests. Normal requests are accepted only if there are no urgent requests pending. Finally, requests in the low category are accepted only if there are no urgent or normal priority requests pending. Within each category requests are accepted in FIFO order.

This scheme is implemented by a task SERVICE that contains the declaration of an entry family REQUEST:

> **task** SERVICE **is**
>   **entry** REQUEST(REQUEST_LEVEL) (D: **in out** DATA);
> **end** SERVICE;

Each member of REQUEST handles one request category. For example, the entry call

> SERVICE.REQUEST(URGENT)(D);   −−D is the data

is a request for urgent service.

The body of task SERVICE is

```
    task body SERVICE is
      --local declarations
    begin
      loop
        select
          accept REQUEST(URGENT)(D: in out DATA) do
            :
            process the request
            :
          end REQUEST;
            :
        or when REQUEST(URGENT)'COUNT = 0 =>
                    --the number of tasks waiting at an entry is
                    --given by the COUNT attribute
          accept REQUEST(NORMAL)(D: in out DATA) do
            :
            process the request
            :
          end REQUEST;
            :
        or when REQUEST(URGENT)'COUNT = 0
                    and REQUEST(NORMAL)'COUNT = 0 =>
          accept REQUEST(LOW)(D: in out DATA) do
            :
            process the request
            :
          end REQUEST;
            :
        end select;
      end loop;

    end SERVICE;
```

Scheduling algorithms such as those for minimizing disk head movement or average process waiting time cannot be implemented with this scheme. To implement a general scheduling scheme, use a two stage process involving two entry calls. First, the task requesting service gets an identification number and issues an entry call indicating that it wants service. This call is accepted immediately and the identification of the calling task is noted by SERVICE—this is the signing-in stage. Next, the caller issues another entry call that is accepted by SERVICE only when it can perform the service—this is the waiting-for-service stage.

The reason for making two entry calls is that SERVICE cannot schedule the calling task, say A, until it rendezvous with A to get information about the request and the resources required. Task A is then given a unique identification number, which it must use to get service. This registering of the request takes place during the first call to SERVICE, at its entry REGISTER_REQUEST. After this, A calls SERVICE again, this time calling a member of the entry family GET_SERVICE corresponding to its identification number. A is then delayed until it gets the requested service. The next task to be served, the task whose call to the entry GET_SERVICE is accepted, is determined by SERVICE using some specified scheduling algorithm.

Task SERVICE is an implementation of the abstract algorithm

```
loop
    Accept all jobs waiting to sign in for service
    Provide service to one job (if any)
end loop
```

It is inconvenient and error prone to let the calling task actually make the two entry calls. Instead, they are encapsulated in a procedure body and the task requesting service issues only one procedure call (which is syntactically similar to an entry call). However, a subprogram specification cannot be in a task specification. Consequently, task SERVICE is enclosed in a package SERVICE_PACKAGE:

```
package SERVICE_PACKAGE is
   --definition of type DATA
   procedure GET_SERVICE(D: in out DATA);
end SERVICE_PACKAGE;

package body SERVICE_PACKAGE is

   subtype ID is INTEGER range 1..100;
   --procedure NEXT_ID, FREE_ID and data to allocate/deallocate
   --identification for tasks requesting service. These are used
   --in procedure GET_SERVICE.

   --other local declarations of SERVICE_PACKAGE

   task SERVICE is
      entry REGISTER_REQUEST(ID)(D: in out DATA);  --sign in
            --Family of entries with index type ID
            --A job that is assigned the unique identification
            --number J of type ID calls entry J for service
      entry SERVE_REQUEST(ID)(D: in out DATA);
   end SERVICE;

   procedure GET_SERVICE(D: in out DATA) is
   begin
      Get a unique identifier I
      --register service request; member I of the entry
      --family REGISTER_REQUEST is called with data D
         SERVICE.REGISTER_REQUEST(I)(D);
      --wait for service
         SERVICE.SERVE_REQUEST(I)(D);
      Free identifier I
   end GET_SERVICE;

   task body SERVICE is
   begin
      loop

         for I in ID loop
               --a loop is used to accept calls of an
               --entry family
            select
                  --poll each member of the entry family;
                  --there can be only one call per member, since
                  --jobs requesting service are assigned unique
```

```
                    --identification numbers
              accept REGISTER_REQUEST(I)(D: in out DATA) do
                  .
                  .
                    --add job I to waiting list
                 end REGISTER_REQUEST;
            else
                null;
            end select;
         end loop;

         if there is any task waiting for service then
            --Let K be the next job to be provided service
            --determined using the specified scheduling algorithm
                 accept SERVE_REQUEST(K)(D:in out DATA) do
                  .
                  .
                 end SERVE_REQUEST;
         end if;

       end loop;

     end SERVICE;

   end SERVICE_PACKAGE;
```

14.5 The Ranked Signals of Modula [WIR77a, WIR77b, WIR77c]

The problem is to implement Modula's primitives for synchronizing concurrent processes. Processes synchronize using signals in Modula. The synchronization primitives allow the specification of a process *delay rank* (the process with the least delay rank has the highest priority). Package SIGNAL_PACKAGE, given earlier, did not allow specification of a delay rank; moreover, it provided only one signal. Using the new package implementing signals, a user will be able to specify the delay rank of a process and declare more than one signal.

The Modula synchronization primitives are

wait(S, R)	Delay the calling process until it gets signal S and give the process delay rank R (a positive integer expression).
wait(S)	Same as *wait (S, 1)*.
send(S)	Send a signal to the process waiting for signal S that has the least delay rank. If several processes have the same delay rank then the process waiting the longest gets the signal. The

process getting the signal resumes execution.

awaited(S)   Function that returns the value TRUE if there is a process waiting for the S signal. Otherwise it returns the value FALSE.

These primitives will be implemented as subprograms in a package SIGNALS_PACKAGE which also provides the limited private type SIGNAL for declaring signals. Type SIGNAL is implemented as a task type whose entries are called by the subprograms of SIGNALS_PACKAGE implementing the Modula primitives. For simplicity, the delay rank will be implemented as an integer value between 1 and 10 of type RANK (instead of an arbitrary integer value).

New signals can be declared as

    S: SIGNALS_PACKAGE.SIGNAL;

(assuming of course that the package is visible at the point of declaration). If the *use* clause

    use SIGNALS_PACKAGE;

has been given then the above declaration for the signal S can be written simply as

    S: SIGNAL;

The specification of SIGNALS_PACKAGE is

```
package SIGNALS_PACKAGE is

    type RANK is range 1..10;
    type SIGNAL is limited private;

    procedure WAIT(S: in SIGNAL; R: in RANK := 1);
        --call WAIT(S) is equivalent to call WAIT(S, 1),
        --because of the default value of formal parameter R
    procedure SEND(S: in SIGNAL);
    function AWAITED(S: in SIGNAL) return BOOLEAN;

private

    task type SIGNAL is
        entry WAIT_SIGNAL(RANK);   --family of entries
        entry SEND_SIGNAL;
        entry AWAITED_SIGNAL(B: out BOOLEAN);
    end SIGNAL;

end SIGNALS_PACKAGE;
```

Each subprogram contains a call to the corresponding entry of the task implementing the specified signal. The implementation of task type SIGNAL is straightforward. Having accepted a SEND_SIGNAL entry call, SIGNAL then accepts the first call to an element of the WAIT_SIGNAL entry family with the lowest index (i.e., lowest delay rank) that has entry calls pending. This allows the task whose entry call was accepted to resume execution. The call AWAITED_SIGNAL is used to query SIGNAL to find out if there are any tasks waiting for a signal. Determining whether or not any task is waiting for a signal is done by examining the COUNT attribute of each member of the WAIT_SIGNAL entry family.

The body of task type SIGNAL is

```
task body SIGNAL is
begin
  loop
    select
      accept SEND_SIGNAL;
                  --accept a send signal and give it to the
                  --process with least delay rank (if any)

      for I in RANK loop
        select
          accept WAIT_SIGNAL(I);
          exit;
        else
          null;
        end select;
      end loop;

    or

      accept AWAITED_SIGNAL(B: out BOOLEAN) do
        B := FALSE;
        for I in RANK loop
          if WAIT_SIGNAL(I)'COUNT /= 0 then
            B := TRUE;
            exit;
          end if;
        end loop;
      end AWAITED_SIGNAL;

    or

      terminate;

    end select;

  end loop;
end SIGNAL;
```

The body of SIGNALS_PACKAGE is

```
package body SIGNALS_PACKAGE is

   procedure WAIT(S: in SIGNAL; R: in RANK := 1) is
   begin
      S.WAIT_SIGNAL(R);
   end WAIT;

   procedure SEND(S: in SIGNAL) is
   begin
      S.SEND_SIGNAL;
   end SEND;

   function AWAITED(S: in SIGNAL) return BOOLEAN is
      B: BOOLEAN;
   begin
      S.AWAITED_SIGNAL(B);
      return B;
   end AWAITED;

   --The body of task type SIGNAL, given earlier,
   --is inserted here

end SIGNALS_PACKAGE;
```

14.6 Shortest Job Next Scheduler

The problem is to implement a task that schedules jobs in the order of increasing execution time, i.e., shortest-job-next order. The scheduler is given jobs (job identification number, of type ID and expected execution time of the job) by several input processes. Several job dispatching processes ask for the next job to be executed from the scheduler. The scheduler selects a job with the shortest-execution-time to give to the next dispatching process requesting a job.

The scheduler uses the package ORDERED_SET declared in Chapter 3 on Packages. The specification of ORDERED_SET is reproduced:

```
package ORDERED_SET is
   procedure INSERT(JOB: in ID; T: in DURATION);
   procedure SMALLEST(JOB: out ID);
   function EMPTY return BOOLEAN;
end ORDERED_SET;
```

The specification of task SCHEDULER is

```
task SCHEDULER is
   entry ADD(JOB: in ID; T: in DURATION);
   entry NEXT(JOB: out ID);
         --return the next job to be executed and delete
         --it from the list of jobs to be scheduled
end SCHEDULER;
```

SCHEDULER accepts jobs from the input processes and inserts them into the ordered set. When there are jobs in the ordered set, SCHEDULER accepts requests from the dispatching processes to which it hands out jobs in increasing execution time order. Assuming that the *use* clause

```
use ORDERED_SET;
```

has been given, the body of SCHEDULER is declared as

```
task body SCHEDULER is
   I: ID;
   PERIOD: DURATION;
begin
   loop
      select
            accept ADD(JOB: in ID; T: in DURATION) do
               I := JOB;
               PERIOD := T;
            end ADD;
            INSERT(I, PERIOD);
      or when not EMPTY =>
            accept NEXT(JOB: out ID) do
               SMALLEST(JOB);
            end NEXT;
      end select;
   end loop;
end SCHEDULER;
```

14.7 The Traffic Light

The problem is to write a task that controls the traffic light at the intersection of a main road and a lightly used side road. Few pedestrians cross the main road. Vehicles must stop when the light is red. Normally the traffic light is green for the main road and red for the side road. The light changes to red for the main road and green for the side road when

1. a sensor detects that a car has arrived at the intersection from the side road.

2. a pedestrian, who wants to cross the main road, presses a button provided for the purpose.

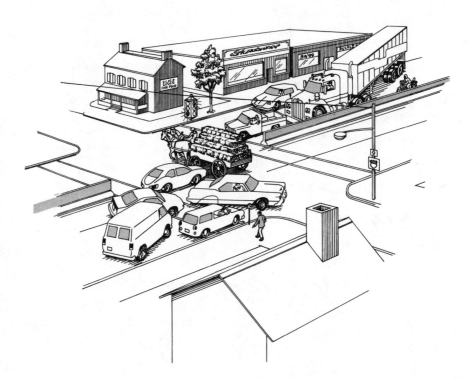

Traffic Light at a Lightly Used Side Road

Both the sensor and the pedestrian button cause an interrupt at location 8#2000# (octal 2000).

The following specifications for the traffic light must be observed.

1. The traffic flow on the main road is to be stopped only if the main road has had the green light for at least 3 minutes.

2. The traffic flow on the main road should be stopped for only 30 seconds at a time.

3. Multiple requests for stopping the flow of traffic on the main road have the same effect as one request. This rule circumvents the unnecessary changes in the traffic light that would otherwise be caused by the repeated pressing of the button by an impatient pedestrian.

A package TRAFFIC_LIGHT with the following specifications is available:

package TRAFFIC_LIGHT **is**

    procedure START_LIGHT;
        ——start the traffic light with green for the main road
    procedure CHANGE_LIGHT;
        ——change the traffic light from green to red in one
        ——direction and red to green in the other

    end TRAFFIC_LIGHT;

Package TRAFFIC_LIGHT encapsulates the physical control of switches so that we need not worry about them.

The implementation of CONTROL_TRAFFIC_LIGHT uses the following abstract algorithm

    Start the traffic light
    loop
        Wait 3.0 minutes
        Accept request to stop main road traffic and change light
        Wait 30.0 seconds
        Clear additional requests to stop main road traffic
        Change light
    end loop

Procedure CONTROL_TRAFFIC_LIGHT is declared as

```ada
with TRAFFIC_LIGHT; use TRAFFIC_LIGHT;

procedure CONTROL_TRAFFIC_LIGHT is

   task LIGHT is
      entry STOP_MAIN;    --pedestrian button and sensor
      for STOP_MAIN use at 8#2000#;
              --an interrupt is an entry call in Ada. The interrupt
              --location is associated with the entry call. This
              --representation specification is implementation dependent
   end LIGHT;

   task body LIGHT is
      CUT_OFF: constant DURATION := 180.0;
         --main road traffic must flow at least 3 minutes
      SIDE_ROAD_OPEN: constant DURATION := 30.0;

   begin
      START_LIGHT;
      loop
         delay CUT_OFF;
         accept STOP_MAIN; CHANGE_LIGHT;
         delay SIDE_ROAD_OPEN;
         --clear out multiple requests to stop main road traffic
            for I in 1..STOP_MAIN'COUNT loop
               accept STOP_MAIN;
            end loop;
         CHANGE_LIGHT;
      end loop;

   end LIGHT;
begin
   null;
end CONTROL_TRAFFIC_LIGHT;
```

The actual times corresponding to the minimum time for which the main road has the green light and the time for which the side road has the green light will be slightly greater than CUT_OFF and SIDE_ROAD_OPEN. This difference occurs, because of the time spent in executing the other statements in the loop; consequently a cumulative time drift occurs in the loop. When performing actions where it is undesirable to have such a cumulative drift, a program segment of the form given below should be used [BAR80]:

```
        INTERVAL: DURATION := ...;
        NEXT_TIME: TIME := ...;
                    --next time the action is to be performed
        :
        :
    loop
        delay NEXT_TIME - CLOCK;
        Action
        NEXT_TIME := NEXT_TIME + INTERVAL;
    end loop;
```

Function CLOCK is from the predefined package CALENDAR [9.6], whose specification is

```
package CALENDAR is
  type TIME is private;

  subtype YEAR_NUMBER is INTEGER range 1901..2099;
  subtype MONTH_NUMBER is INTEGER range 1..12;
  subtype DAY_NUMBER is INTEGER range 1..31;
  subtype DAY_DURATION is DURATION range 0.0 .. 86_400.0;

  function CLOCK return TIME;

  function YEAR(DATE: TIME) return YEAR_NUMBER;
  function MONTH(DATE: TIME) return MONTH_NUMBER;
  function DAY(DATE: TIME) return DAY_NUMBER;
  function SECONDS(DATE: TIME) return DAY_DURATION;

  procedure SPLIT(DATE: in TIME;
                  YEAR: out YEAR_NUMBER;
                  MONTH: out MONTH_NUMBER;
                  DAY: out DAY_NUMBER;
                  SECONDS: out DAY_DURATION);

  function TIME_OF(YEAR: YEAR_NUMBER;
                  MONTH: MONTH_NUMBER;
                  DAY: DAY_NUMBER;
                  SECONDS: DAY_DURATION := 0.0) return TIME;

  function "+"(LEFT: TIME; RIGHT: DURATION) return TIME;
  function "+"(LEFT: DURATION; RIGHT: TIME) return TIME;
  function "−"(LEFT: TIME; RIGHT: DURATION) return TIME;
  function "−"(LEFT: TIME; RIGHT: TIME) return DURATION;

  function "<"(LEFT, RIGHT: TIME) return BOOLEAN;
  function "<="(LEFT, RIGHT: TIME) return BOOLEAN;
  function ">"(LEFT, RIGHT: TIME) return BOOLEAN;
  function ">="(LEFT, RIGHT: TIME) return BOOLEAN;

  TIME_ERROR: exception; −−can be raised by TIME_OF, "+" and "−"

private
  −−implementation-dependent
end CALENDAR;
```

14.8 The Mortal Dining Philosophers

This problem is an adaptation of the one posed by E. W. Dijkstra. Five philosophers spend their lives eating spaghetti and thinking. They eat at a circular table in a dining room. The table has five chairs around it and chair number I has been assigned to philosopher number I ($1 \leqslant I \leqslant 5$). Five forks have also been laid out on the table so that there is one fork between every two chairs. Consequently there is one fork to the left of each chair and one to its right. Fork number I is to the left of chair number I.

The Five Philosophers

In order to be able to eat, a philosopher must enter the dining room and sit in the chair assigned to him. A philosopher must have two forks to eat (the forks are placed to the left and right of every chair). If he cannot get two forks immediately then the philosopher must wait until he gets them before he can eat. The forks are picked up one at a time with the left fork being picked up first. When a philosopher is finished eating (after a finite amount of time), he puts the forks down and leaves the room.

The dining philosophers problem has been studied extensively in the computer science literature. It is used as a benchmark to check the appropriateness of the facilities for concurrent programming and proof techniques for concurrent programs. It is interesting, because, despite its apparent simplicity, it illustrates many of the problems encountered in concurrent programming such as shared resources and *deadlock*. The forks are the resources shared by the philosophers who represent the concurrent processes.

The five philosophers and the five forks will be implemented as tasks using two arrays of tasks in the procedure DINING. On activation, each philosopher first gets an identification number (equal to the array index he is associated with). Using this number, a philosopher can determine the identification numbers of the forks on either side of him. Each philosopher is mortal and passes on to the next world soon after having eaten 100,000 times.

```
procedure DINING is
   subtype ID is INTEGER range 1..5;

   task type PHILOSOPHER is
      entry GET_ID(J: in ID);
            --get an identification number
   end PHILOSOPHER;

   task type FORK is
      entry PICK_UP;
      entry PUT_DOWN;
   end FORK;

   F: array(ID) of FORK;              --the 5 forks
   P: array(ID) of PHILOSOPHER;     --the 5 philosophers

   task body FORK is
            --A fork can be picked up by one philosopher at a time.
            --It must be put down before it can be picked up again.
            --The forks terminate when the philosophers terminate.
   begin
      loop
         select
               accept PICK_UP;
               accept PUT_DOWN;
```

```
               or
                    terminate;
               end select;
          end loop;
     end FORK;

     task body PHILOSOPHER is
          I: ID;  --index or number of this philosopher
          LIFE_LIMIT: constant := 100_000;
          TIMES_EATEN: INTEGER := 0;
          LEFT, RIGHT: ID;        --fork numbers
     begin
          accept GET_ID(J: in ID) do
                              --get the identification number
               I := J;
          end GET_ID;

          LEFT := I;     --number of the left fork
          RIGHT := I mod 5 + 1;   --number of the right fork

          while TIMES_EATEN /= LIFE_LIMIT loop
               --think for a while; then enter dining room and sit down
               --pick up forks
                  F(RIGHT).PICK_UP;
                  F(LEFT).PICK_UP;
               --eat
               --put down forks
                  F(LEFT).PUT_DOWN;
                  F(RIGHT).PUT_DOWN;

               TIMES_EATEN := TIMES_EATEN + 1;
               --get up and leave dining room
          end loop;
     end PHILOSOPHER;

begin
     for K in ID loop
               --give identification numbers to the philosophers
          P(K).GET_ID(K);
     end loop;
end DINING;
```

Philosophers and forks were both implemented as arrays of tasks. It would have been convenient if Ada had allowed a task that is an element of an array to determine its index in the array so that it could distinguish itself from the other elements of the array. The above program would then become simpler, since there would be no need to supply the identification numbers explicitly to the philosophers.

A variation of the above problem for the reader to try is to allow a philosopher to sit on any chair. This variation will result in a smaller average waiting time for eating for the philosophers. *Hint*: this scheme can be implemented by declaring a new task that is called by every philosopher to request a chair (preferably one with free forks). On leaving the dining room a philosopher informs this task that the chair is vacant.

Who Eats Next?

In the solution given, no individual philosopher will be blocked indefinitely from eating, i.e., *starve*, because the philosophers pick up the forks in first-in first-out order (the discipline associated with all entry queues). However, there is a possibility of deadlock in the solution given above, e.g., each philosopher picks up one fork and waits to get another fork so that he can start to eat. Assuming that all the philosophers are obstinate and that none of them will give up his fork until he gets another fork and has eaten, everything will be in a state of suspension.

Deadlock can be avoided in several ways, for example, a philosopher may pick up the two forks needed by him only when both the forks are available (*Hint*: by using *when* conditions in the *select* statement). Alternatively, one could add another task called the HOST that makes sure that there are at most four philosophers in the dining room at any given time. Each philosopher must request permission to enter the room from the HOST and must inform it on leaving.

Task HOST is declared as

```
task HOST is
   entry ENTER;
   entry LEAVE;
end HOST;

task body HOST is
   I: INTEGER := 0;    --number of philosophers in the room
   begin
      loop
         select
            when I < 4 =>
                  --a philosopher can enter if there are less
                  --than 4 philosophers in the dining room
               accept ENTER;
               I := I + 1;
         or
               accept LEAVE;    --philosopher is leaving
               I := I - 1;
         or
               terminate;
         end select;
      end loop;
end HOST;
```

Clearly there is no possibility of a deadlock with this change, since there will be at least one philosopher in the room who will be able to eat. Since they all eat for a finite time, he will leave and some other philosopher will be able to eat.

14.9 Elevator Control

This example of a real-time application illustrates just about all the facilities in Ada discussed so far—packages, tasks, *delay* statements and representation specifications. The problem is to design a procedure RUN_ELEVATOR that controls an elevator serving 8 floors of a building, numbered from 1 to 8 (no basement).

At each floor in the building are two elevator call buttons—UP and DOWN (except for the first floor which does not have a DOWN button and the top floor which does not have an UP button). Inside the elevator there are 8 FLOOR buttons, one for each of the 8 floors and an OPEN button. FLOOR button marked I is depressed by a passenger to get off at floor I and the OPEN button is depressed to prolong the period the elevator door is open.

The Elevator Entrance

The Request Buttons Inside the Elevator

14.9.1 Elevator Specification: The elevator car behaves as follows:

1. It services the 8 floors carrying, passengers up and down. Its *home* floor is the first floor (the building lobby). Whenever there are no requests for use, it stations itself at the home floor.

2. When going up, the elevator services all requests for stops on floors above its current position; similarly when it is going down. The elevator tries to minimize the number of changes in direction. (No person waits forever.)

3. The elevator opens its door for 5 seconds. Every time the OPEN button is pressed, the door is kept open for one extra second. However, pressing the OPEN button when the door is closed has no effect.

14.9.2 Physical Details of the Elevator: Depressing an elevator button causes a hardware interrupt (with a possible parameter) on the computer associated with the elevator. These interrupts are queued automatically. Hardware addresses corresponding to these interrupts are

Button	Address	Function
DOWN(I)	8#1000#	Request to go down from floor I
UP(I)	8#1010#	Request to go up from floor I
FLOOR(I)	8#1020#	Stop at floor I
OPEN	8#1030#	Delay closing door by one second

A package ELEVATOR with the following specification is available.

```
package ELEVATOR is
   procedure MOVE_UP_ONE_FLOOR;
   procedure MOVE_DOWN_ONE_FLOOR;
   procedure CLOSE_DOOR;
   procedure OPEN_DOOR;
end ELEVATOR;
```

14.9.3 Elevator Movement Timing Characteristics: The elevator movement consists of three phases—the car first accelerates to steady speed, then travels at steady speed and, finally, decelerates to a stop. The elevator takes 1.80 seconds to go from a stationary position at floor I to a stationary position at floor I+1 (the characteristics are the same whether the elevator is going up or down)—0.40 seconds to accelerate to steady speed while covering the distance $A_I B_I$, 1.00 seconds traveling at steady speed to cover the distance $B_I C_I$, and 0.40 seconds decelerating to a stop while covering the distance $C_I D_I$. $A_I B_I$ is equal to $C_I D_I$, A_I coincides with D_{I-1} and D_I coincides with A_{I+1}.

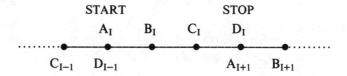

The distance between floor I and I+1 is represented by $A_I D_I$. The elevator will start declerating at point C_I unless a signal to skip floor I+1 is given.

If there is no need for the elevator to stop at the next floor then it must be given another move command before it starts decelerating, i.e., at or before position C_I. There are two cases:

1. Suppose the elevator is in a stationary position at the time the first move command is given. Then the elevator should be given the next move command at most 1.40 seconds after the previous move command.

2. Suppose the elevator starts from floor $I-1$ or earlier. It does not stop at floor I and is not to stop at floor $I+1$ either. It was last instructed to keep moving at position C_{I-1}. It must now be instructed to keep moving at C_I. Traveling at steady speed the elevator covers the distance $A_I B_I$ or $C_I D_I$ in half the time it takes when accelerating or decelerating. Consequently, it covers the distance $C_{I-1} C_I$ in 1.40 seconds. The next move command, as in the first case, must be given at most 1.40 seconds after the previous move command.

The timing characteristics of a real elevator will be considerably different. For example, a real elevator might take less time to go down a floor and the time it takes to traverse a floor might depend on the load it is carrying. The timing characteristics given here have been simplified considerably so as to focus on those aspects that illustrate interesting facets of Ada.

14.9.4 Solution: In reading the solution, the reader is urged to keep in mind how reasonable elevators operate. Requests for elevator service, to go up or down, or to get off, are accepted by a task REQUEST_DB (requests data base), which also keeps track of these requests. Task ELEVATOR_CONTROL controls the elevator using commands provided in the package ELEVATOR. It also accepts requests from passengers, made by depressing the OPEN button, to keep the elevator door open longer than the normal period. Task ELEVATOR_CONTROL interacts with the task REQUEST_DB to

1. determine the next elevator destination based on pending requests for elevator service, and

2. supply information specifying the floors that have been serviced.

The interaction between tasks ELEVATOR_CONTROL, REQUEST_DB, package ELEVATOR and the elevator itself is illustrated in Figure 4.4:

At any time, the elevator will be in one of three states—UP, DOWN or NEUTRAL. States UP and DOWN indicate that the elevator is going in the direction implied by its state in response to passenger requests. The NEUTRAL state indicates that the elevator is not responding to a request but that it might be headed toward its home floor if it is not already there.

The Elevator System

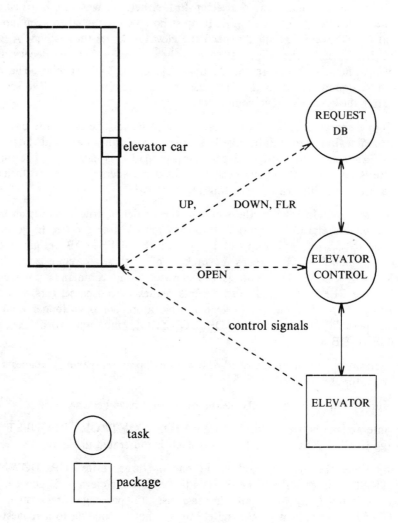

Figure 4.4

Some constant and type declarations used in the implementation are

```
HOME: constant := 1;
N: constant := 8;    --number of floors

subtype STORIES is INTEGER range 1..N;
type STATE is (UP, DOWN, NEUTRAL);

NORMAL_OPEN_TIME: constant DURATION := 5.0;
EXTRA_OPEN_TIME: constant DURATION := 1.0;
NEXT_MOVE_TIME: constant DURATION := 1.39
        --the next move command must be given at most
        --1.40 seconds after the previous move command;
        --selection of 1.39 is arbitrary except for the
        --above constraint
```

The specification of task ELEVATOR_CONTROL is

```
task ELEVATOR_CONTROL is
    entry OPEN;    --keep the door open one second longer
    --associate hardware interrupt location with entry OPEN
        for OPEN use at 8#1030#;
end ELEVATOR_CONTROL;
```

The specification of task REQUEST_DB is

```
task REQUEST_DB is
    entry DEST(CUR_STATE: in STATE; CUR_FLOOR: in STORIES;
                    NEW_STATE: out STATE;
                    NEW_FLOOR: out STORIES);
        --computes the new destination and direction
        --based on the current location, current
        --direction and pending requests
    entry REQUESTS(B: out BOOLEAN);
        --TRUE returned in B if there is any pending request
        --for elevator service and FALSE otherwise
    entry CLEAR_GO(DIR: in STATE; I: in STORIES);
        --picked up passenger(s) going up or down from floor I
    entry CLEAR_OFF(I: in STORIES);
        --passenger(s) let off at floor I

    --the following entries correspond to passenger
    --requests for elevator service
        entry DOWN(I: in STORIES);
        entry UP(I: in STORIES);
        entry FLOOR(I: in STORIES);

    --associate hardware interrupt locations with entries
        for DOWN use at 8#1000#;
        for UP use at 8#1010#;
        for FLOOR use at 8#1020#;
end REQUEST_DB;
```

The procedure used by task ELEVATOR_CONTROL to control the elevator is described abstractly as

P_0:
```
loop
    Respond to requests, if any; otherwise position
      car at the home floor
end loop
```

The statement *Respond to requests, ...* is refined as

P_1:

    if There are no requests pending **then**

        If at home floor then sleep for 1 second (to avoid *busy waiting*); otherwise, move elevator toward home floor and wait till it is time to give the next move instruction

    else

        Compute destination (it might have changed)

        if Elevator is not responding to a request or
            is not about to reach its destination **then**

            Give a move instruction to the elevator and wait until it is time to give the next move instruction

      else

            Let passengers get off and on; respond to requests to keep door open longer and clear requests to get off

            if There are requests pending **then**

                Compute destination

                Give a move instruction to the elevator and wait until it is time to give the next move instruction

            end if

      end if

    end if

When at the home floor, the program controlling the elevator delays itself by one second every time to minimize needless execution (busy waiting). This delay will allow additional execution time to be allocated to REQUEST_DB and other programs or tasks on the computer.

The following variables will be used in further refinements of the task ELEVATOR_CONTROL and in the final program:

CUR_FLOOR	The floor the elevator is at or about to reach.
CUR_STATE	The current state of the elevator.
NEW_STATE	The new state of the elevator.
NEW_FLOOR	The elevator destination.

Continuing the refinement, the boolean expression *There are no requests pending* is refined to be the expression

    not REQUESTS

where REQUESTS is declared as

```
function REQUESTS return BOOLEAN is
   B: BOOLEAN;
begin
   REQUEST_DB.REQUESTS(B);    --entry call
   return B;
end REQUESTS;
```

The statement *If at home floor then sleep for 1 second ...* of P_1 is refined as

```
CUR_STATE := NEUTRAL;    --not responding to any requests
if CUR_FLOOR = HOME then
   delay 1.0;    --sleep for one second
else
   MOVE(CUR_STATE);
   delay NEXT_MOVE_TIME;
end if;
```

Procedure MOVE is declared as

```
procedure MOVE(DIR: in STATE) is
begin
   case DIR is
      when UP =>
          MOVE_UP_ONE_FLOOR;
          CUR_FLOOR := CUR_FLOOR + 1;
      when DOWN | NEUTRAL =>
          MOVE_DOWN_ONE_FLOOR;
          CUR_FLOOR := CUR_FLOOR - 1;
   end case;
end MOVE;
```

The statement *Compute destination* is replaced by the entry call

```
REQUEST_DB.DEST(CUR_STATE, CUR_FLOOR,
                NEW_STATE, NEW_FLOOR);
```

The boolean expression *Elevator is not responding to a request or is not about to reach its destination* is refined as

```
CUR_STATE = NEUTRAL or else CUR_FLOOR /= NEW_FLOOR
```

The statement *Give a move instruction to the elevator and wait...* of the abstract algorithm P_1 is refined as

```
CUR_STATE := NEW_STATE;
        ——new floor and direction were computed just before reaching
        ——the current floor; no new calls have been accepted since
MOVE(CUR_STATE);
delay NEXT_MOVE_TIME;
```

Requests to keep the elevator door open are honored only when the elevator door is open; when the door is closed they are ignored.

The statement *Let the passengers get off and ...* is refined as

> Clear any previous requests to open the door for extra time and
> open the door for the normal time.
> Close the door but delay closing if the open button has been pressed
> Clear requests to get off and on

These three statements are refined as

(1) *Clear any previous requests to open the door for ...*

```
for I in 1..OPEN'COUNT loop
    accept OPEN;
end loop;
OPEN_DOOR;
delay NORMAL_OPEN_TIME;
```

(2) *Close the door but delay closing if the open button ...*

```
while OPEN'COUNT /= 0 loop
    accept OPEN;
    delay EXTRA_OPEN_TIME;
end loop;
CLOSE_DOOR;
```

(3) *Clear requests to get off and on*

```
CLEAR_OFF(CUR_FLOOR);
if There are requests pending then
    Compute destination
    CLEAR_GO(NEW_STATE, CUR_FLOOR);
end if;
```

Just before reaching a floor, the elevator indicates to the would be passengers the direction in which it will be going next[40] so that the passengers going in that direction may get on.

The boolean expression *There are requests pending* is refined to be just the function call

REQUESTS

These refinements when collected together make up the executable part of the task ELEVATOR_CONTROL body. The job of collecting the refinements is left to the reader. Procedure RUN_ELEVATOR, which contains the tasks ELEVATOR_CONTROL and REQUEST_DB, is now declared:

---

40. The direction may be indicated by means of colored lights. Direction indicators are not implemented in this algorithm.

```
with ELEVATOR; use ELEVATOR;
      --ELEVATOR is compiled separately (see Chapter 7
      --on Program Structure and Separate Compilation)
procedure RUN_ELEVATOR is

   N: constant := 8;    --number of floors
   subtype STORIES is INTEGER range 1..N;
   type STATE is (UP, DOWN, NEUTRAL);
   HOME: constant := 1;

   NORMAL_OPEN_TIME: constant DURATION := 5.0;
   EXTRA_OPEN_TIME: constant DURATION := 1.0;
   NEXT_MOVE_TIME: constant DURATION := 1.39;

   --specification and body of the task REQUEST_DB
   --specification of task ELEVATOR_CONTROL

   task body ELEVATOR_CONTROL is
      CUR_FLOOR: STORIES := HOME;
            --the elevator starts out positioned at its home floor
      NEW_FLOOR: STORIES;
      CUR_STATE: STATE := NEUTRAL;
      NEW_STATE: STATE;

      --the body of the procedure MOVE
      --the body of the function REQUESTS

   begin
      --The body of this task which was developed by stepwise
      --refinement is inserted here.
   end ELEVATOR_CONTROL;

begin
   null;
end RUN_ELEVATOR;
```

14.9.5 REQUEST_DB: Task REQUEST_DB accords entry calls made by task ELEVATOR_CONTROL a higher priority than requests from passengers for elevator service. It is important that task ELEVATOR_CONTROL be serviced as promptly as possible so that it can control the movement of the elevator within the constraints of the elevator's timing characteristics.

The infinite loop executed by REQUEST_DB can be abstractly described as

```
loop
  select
      Accept request to compute new destination
  or
      Accept information regarding the passengers
       picked up at floor I
  or
      Accept information specifying that passengers
       were let off at floor I
  or
      Accept an inquiry to find out if any elevator
       service requests are pending
  else
      Accept passenger requests for elevator service
  end select
end loop
```

Task REQUEST_DB will use BOOLEAN arrays F, U and D to record requests from passengers to get off at floors, and to go up or down.

F(I)	a TRUE value indicates that a passenger wants to get off at floor I
U(I)	a TRUE value indicates that a passenger wants to go up from floor I
D(I)	a TRUE value indicates that a passenger wants to go down from floor I

The statement *Accept request to compute new destination* is refined as

```
accept DEST(CUR_STATE: in STATE; CUR_FLOOR: in STORIES;
            NEW_STATE: out STATE;
            NEW_FLOOR: out STORIES) do
  DESTINATION(CUR_STATE, CUR_FLOOR,
            NEW_STATE, NEW_FLOOR);
end DEST;
```

The statement *Accept information regarding the passengers picked up at floor I* is refined to be

```
    accept CLEAR_GO(DIR: in STATE; I: in STORIES) do
        case DIR is
            when UP => U(I) := FALSE;
            when DOWN => D(I) := FALSE;
            when NEUTRAL => raise PROGRAM_ERROR;
                    --raise the predefined exception PROGRAM_ERROR;
                    --raising this exception will result in the
                    --execution of the program being abandoned.
                    --Exceptions are discussed in Chapter 5
        end case;
    end CLEAR_GO;
```

The statement *Accept information specifying that passengers were let off at floor I* is refined as

```
    accept CLEAR_OFF(I: in STORIES) do
        F(I) := FALSE;
    end CLEAR_OFF;
```

The statement *Accept an inquiry to find out if any elevator service requests are pending* is refined as

```
    accept REQUESTS(B: out BOOLEAN) do
        B := ANY(F) or ANY(U) or ANY(D);
    end REQUESTS;
```

where ANY is a user-defined function that returns TRUE if any one of the elements of its array actual parameter has the value TRUE.

Finally, the statement *Accept passenger requests for elevator service* is refined as

```
select
   accept UP(I: in STORIES) do
      U(I) := TRUE;
   end UP;
or
   accept DOWN(I: in STORIES) do
      D(I) := TRUE;
   end DOWN;
or
   accept FLOOR(I: in STORIES) do
      F(I) := TRUE;
   end FLOOR;
else
   null;
end select
```

The body of the task REQUEST_DB is now given:

```
task body REQUEST_DB is

   type STATUS is array(INTEGER range <>) of BOOLEAN;
   F, U, D: STATUS(1..N) := (STORIES => FALSE);
      --F, U, & D contain requests to get off, go up
      --and down, respectively

   function ANY(A: in STATUS) return BOOLEAN is
      --returns TRUE if any element of A is true and false otherwise
   begin
      for I in A'RANGE loop
         if A(I) then
            return TRUE;
         end if;
      end loop;
      return FALSE;
   end ANY;

   function LOWEST(A, B : in STATUS) return STORIES is
      --call only when at least 1 element of A or B is TRUE; returns
      --lowest index in the 2 arrays such that element is TRUE
   begin
      for I in A'RANGE loop
         if A(I) or B(I) then return I; end if;
      end loop;
   end LOWEST;
```

```
function HIGHEST(A, B : in STATUS) return STORIES is
    ——call only when at least 1 element of A or B is TRUE; returns
    ——highest index in the 2 arrays such that element is TRUE
begin
    for I in reverse A'RANGE loop
        if A(I) or B(I) then
            return I;
        end if;
    end loop;
end HIGHEST;
```

——the body of procedure DESTINATION (developed
——following this task)

```
begin
```

——the infinite loop whose refinements were given above

```
end REQUEST_DB;
```

Task REQUEST_DB is executed continuously without ever delaying itself. If REQUEST_DB is modified to eliminate busy waiting, care must be taken to ensure that ELEVATOR_CONTROL is always serviced in time for it to control the elevator properly.

Procedure DESTINATION computes the new destination depending upon the current direction of the elevator. While doing so it tries to minimize changes in elevator direction. It will not suggest a change in the elevator direction if there exists a request for elevator service that does not require changing direction. This means that when the elevator is going up, it will not stop on intermediate floors for requests to go down; it will stop for them on its way down. The elevator behaves in a similar fashion when it is going down.

Procedure DESTINATION should be called only after ensuring that there is at least one request for elevator service. It is specified as

```
procedure DESTINATION(CUR_STATE: in STATE;
                CUR_FLOOR: in STORIES;
                NEW_STATE: out STATE; NEW_FLOOR: out STORIES);
```

and implements the following abstract algorithm:

if If the elevator is not responding to requests or is going up **then**
　　Process requests from the current floor or above to compute the new
　　destination such that a change of the elevator direction is not
　　required; if there are no such requests then change the direction
　　to down and compute the new destination
else
　　Process requests from the current floor or below to compute the new
　　destination such that a change of direction is not required;
　　if there are no such requests then change the direction to up and
　　compute the new destination
end if

This algorithm is further refined as

if Current direction is NEUTRAL or UP **then**
　　if There are requests from current floor or above to go up
　　　　　　or from passengers to get off above **then**
　　　　NEW_FLOOR is the lowest floor up (current floor or above)
　　　　requiring service
　　　　NEW_STATE is UP
　　elsif There are requests to come down from above **then**
　　　　NEW_FLOOR is the highest floor up requiring service
　　　　NEW_STATE is UP
　　else ――change directions and compute recursively
　　　　DESTINATION(DOWN, CUR_FLOOR,
　　　　　　　　　　　　NEW_STATE, NEW_FLOOR)
　　end if
else
　　if There are requests from current floor or below to go down
　　　　　　　from passengers to get off below **then**
　　　　NEW_FLOOR is the highest floor down (current floor or below)
　　　　requiring service
　　　　NEW_STATE is DOWN
　　elsif There are requests to come up from below **then**
　　　　NEW_FLOOR is the lowest floor down requiring service
　　　　NEW_STATE is DOWN
　　else ――change directions and compute recursively
　　　　DESTINATION(UP, CUR_FLOOR, NEW_STATE, NEW_FLOOR)
　　end if
end if

As mentioned before, DESTINATION should be called only when there is at
least one request for elevator service. Termination of recursion can be shown
easily if there is at least one request. There will be at most one recursive call.

This procedure, as designed, gives preference to requests in the upward direction (because when direction is NEUTRAL it looks for requests on the floors above the current floor).

The Ada version of procedure DESTINATION is

```
procedure DESTINATION(CUR_STATE: in STATE;
                      CUR_FLOOR: in STORIES;
                      NEW_STATE: out STATE;
                      NEW_FLOOR: out STORIES) is
    --uses global variables U, F, D but does not change them.
begin
  if CUR_STATE = NEUTRAL or CUR_STATE = UP then
    if ANY(U(CUR_FLOOR..U'LAST)) or
              ANY(F(CUR_FLOOR..F'LAST)) then
    NEW_FLOOR := LOWEST(U(CUR_FLOOR..U'LAST),
                 F(CUR_FLOOR..F'LAST));
    NEW_STATE := UP;
    elsif ANY(D(CUR_FLOOR..D'LAST)) then
      NEW_FLOOR := HIGHEST(D(CUR_FLOOR..D'LAST),
                 (CUR_FLOOR..D'LAST => FALSE));
        NEW_STATE := UP;
    else
      DESTINATION(DOWN, CUR_FLOOR,
                 NEW_STATE, NEW_FLOOR);
    end if;

  else
    if ANY(D(D'FIRST..CUR_FLOOR)) or
              ANY(F(F'FIRST..CUR_FLOOR)) then
    NEW_FLOOR := HIGHEST(D(D'FIRST..CUR_FLOOR),
                 F(F'FIRST..CUR_FLOOR));
      NEW_STATE := DOWN;
    elsif ANY(U(U'FIRST..CUR_FLOOR)) then
      NEW_FLOOR := LOWEST(U(U'FIRST..CUR_FLOOR),
                 (U'FIRST..CUR_FLOOR => FALSE));
      NEW_STATE := DOWN;
    else
      DESTINATION(UP, CUR_FLOOR,
                 NEW_STATE, NEW_FLOOR);
    end if;
  end if;
end DESTINATION;
```

14.9.6 Extensions to the Elevator Problem: When moving to the home floor, the elevator stops at every floor although it does not open the door. These unnecessary stops causes additional wear and tear on the machinery. Modification of task ELEVATOR_CONTROL to eliminate this characteristic is left for the reader.

From the user's viewpoint, the elevator can be made more sophisticated by adding buttons for *emergency stop*, quick closing of the door and indicator lights at each floor. The home floor for the elevator is the first floor. The algorithm given exploits this information, since the elevator is always instructed to go down if it is not at the home floor and there are no requests. Selecting a floor different from the top or the bottom floors as the home floor will make the algorithm slightly more complicated, since the elevator may have to go up or down to reach its home floor instead of just going down.

Another dimension of complexity can be added to this problem by extending it to handle a bank of elevators. The elevators do not work independently and must be scheduled appropriately by a central scheduler. A possible approach is to define an array of tasks, one for each elevator, and a scheduler task. Each elevator task controls the physical movement of one elevator and communicates with the scheduler to find out where the elevator is to go next.

14.10 Disk Scheduler

The disk scheduler algorithm [HOA74] is similar to the above elevator algorithm, but simpler. Unlike the elevator, requests are only of one kind (to access some part of the disk), and there is more flexibility in handling them. For example, short requests may be given priority over large ones or requests may be accepted in FIFO order.

Prior to doing a disk read/write, a task asks the disk scheduler for permission to access a specific cylinder of the disk. When the request is granted, the task is free to access the disk. On completion, it informs the scheduler that it is done. The scheduler task has the specifications

```
task DISK_SCHEDULER is
    entry REQUEST(CYLINDER);      ——one entry for each cylinder
    entry DONE;
end DISK_SCHEDULER;
```

where the subtype CYLINDER is declared as

```
subtype CYLINDER is INTEGER range 1..MAX_CYLINDER;
```

It is left to the reader to implement the body of the task DISK_SCHEDULER.

Chapter 5: **Exceptions** [11]

1. Introduction

An *exception* is an event that occurs unexpectedly or infrequently, for example, an error or exhaustion of data. Specific examples of exceptions are

1. symbol table overflow,

2. division by zero,

3. bad input caused by a non-numeric character in data that is supposed to be numeric and

4. overheating of a car caused by lack of sufficient coolant.

The ability to respond to exceptions is particularly essential for the reliability of real-time systems. In many cases systems are designed to run forever. Design of such programs requires an ability to handle, without program termination, the exceptions that will occur sooner or later.

Exception handling has been classified into two categories:

1. A normal programming technique used for infrequent events that are not necessarily errors or boundary conditions [GOO75]. The passing of control to an exception handler is like a subprogram call, as is the case with PL/I's ON conditions [IBM70].

2. A programming technique used for handling errors and limiting conditions [BRO76]. Normal program execution is terminated when an exception occurs and execution of an exception handler is initiated. After the exception has been handled, execution is not resumed at or near the point in the program where the exception occurred.

Exception handling in Ada falls into the second category. The occurrence of an exception results in suspension[41] of execution of the *normal* part of a program. Bringing the exception to the attention of the appropriate program statements that must respond to this unusual situation is called *raising* the

---

41. Charles Wetherell, a colleague at Bell Labs, prefers the term *interruption* to *suspension*, the term used by the Ada designers, since it does not suggest any return to the point of error.

exception. These statements, which are specified in an *exception handler*, are then executed to *handle* the exception. Exception handlers are specified at the end of a block, a subprogram, a package or a task. Execution of an exception handler completes execution of the block, subprogram, package and task. After the exception has been handled, execution is not resumed at or near the point where the exception was raised.

If no exception handlers are provided, then execution of the program segment (which may be a block, subprogram, package, or task) in which the exception was raised is abandoned and the responsibility of responding to the exception is transferred to another part of the program. This transferring of responsibility is called *propagating* the exception.

A language does not need to provide a special mechanism for handling exceptions (most programming languages do not), since explicit tests can be used to detect the occurrence of an exception.[42] These tests must be placed at all places in the program where the exception might occur. However, the lack of an exception handling facility in a programming language results in [LEV77, BLA80]

1. *reduced program clarity*: Program clarity suffers, because the processing of all events, both normal computation and exceptions, is intermingled and not identified as different. Consequently, the reader of a program may experience difficulty in distinguishing the normal part of the program from the exception handler.

2. *impracticality*: For some classes of exceptions (e.g., numeric errors and I/O completions) the exception may occur anywhere in the program—in the middle of a statement, for example. For such exceptions it is clearly impractical to test explicitly for their occurrence at all possible points in a program.

3. *inefficient implementation*: Consider a function SEARCH that searches a one-dimensional array A with positive integer subscripts for a value X. SEARCH returns as its result an integer that is the index of X in A if X is present and −1 otherwise. This specification of a search function is reasonable for a language like FORTRAN or C. The result can be used to index A but only after explicitly checking to ensure that it does not have the value −1.

---

42. Even these tests are usually not provided in most programming languages!

Such a search function can be better designed in Ada by using an exception. For example, the range of SEARCH can be specified more precisely to be the domain of the subscripts of A. If X is present in the array, then SEARCH returns the index of X in A; if X is not present, then this is indicated to the calling subprogram by raising an exception. The compiler can now use a more compact representation for the result type of SEARCH, since it does not include the failure value. Explicit subscript checks, when the result of SEARCH is used to index into A, are no longer required, since SEARCH always returns a valid subscript when X is present. When X is not present control transfers to the exception handler. Thus the lack of an exception facility could result in inefficiency.

2. Declaring Exceptions [11.1]

Exceptions are declared using declarations of the form

    list of exception names: **exception**;

Some examples of exception declarations are

    TEMP_OUTSIDE_LIMITS: **exception**;
    FIRE, BREAK_IN: **exception**;
    STACK_OVERFLOW, STACK_UNDERFLOW: **exception**;

The identity of the exceptions is established at compile time (instead of run time). This treatment of exception identity is similar to the treatment of procedure and package declarations but different from the treatment of variable declarations in procedures—new new local variables are allocated every time a procedure is called. Consequently, different calls to a subprogram or different instances of a recursive subprogram do not result in new exceptions being declared. Different *instantiations* of generic subprograms and packages, however, do result in different exceptions being defined.

All user-defined exceptions must be raised explicitly when conditions warrant. Ada provides some *predefined exceptions* defined in the package STANDARD (Appendix C of the Ada Reference Manual). These are generally raised automatically by Ada when the conditions stated below are satisfied, but they may also be raised explicitly by the user. The predefined exceptions are

exception	**when raised**
CONSTRAINT_ERROR	This exception is raised when a range, index, or discriminant constraint is violated. It is also raised when an attempt is made to reference a nonexistent component of an array or a record, or when an access object with the value **null**

is used to refer to an object.

NUMERIC_ERROR — This exception is raised when the result of a predefined numeric type does not lie within the implemented range of the numeric type, e.g., division by 0, multiplication of two large numbers. (Raising this exception is implementation dependent.)

PROGRAM_ERROR — This exception is raised to indicate a variety of errors not covered by the other predefined exceptions, e.g., when a *select* statement without an *else* part has no open alternatives, the exception PROGRAM_ERROR is raised.

STORAGE_ERROR — This exception is raised during the execution of the storage allocator when all available space for the specified access type has been exhausted.

TASKING_ERROR — Problems during task communication cause this exception to be raised.

3. Raising Exceptions [11.3]

Exceptions are raised explicitly by means of the *raise* statement, which has the form

        raise [exception_name];

Some examples are

        raise TEMP_OUTSIDE_LIMITS;
        raise NUMERIC_ERROR;   ——predefined exception is raised
        raise STACK_OVERFLOW;
        raise;   ——reraise the exception in question

A *raise* statement without an exception name can appear only in an exception handler (if the exception handler is not in a nested subprogram, package or a task). It causes reraising of the exception that caused the exception handler containing the *raise* statement to be activated.

4. Specifying Exception Handlers [11.2]

Exception handlers are specified at the end of a block, a subprogram, package and a task body following the key word **exception**. Each exception handler contains a sequence of one or more statements to handle the associated exceptions. Exception handlers have the form

> **when** exception_choice {| exception_choice} =>
> > sequence_of_statements

where *exception_choice* is the name of an exception or the keyword **others**.

If the exception choice **others** appears, it must appear by itself in an exception handler and this handler must be the last one specified in the block, subprogram, package or task. The choice **others** stands for all exceptions that may be raised in the block, subprogram, package or task but for which an exception handler has not been explicitly specified. It also represents exceptions that are not visible, that is, those defined, raised and propagated from other parts of a program but for which no handlers were provided.

If an exception is to be reraised in an exception handler associated with the choice **others**, so that the exception is propagated to some other part of the program and the execution of the handler terminated, then the abbreviated *raise* statement

> **raise;**

must be used. Using this form of the *raise* statement is necessary, because the name of the exception activating the handler is not known in the handler—it is anonymous.

When an exception is raised, the remainder of the statements in the block, subprogram, package or task are not executed. Instead execution of the appropriate exception handler, if any, is initiated. If no exception handler is provided for an exception (explicitly or implicitly using the choice **others**), execution of the block, subprogram, package or task is abandoned and the exception is propagated. If an exception cannot be handled in the main program, then the program is terminated.

The exception handler has the same rights and capabilities as the block, subprogram, package or task in which the exception is raised. For example, an exception handler associated with a subprogram has access to the local variables and parameters of the subprogram, and can contain the *return* statement.

Some examples of exception handlers are

when NUMERIC_ERROR **=>** **return** INTEGER'LAST;

when TEMP_OUTSIDE_LIMITS **=>**
    ——call the appropriate procedures to initiate
    ——IMMEDIATE SHUT DOWN of the reactor
    ——give reason for shut down
      if T < T_MIN **then**
        PUT("SHUT DOWN **=>** Vessel OVERCOOLING");
      else
        PUT("SHUT DOWN **=>** Vessel OVERHEATING");
      end if;

5. Activation of Exception Handlers [11.4]

The specific exception handler activated to take care of an exception depends upon the execution path of the program and not the textual layout of the program—the association of a handler with an exception is dynamic and not static. Suppose no exception handler is provided in a subprogram S for an exception E. Exception E, when raised, will be propagated to the caller of S and handled there instead of being handled in the part of the program containing the declaration of S.

The selection of a handler for an exception also depends upon whether the exception was raised during execution of a statement or during elaboration (processing) of a declaration.

5.1 Exceptions Raised During Statement Execution

If an exception is raised during execution of a statement, then execution of local exception handler, if any, replaces execution of the remainder of the block, subprogram, package or task in which the exception occurs. Otherwise, if no local exception handler has been specified, the exception is propagated to other parts of the program as explained below.

If the exception is raised in

1. a *subprogram*, then execution of the subprogram is abandoned and the exception raised at the point at which the subprogram was called. If the subprogram is a main program then execution of the program is terminated.

2. a *block*, then execution of the block is abandoned and the exception raised immediately following the block in the surrounding program.

3. a *package body*, then elaboration of the package body is abandoned. If the package is a library unit, then execution of the main program is abandoned. Otherwise, the exception is raised in the part of the program containing the package body or its *stub* (stubs are discussed in Chapter 7

on Program Structure and Separate Compilation).

4. a *task*, then the execution of task is completed.

5. the sequence of statements of an *exception handler* (but not in a block nested in the exception handler), then execution of the exception handler is terminated and the new exception propagated, depending upon whether the exception handler was in a block, subprogram, package or task (following these rules).

5.2 An Example

Consider a procedure ROOTS that computes the roots r_1 and r_2 of a quadratic equation; the roots are given by the equations

$$r_1 = \frac{-b + \sqrt{b^2 - 4ac}}{2a}$$

and

$$r_2 = \frac{-b - \sqrt{b^2 - 4ac}}{2a}$$

where $a \neq 0$ and $b^2 - 4ac > 0$.

ROOTS uses function SQRT (defined in Chapter 1) to compute the roots. The exception CONSTRAINT_ERROR is propagated to ROOTS from the function SQRT. CONSTRAINT_ERROR is raised in SQRT when SQRT is called with a negative actual parameter. It is propagated because SQRT does not contain any exception handlers. The exception NUMERIC_ERROR is raised in ROOTS when an attempt is made to divide by zero (this happens when the coefficient *a* is zero) or when multiplication results in a very large number. ROOTS propagates an indication of an abnormal condition by raising the exception ERROR in the caller after having handled any exception raised in it:

```
with TEXT_IO; use TEXT_IO;
        −−makes string I/O available and directly visible in ROOTS
with SQRT;
        −−make the separately compiled SQRT available inside ROOTS
procedure ROOTS (A, B, C: FLOAT; R1, R2: out FLOAT) is
    TEMP: FLOAT;
    ERROR: exception;
                −−to be propagated to the caller of ROOTS if an
                −−exception is raised in ROOTS or propagated to ROOTS
begin
    TEMP := SQRT(B * B − 4.0 * A * C);
    R1 := (−B + TEMP ) / (2.0 * A);
    R2 := (−B − TEMP ) / (2.0 * A);
exception
    when NUMERIC_ERROR =>
        PUT("ERROR******* OVERFLOW or DIVIDE BY ZERO");
        raise ERROR;
    when CONSTRAINT_ERROR =>
        PUT("ERROR******* B*B−4*A*C is negative");
        raise ERROR;
end ROOTS;
```

Exception ERROR must be handled by the caller of the subprogram ROOTS by means of an exception handler with the keyword **others**, because the name ERROR is not visible outside ROOTS.

The caller of ROOTS will not be able to determine the cause of the exception, i.e., whether the exception was raised due to a constraint error or a numeric error, since the same exception ERROR is raised at the point of call. This information can be provided to the caller of ROOTS by having ROOTS reraise the exceptions NUMERIC_ERROR or CONSTRAINT_ERROR (instead of raising ERROR) by using the statement

> **raise**;

These exceptions, being predefined, would be visible to the caller of ROOTS.

5.3 Exceptions Raised During Declaration Processing

The occurrence of an exception in the processing of a declarative part, or in the declaration of a subprogram, package or a task, causes the processing to be abandoned. Propagation of the exception depends upon where it was raised. If the exception is raised in a

1. declaration in a *subprogram body*, then the exception is propagated to the part of the program calling the subprogram. If the subprogram is a main program, then execution of the program is terminated.

2. declaration in a *block*, then the exception is propagated to the surrounding program.

3. declaration in a *package body*, then the exception is propagated to the part of the program containing the package. If the package is a library unit then execution of the main program is terminated.

4. declaration in a *task body*, then the exception TASKING_ERROR is propagated to the part of the program that caused activation of the task; the task becomes completed.

5. *subprogram, package or task declaration (i.e., specification)*, then the exception is propagated to the part of the program containing the declaration. If the declaration is that of a library unit, then execution of the main program is terminated.

6. Exceptions and Tasks [11.5]

During a rendezvous or a rendezvous attempt, the following situations cause exceptions to be raised or propagated:

1. *The called task completes before accepting an entry call or is already completed at the time of the call.* Exception TASKING_ERROR is raised in the calling task at the point of the entry call.

2. *The called task becomes abnormal during rendezvous.* Exception TASKING_ERROR is raised in the calling task at the point of the entry call.

3. *An exception raised in the accept statement is not handled locally.* The exception is propagated to the calling task at the point of the entry call and to the part of the program containing the *accept* statement.

Abnormal termination of the calling task does not affect the called task. If the rendezvous has not started then the rendezvous is canceled. Otherwise, the rendezvous is allowed to complete normally.

7. Retrying an Operation Raising an Exception

When an exception occurs, execution cannot be resumed just before, at or just after the point at which the exception is raised. Execution of an appropriate handler replaces the execution of the remainder of the block, subprogram or task in which the exception occurred; if no exception handler has been specified then execution of the block, subprogram or task in which the exception occurred is terminated. However, the statement in which the exception occurred can be re-executed by enclosing the statement in a block with a local exception handler and enclosing the block in a loop.

Sometimes errors (i.e., exceptions) in interacting with input and output devices, such as tape drives, are caused by transient conditions such as those resulting from electrical noise. In these cases it often suffices to retry the unsuccessful operation a few times until it works right. In other situations it may be desirable to retry an operation after the exception handler has rectified some of the conditions that may have caused the exception. For example an operation may result in the exception STORAGE_ERROR, because no more free storage is available. The operation is retried after storage is freed in the exception handler, by explicitly deallocating storage or by calling a garbage collector.

The following program segment [ICH80] illustrates how an attempt is made to read a tape 10 times before giving up, assuming that the tape drive malfunction is not due to transient errors.

```
--in case of errors try again to read the tape
--but give up after 10 attempts

for I in 1..10 loop
   begin
      READ_TAPE(BLOCK);
      exit;
         --an appropriate use of the exit statement
   exception
      when TAPE_ERROR =>
         if I = 10 then
            raise TAPE_DRIVE_MALFUNCTION;
         else
            BACK_SPACE;    --back up to beginning of last block
         end if;
   end;
end loop;
```

8. Suppressing Exceptions [11.7]

Normally, exceptions are automatically raised when detected, but the raising of some predefined exceptions may be suppressed by requesting the compiler to not check for certain conditions (e.g., division by zero or uninitialized variables). The pragma SUPPRESS is used to make requests for suppressing checks. The compiler may choose to ignore the request if the suppression of the specified check is impossible or too expensive.

Suppression of checks may lead to a program that will run faster and use less storage, since code for performing the checks need not be inserted into the program. For example, the code to check whether or not array subscripts are legal may be left out if the check INDEX_CHECK is suppressed. *The user must be very careful, especially in critical applications, of the ramifications of suppressing checks.* Checks should be suppressed only after ensuring that the corresponding conditions will not arise during program execution.

The scope of suppressing the checks is the block, the body of the subprogram, the package or the task in whose declarative part the SUPPRESS pragma appears. The SUPPRESS pragma has the form

   pragma SUPPRESS(check_name [,[ON =>] name]);

The second parameter is an object or type name for which the check is to be suppressed. If the second parameter is left out then the check specified will be suppressed throughout the unit containing the pragma.

Checks that can be suppressed and the associated exceptions are given in the table below:

Check Suppressed	Exception Affected
ACCESS_CHECK DISCRIMINANT_CHECK INDEX_CHECK LENGTH_CHECK RANGE_CHECK	CONSTRAINT_ERROR
DIVISION_CHECK OVERFLOW_CHECK	NUMERIC_ERROR
ELABORATION_CHECK	PROGRAM_ERROR
STORAGE_CHECK	STORAGE_ERROR

9. Examples

The examples in this section illustrate the handling of exceptions in the context of packages, subprograms and tasks. The first example discusses how package FIFO, declared in Chapter 3 on Packages, can be modified to handle limiting conditions by the use of exceptions. The next example illustrates the differences, with respect to exceptions, between an iterative and a recursive formulation of a program to compute factorials. The next two examples illustrate the use of exceptions in tasks monitoring a nuclear reactor for overheating or overcooling and a house for fires and break-ins. The example on merging two sorted files shows the use of exceptions in file handling, how a program should clean up after handling an exception and how to identify the operation raising a predefined exception. The next example illustrates how subprograms may be written so that they can express their *last wishes* before being terminated, because of the occurrence of an exception. Finally, there is an example from parsing that shows the use of a user-defined exception to abandon execution of the parser when the parser cannot continue in a meaningful way.

9.1 The package FIFO (from the Set of Priority Queues example given in Chapter 3 on Packages)

The problem is to modify the package FIFO used in the *Set of Priority Queues* example so that appropriate exceptions are raised when an attempt is made to add an item to a full queue or to remove an item from an empty queue.

The following changes are made to the package FIFO to handle the limiting conditions:

1. The exceptions FULL and EMPTY are declared in the specification of FIFO.

2. The procedures Q_ADD and Q_FIRST are modified by replacing the *if* statements printing messages that the queue is full or the queue is empty by *if* statements raising the appropriate exceptions. For example, the *if* statement

```
if Q.CUR_SIZE = MAX_SIZE then
    PUT("ERROR: Queue Full");
    NEW_LINE;
    return;
end if;
```

in Q_ADD is replaced by the *if* statement

```
if Q.CUR_SIZE = MAX_SIZE then
    raise FULL;
end if;
```

Of course, it is the responsibility of the user of FIFO (the package PRIORITY_QUEUES in this case) to handle the exceptions FIFO.FULL and FIFO.EMPTY. For example, procedure ADD in the body of the package PRIORITY_QUEUES

```
procedure ADD(P: in PRIORITY; J: in JOB_ID) is
begin
    Q_ADD(P_Q(P), J);
end ADD;
```

is modified to

```
    procedure ADD(P: in PRIORITY; J: in JOB_ID) is
    begin
       Q_ADD(P_Q(P), J);
    exception
       when FULL =>
              --take appropriate actions to handle the case
              --when the queue is full
    end ADD;
```

9.2 Factorial

The problem is to write a function that computes the factorial of a number n ($\geqslant 0$). This function must return the largest value of type INTEGER if the exception NUMERIC_ERROR is raised, because the factorial is too large.

The iterative version FACT_ITER is

```
    function FACT_ITER(N: NATURAL) return INTEGER is
       FACT: INTEGER := 1;
    begin
       for I in 2..N loop
          FACT := FACT * I;
       end loop;
       return FACT;
    exception
       when NUMERIC_ERROR => return INTEGER'LAST;
    end FACT_ITER;
```

The recursive version FACT_REC is

```
    function FACT_REC(N: NATURAL) return INTEGER is
    begin
       if N = 0 then
          return 1;
       else
          return N * FACT_REC(N - 1);
       end if;
    exception
       when NUMERIC_ERROR => return INTEGER'LAST;
    end FACT_REC;
```

The raising and handling of exceptions in the iterative and recursive versions of the function to compute the factorial differ in an interesting way. In case of FACT_ITER, as soon as overflow occurs the exception NUMERIC_ERROR is raised, execution of the normal part of FACT_ITER is abandoned and INTEGER'LAST returned via the exception handler.

On the other hand, in case of FACT_REC, the currently active instantiation of FACT_REC is abandoned as soon as overflow occurs with INTEGER'LAST returned to the previous activation. Overflow occurs again causing the exception NUMERIC_ERROR to be raised again. This exception raising cascades to the first activation, which eventually returns INTEGER'LAST as the factorial of N.

The number of times the exception NUMERIC_ERROR is raised in the iterative version is at most one, while in case of the recursive version it can be raised several times.[43]

9.3 Controlling a Nuclear Reactor

The problem is to design a task VESSEL_MONITOR that monitors and controls the temperature of the walls of the pressure vessel of a nuclear reactor. This task is given control of the pressure vessel (i.e., the task is activated) by a startup task, called START_REACTOR, but only after the pressure vessel has reached a steady state and its temperature is near the optimal operating temperature T_OPT.

The temperature of the pressure vessel must be maintained between T_MIN and T_MAX, and as close to T_OPT as possible (T_MIN < T_OPT < T_MAX). *If the pressure vessel temperature goes outside these limits, the reactor must be shut down first and questions asked and answered later.*

The pressure vessel temperature can be increased or decreased by an amount DELTA_T by decreasing or increasing the coolant flow by an amount DELTA_F. Larger changes in the pressure vessel temperature can be obtained by increasing or decreasing the coolant flow by a proportionally larger amount.

A package PRESSURE_VESSEL is available with procedures to control the coolant flow around the pressure vessel, read the latest pressure vessel temperature and so on. It also has the appropriate constant definitions. The specification of PRESSURE_VESSEL is

---

43. Up to N−7 times if 16 bit words are used to implement values of type INTEGER with one bit being reserved for the sign, and up to N−12 times if a 32 bit word is used.

```
package PRESSURE_VESSEL is

    subtype TEMPERATURE is FLOAT;

    DELTA_F: constant := 1000.0;
    DELTA_T: constant TEMPERATURE := 1.0;
        --A unit change in temperature is caused by changing the
        --coolant flow by DELTA_F/DELTA_T. The temperature
        --change is negative or positive depending on whether the
        --coolant flow change is positive or negative

    T_MIN: constant TEMPERATURE := 400.0;
    T_MAX: constant TEMPERATURE := 500.0;
    T_OPT: constant TEMPERATURE := 450.0;

    procedure CHANGE_FLOW(F: in FLOAT);
        --To change the temperature by an amount T the
        --flow should be changed by an amount equal to
        --T * (-DELTA_F/DELTA_T).
        --The - sign indicates that the flow is to be decreased
        --when T is positive and increased when T is negative

    --specifications of other procedures such as START_FLOW
    --and STOP_FLOW to start and stop the coolant flow
    procedure READ_TEMP(T: out TEMPERATURE);

end PRESSURE_VESSEL;
```

Task START_REACTOR takes care of the pressure vessel until it reaches a steady state and then hands over control of the pressure vessel to the task VESSEL_MONITOR. VESSEL_MONITOR is defined abstractly as

```
Wait until START_REACTOR gives the go ahead
loop
    Read the temperature
    if The temperature is not within the limits then
        First initiate reactor shut down by raising the
        exception TEMP_OUTSIDE_LIMITS.
        Follow up by appropriate messages
    end if;
    Adjust coolant flow so as to move the vessel temperature
        toward the optimum temperature
end loop;
```

These two tasks are enclosed in a procedure RUN_REACTOR declared as

```
with PRESSURE_VESSEL, TEXT_IO;
use PRESSURE_VESSEL, TEXT_IO;
procedure RUN_REACTOR is
    pragma PRIORITY(10);
        --highest priority provided by the implementation
        --is given to executing this task
    task START_REACTOR is
        .
        .
    end START_REACTOR;

    task VESSEL_MONITOR is
        entry START;
    end VESSEL_MONITOR;

    task body START_REACTOR is
        .
        .
    begin
        .
        .
        VESSEL_MONITOR.START;
        .
        .
    end START_REACTOR;

    --body of the task VESSEL_MONITOR is placed here
begin
    null;
            --a procedure must have one statement even
            --even if it is the null statement
end RUN_REACTOR;
```

The procedure RUN_REACTOR has been given the highest priority supported by an implementation, because it is of the utmost important that such a critical program be scheduled before all the other programs or tasks. It would be desirable if no other task or program on the system were given this high priority. It would be better if a computer were dedicated to running the program RUN_REACTOR. Of course, if the computer is dedicated to running RUN_REACTOR then the specification of the priority will not make any difference.

The body of the task VESSEL_MONITOR is

```
      task body VESSEL_MONITOR is
        T: TEMPERATURE;
        TEMP_OUTSIDE_LIMITS: exception;
        DELTA_FT: constant FLOAT := − DELTA_F/DELTA_T;
              −−flow decrease required per unit temperature increase;
              −−the flow increase required for a unit
              −−temperature decrease is −DELTA_FT
   begin
      accept START;
      loop
        READ_TEMP(T);
        if T >= T_MIN and T <= T_MAX then
          CHANGE_FLOW((T_OPT−T) * DELTA_FT);
                      −−move temperature toward T_OPT
        else
          raise TEMP_OUTSIDE_LIMITS;
        end if;
      end loop;
   exception
      when TEMP_OUTSIDE_LIMITS =>

          −−call the appropriate procedures to initiate
          −−IMMEDIATE SHUT DOWN of the reactor

        if T < T_MIN then
              −−note that any identifier accessible in the
              −−main program is accessible here
          PUT("SHUT DOWN => Vessel OVERCOOLING");
        else
          PUT("SHUT DOWN => Vessel OVERHEATING");
        end if;

          −−Task terminates after the exception is handled
      end VESSEL_MONITOR;
```

9.4 Home Fire/Energy/Security Monitoring

The use of computers at home is becoming common. One of their uses will be to monitor the state of a house, which includes routine tasks such as keeping track of the energy usage, and being on the alert for exceptional situations like fires and break-ins. The computer will be programmed to respond to exceptional situations.

This example illustrates a task ALARM that is used to monitor fires or break-ins. The presence of a fire or break-in is indicated by interrupts at locations 8#100# and 8#110# by the heat sensors and the movement detectors. The interrupts supply an integer value (of subtype LOCATION) identifying the location in the house where the fire or break-in has been detected. If there are no interrupts, thus indicating that everything is fine, then the task ALARM informs a task STATUS that all is well by calling its entry NO_FIRE_OR_BURGLAR at least once every 5 seconds. The task STATUS may be executing on a computer different from the one running ALARM. In this case, not getting an entry call from ALARM within 5 seconds could imply that the computer running the task ALARM has failed or been tampered with and that these possibilities should be checked.

The specification of the task ALARM is

```
task ALARM is
   entry HEAT_SENSOR(I: in LOCATION);
   entry MOVEMENT_DETECTOR(I: in LOCATION);

   for HEAT_SENSOR use at 8#100#;
   for MOVEMENT_DETECTOR use at 8#110#;
end ALARM;
```

ALARM implements the abstract algorithm

```
loop
   select
      Sound the fire alarm if the temperature of some part
      of the house has exceeded the ignition point
   or
      Sound the burglar alarm if suspicious movement
      has been detected
   else
      Wait for 4.5 seconds and signal all is well
   end select
end loop
```

The body of the task ALARM is

```
task body ALARM is
  X: LOCATION;
  FIRE, BREAK_IN: exception;
begin
  loop
    select
      accept HEAT_SENSOR(I: in LOCATION) do
        X := I;
      end HEAT_SENSOR;
      raise FIRE;
    or
      accept MOVEMENT_DETECTOR(I: in LOCATION) do
        X := I;
      end MOVEMENT_DETECTOR;
      raise BREAK_IN;
    or
      delay 4.5;     --Must acknowledge within 5 second intervals
      STATUS.NO_FIRE_OR_BURGLAR;
    end select;
  end loop;
exception
  when FIRE =>
    --SOUND the FIRE ALARM and call the fire department
    --with the address of the house and the location of fire
  when BREAK_IN =>
    --SOUND the BURGLAR ALARM and call the police with
    --the address of the house and the location of the burglar
end ALARM;
```

The task ALARM is terminated after it finishes handling the FIRE or BREAK_IN exception. ALARM must be restarted.

9.5 Merging Sorted Files

This example illustrates how subprograms *clean up* after an exception has been raised and how programs can be written to identify the statements that caused a predefined exception to be raised. Also illustrated in this example is the use of files and the exceptions raised by file operations.

The problem is to write a subprogram that merges two non-empty files, sorted in increasing order, to produce another file also sorted in increasing order. The input files have the *external* names A and B while the output file is named C (external names are the system names). Each of the files A and B contains elements of the type STUDENT_DATA. The comparison operation "<" is defined for elements of type STUDENT_DATA and is available in the context of the subprogram MERGE_SORT.

There are quite a few problems in writing MERGE_SORT. For example, occasionally an empty file is mistakenly given as input, which causes the exception END_ERROR to be raised. The underlying hardware (e.g., a tape drive) may malfunction, causing the exception DEVICE_ERROR to be raised. Also, there is some possibility that the files may contain elements of the wrong type (i.e., not STUDENT_DATA), which causes the exception DATA_ERROR to be raised. These exceptions are all raised when trying to read a tape. *When any of these exceptions is raised, prior to abandoning the sort, all the open files must be closed and appropriate error messages printed.*

The algorithm for merging two sorted files A and B to produce a sorted file C can be abstractly described as

```
Name the files P, Q, and R and open them
READ(P, X); READ(Q, Y);
loop
   if X < Y then
      WRITE(R, X);
      if file P is empty then
         WRITE(R, Y);
         Copy rest of Q onto R
         exit;
            ――an appropriate use of the exit statement
      end if;
      READ(P, X);
   else
      WRITE(R, Y);
      if file Q is empty then
         WRITE(R, X);
         Copy rest of P onto R
         exit;
      end if;
      READ(Q, Y);
   end if;
end loop;
```

In procedure MERGE_SORT, an instantiation of the predefined generic package SEQUENTIAL_IO [14.2.3] will be used for reading and writing elements of type STUDENT_DATA. This will allow the declaration of files with elements of type STUDENT_DATA and will also supply the file operations, such as OPEN, CLOSE, READ and END_OF_FILE.

```
with SEQUENTIAL_IO, TEXT_IO;
with STUDENT; use STUDENT;
        --package STUDENT contains type declarations
        --relevant to students such as STUDENT_DATA
        --and appropriate operations
procedure MERGE_SORT(A, B, C: STRING) is
   package STUDENT_DATA_IO is
                    new SEQUENTIAL_IO(STUDENT_DATA);
   use STUDENT_DATA_IO;

   P, Q, R: FILE_TYPE;
            --internal files corresponding to the external
            --files A, B, C

   X, Y: STUDENT_DATA;

begin
   --associate the internal names for the files with the external ones
   --and specify their modes
      OPEN(FILE => P, MODE=IN_FILE, NAME => A);
                --named notation used
      OPEN(Q, IN_FILE, B); OPEN(R, OUT_FILE, C);
                --positional notation used for illustration

   READ(P, X); READ(Q, Y);
                    --exception END_ERROR will be raised if
                    --either P or Q is empty to start with

   loop
      if X < Y then
         WRITE(R, X);
         if END_OF_FILE(P) then
            WRITE(R, Y);
            while not END_OF_FILE(Q) loop
               READ(Q, Y);
               WRITE(R, Y);
            end loop;
            exit;
         end if;
         READ(P, X);
      else
         WRITE(R, Y);
         if END_OF_FILE(Q) then
            WRITE(R, X);
```

```
            while not END_OF_FILE(P) loop
                READ(P, X);
                WRITE(R, X);
            end loop;
            exit;
        end if;
        READ(Q, Y);
    end if;
end loop;

exception
    when END_ERROR =>
        TEXT_IO.PUT("ERROR: One of the files "
                & A & " or " & B & " was empty");
        CLOSE(P); CLOSE(Q); CLOSE(R);
    when DEVICE_ERROR =>
        TEXT_IO.PUT("ERROR: hardware device with files "
                & A & " or " & B & " malfunctioning");
        CLOSE(P); CLOSE(Q); CLOSE(R);
    when DATA_ERROR =>
        TEXT_IO.PUT("ERROR: One of the files "
                & A & " or " & B & " has bad data");
        CLOSE(P); CLOSE(Q); CLOSE(R);
end MERGE_SORT;
```

The problem with Ada's treatment of exceptions is that it is not easy to pinpoint the statement that causes an exception to be raised. For example, in the above program it cannot be determined which read operation raised the exception, so the bad file or the malfunctioning device cannot be pinpointed.

This problem can be solved by modifying MERGE_SORT as follows:

1. Encapsulate the READ operation in a procedure, say CLEAR_READ, which does its own exception handling. Procedure CLEAR_READ is

```
                    procedure CLEAR_READ(F: in IN_FILE;
                                          V: out STUDENT_DATA) is
                    begin
                      READ(F, V);
                    exception
                      when END_ERROR =>
                        TEXT_IO.PUT("ERROR: File "
                                        & NAME(F) & " was empty");
                        raise;
                      when DEVICE_ERROR =>
                        TEXT_IO.PUT("ERROR: hardware device with file "
                                        & NAME(F) & " malfunctioning");
                        raise;
                      when DATA_ERROR =>
                        TEXT_IO.PUT("ERROR: File "
                                        & NAME(F) & " has bad data");
                        raise;
                    end CLEAR_READ;
```

An exception in CLEAR_READ is handled by CLEAR_READ itself.
Since the name of the file involved in the read operation is known there is
no problem in identifying the file (or the device it is on) that caused the
exception to be raised. CLEAR_READ raises the exception again for the
benefit of MERGE_SORT, which can then close all the files.

2. Replace all calls to READ by calls to CLEAR_READ.

3. Change the *exception* section of MERGE_SORT to contain just the
    following exception handler.

```
          when END_ERROR | DEVICE_ERROR | DATA_ERROR =>
              CLOSE(P); CLOSE(Q); CLOSE(R);
```

This example also illustrated an appropriate use of the *exit* statement. The
program could have been written without the *exit* statement,[44] albeit
inelegantly, by using one of the alternative formulations:

1. Using a *while* loop along with some additional BOOLEAN variables.

2. Allowing the READ statements in the loop to raise END_ERROR
    exception and do all the final processing in the corresponding exception

---

44. As an *exit* statement is a restricted form of the *goto* statement, a programmer should justify
    each use of *exit*.

handler (copying one of the non-empty input files to the output file and closing the files). This would, of course, require explicit checks for empty input files. This solution moves some of the normal computation, i.e., the final processing occurs when the end of one of the two input files has been reached, into the exception handler. Using exception handlers to do the final processing in a program is not good style, because an exception handler is meant processing exceptional situations only.

An elegant and succinct solution, that does not require the use of *exit* statements, can be easily arrived at in a language like Pascal [JEN74] that provides the user with a one element look-ahead for all input files.[45]

while neither file P nor Q is empty **loop**

P and Q are the look-ahead variables associated with files P and Q.
Set H to be the appropriate of P or Q and advance
the file (this advancing is the read but it is done
after examining the variable)

Write H on the output file R

end loop;

Copy the rest of the non-empty file (one of P or Q) to R

9.6 Example Illustrating the Last Wishes of a Subprogram [DOD79b]

Suppose that during execution of a subprogram several exceptions may occur which are not handled locally but are propagated to the caller. Prior to termination, the subprogram should have an opportunity to fulfill its last wishes, such as cleaning up and undoing the unwanted effects caused by its partial execution. This opportunity can be given to the subprogram by incorporating in it an exception handler with the choice **others**. The handler will contain the last wishes of the subprogram followed by the *raise* statement to propagate the exception to the caller of the subprogram.

Assume that the generic package DIRECT_IO has been appropriately instantiated and its entities made directly visible by a *use* clause. Now consider, as an example, the subprogram FILE_PROCESS that is used to process a file in some way:

---

45. This look ahead strategy causes problems when doing interactive input [FEU82].

```
procedure FILE_PROCESS(FILE_NAME: STRING) is
   F: FILE_TYPE;
begin
   Initial actions
   OPEN(F, INOUT_FILE, FILE_NAME);
   Process file
   CLOSE(F);
   Final actions
end FILE_PROCESS;
```

An exception occurring during the processing of the file will cause it to be left in the open state, since execution of the operation FILE_PROCESS will be immediately terminated, with the exception being propagated to the caller of FILE_PROCESS. Before terminating, operation FILE_PROCESS, as its last wish, would like to close the input file. Execution of last wishes can provided by writing FILE_PROCESS as the subprogram SAFE_FILE_PROCESS:

```
procedure SAFE_FILE_PROCESS(FILE_NAME: STRING) is
   F: FILE_TYPE;
begin
   Initial actions
   OPEN(F, INOUT_FILE, FILE_NAME);
   begin
      Process file
   exception
      when others =>
         CLOSE(F);
         raise;
   end;
   CLOSE(F);
   Final actions
end SAFE_FILE_PROCESS;
```

All exceptions that occur during the execution of SAFE_FILE_PROCESS are propagated to its caller. Exceptions that occur during the processing of the file are first handled locally. The local handler closes the file and reraises the exception for the caller.

9.7 An Example from Parsing

In parsing, situations arise when the parser is no longer able to make head or tail of the input program, because of the large number of errors present in the program. In these cases the parser gives up further analysis of the input program and quits. The skeleton of a parsing procedure PARSE shows that the exception CANNOT_RECOVER is raised when there is no point continuing the parse. The exception handler for CANNOT_RECOVER closes the files and prints appropriate messages.

```
procedure PARSE is
    .
    .
    CANNOT_RECOVER: exception;
    .
    .
begin
    .
    .
    if Error then
        if Can recover then
            Recover correcting error in best possible way
        else
            raise CANNOT_RECOVER;
        end if;
    end if;
    .
    .
exception
    .
    .
    when CANNOT_RECOVER =>
        Print messages including one indicating where the parsing
        was abandoned, close all files, ...
    .
    .
end PARSE;
```

Chapter 6: **Generic Facilities** [12]

1. Introduction

Subprograms and packages in Ada can be generic, that is, they can be templates of ordinary subprograms and packages. Generic subprograms and packages are often parameterized and can accept, in addition to normal parameters, types and subprograms as parameters. Generic subprograms and packages constitute the fourth form of a program unit from which programs are composed—the others being subprograms, packages and tasks.

Generic subprograms and packages have two parts—a generic specification and a body. They are specified by means of a generic declaration. A generic declaration consists of a generic part, where the generic formal parameters are declared, followed by the specification of the subprogram or the package. The body of a generic subprogram or a package has the same form as the body of an ordinary subprogram or a package.

Generic subprograms and packages cannot be used directly, since they are templates from which usable subprograms and packages are created. A generic subprogram or a package must first be instantiated (by means of a declaration) for some set of generic actual parameters. The instantiation creates a new subprogram or package, which can then be used just like any other subprogram or package. Many such instantiations can be created.

Generic subprograms and packages simplify some of the tedious aspects of programming. As an example, suppose we have to sort several arrays each with elements of a different type, e.g., reals, enumeration types, integers and characters. Without generic facilities, a sort procedure has to be written for each element type. With generic facilities, one sort procedure can be written to sort all arrays regardless of their element type. The generic sort procedure will have the array element type, the array type and the comparison operator < (defined for the array element type) as its formal parameters. This generic procedure can be instantiated for any element type that has < defined for it.

The advantages of having generic facilities in a programming language include [GEH80, GRI77]

1. *Reduced Programming Effort*: Only one generic subprogram or package need be written for subprograms and packages that are identical except for the types of their formal parameters and associated local variables, and the subprograms used by them.

2. *More Manageable Programs*: Program listings become smaller and less storage is required for the source code, since there will be fewer subprograms and packages. Program correctness proofs also become smaller, but these proofs, unlike those for normal subprograms and packages, must also take into consideration the restrictions and conditions on the generic formal parameters of the generic subprograms or packages being verified.

3. *Abstraction*: Generic subprograms and packages are abstractions of ordinary subprograms and packages. Generic facilities are therefore in accordance with the strategy of developing programs using stepwise refinement. Stepwise refinement encourages the programmer to concentrate on the algorithm without worrying about the details. In this case, the details are the actual types and subprograms used in the generic subprogram or the package body.

4. *Portability Across Types*: Changes to type declarations in a program will not require any changes to the generic subprogram or package, provided the subprograms used in the generic program unit are declared for the modified types. For example, suppose a program uses an instantiation of the generic sort procedure to sort an array with elements of type T. Type T was initially declared to be an integer but is now modified to be a real. As a result of this modification, no change is necessary for the generic subprogram or its instantiation for sorting an array with elements of type T.

2. Generic Specifications and Bodies [12.1-2]

A generic subprogram or package specification has the form

> **generic**
> generic formal parameters
> subprogram or package specification

A generic formal parameter can be an ordinary parameter declaration, a generic type definition, or a generic formal subprogram. Generic subprograms or packages are not required to have any parameters. Some examples of generic declarations are

```
generic
   type ELEM is private;
            --The generic actual parameter corresponding to ELEM
            --cannot be a limited private type, since it would not have
            --the assignment and equality operations. The assignment
            --operation will be used in sorting
   type VECTOR is array(INTEGER range <>) of ELEM;
   with function ">"(A, B: in ELEM) return BOOLEAN is <>;
            --the box <> allows for an identical subprogram visible
            --at the point of instantiation to be used if this generic
            --actual parameter is not supplied

   procedure INSERTION_SORT_G(A: in out VECTOR);
```

A normal (nongeneric) sort procedure is derived from the generic procedure INSERTION_SORT_G by instantiating it with three generic actual parameters—the element type, the array type and the comparison function ">":

```
procedure BOOLEAN_SORT is new
            INSERTION_SORT_G(BOOLEAN,
            BOOLEAN_ARRAY, ">");
```

Another example is the specification of a generic package STACK_G that implements a stack [DOD83]:

```
generic
    SIZE: POSITIVE;
    type ELEM is private;
package STACK_G is
    procedure PUSH(E: in ELEM);
    procedure POP(E: out ELEM);
    STACK_OVERFLOW, STACK_UNDERFLOW: exception;
end STACK_G;
```

STACK_G is instantiated with two generic actual parameters—the size of the desired stack and the type of the stack elements.

The specification of a generic subprogram, unlike for ordinary subprograms, must always be given. For ordinary subprograms, the subprogram body can also act as the specification of the subprogram. As another example, consider the following generic procedure SWAP_G, which is a generic version of procedure SWAP given in Chapter 1. The specification of SWAP_G is

```
generic
    type ELEM is private;
procedure SWAP_G(X, Y: in out ELEM);
```

As mentioned before, bodies of generic subprograms and packages are similar to those of ordinary subprograms and bodies. For example, the body of SWAP_G is

```
procedure SWAP_G(X, Y: in out ELEM) is
    T: ELEM;    --ELEM is the generic formal parameter type
begin
    T := X;
    X := Y;
    Y := T;
end SWAP_G;
```

2.1 Generic Subprogram Names

Within the body of a generic subprogram, its name can be used in a subprogram call—a recursive call to the current instantiation of the generic subprogram.

3. Generic Formal Parameters [12.1.1-3]

Generic formal parameters can be ordinary parameters but their modes are restricted to **in** or **in out**. The default mode is **in**. A generic formal parameter with the mode **in** behaves as a constant. On the other hand, a generic formal parameter with the mode **in out** renames the corresponding generic actual parameter.

A generic formal parameter type definition can be one of

1. an array type,

2. an access type,

3. a private type definition,

4. any discrete type (denoted (<>)),

5. any integer type (denoted **range** <>),

6. any floating point type (denoted **digits** <>),

7. any fixed point type (denoted **delta** <>).

Some examples of generic type declarations are

```
type ELEM is private;
type BUFFER(LENGTH: POSITIVE) is limited private;
type ELEM is (<>);
type VECTOR is array (INTEGER range <>) of ELEM;
```

In Ada, subprograms cannot be passed as ordinary parameters. However, the same effect can be achieved by using generic facilities and specifying a subprogram to be a generic formal parameter, as is illustrated by generic function INTEGRATE_G:

> **generic**
> **type** REAL **is digits** < >;
> **with function** F(X: **in** REAL) **return** REAL;
> **procedure** INTEGRATE_G(A, B, EPS: **in** REAL);

A subprogram corresponding to a generic formal subprogram parameter need not be supplied when instantiating a generic subprogram or package provided that

1. the generic formal subprogram declaration is followed by the keyword **is** and the name of a subprogram, in which case this subprogram is used by default, or

2. the generic formal subprogram declaration is followed by the keyword **is** and a *box* (i.e., < >). Then, by default, a subprogram with the same name as the generic formal subprogram is taken from the context in which the generic formal subprogram or package is instantiated. Such a subprogram must exist in the context of the instantiation; otherwise there is an error.

An example of generic formal parameter with a default value is

> **with function** ">"(A, B: **in** ELEM) **return** BOOLEAN **is** < >;

4. Instantiation of Generic Subprograms and Packages [12.3]

Generic subprograms and packages must be instantiated with actual parameters that match the generic formal parameters prior to being used. An instantiation is a declaration of the form

> [**procedure** | **function** | **package**] name **is**
>   **new** generic_name [(generic actual parameter list)] ;

where *name* is the name given to the instantiation and *generic_name* is the name of the generic subprogram or package instantiated. The name associated with the instantiation can be an operator [6.7] if a generic function with one or two formal parameters (the ordinary parameters and not the generic parameters) is being instantiated. The generic actual parameters may be specified using the positional or named notation as in subprogram calls. A generic actual parameter can be an expression, a variable name, a subprogram name, an entry name, a type name or a subtype name.

Some examples of instantiation are

procedure INTEGER_SORT **is new**
          INSERTION_SORT_G(ELEM **=>** INTEGER,
          VECTOR **=>** INTEGER_ARRAY);
                    ――named parameter notation is used;
                    ――the comparison operator > for type INTEGER
                    ――must be present in the context of the instantiation,
                    ――since it has not been explicitly supplied

procedure MATRIX_SWAP **is new** SWAP_G(MATRIX);
                    ――positional parameter notation is used

package INTEGER_STACK **is new** STACK_G(100, INTEGER);

Each instantiation of a generic subprogram or package results in a new set of
declarations for the instantiation (including exceptions).

5. Generic Packages Without Parameters

Package ORDERED_SET given in Chapter 3 on Packages provided only one
ordered set to the user. To circumvent this limitation it was reimplemented as
package ORDERED_SET2 with limited private type ORD_SET. More than
one ordered set could then be declared by just declaring objects of type
ORD_SET. The generic facilities can also be used to create more than one
instance of an object being implemented by a package. For example, by
declaring ORDERED_SET as a generic package without parameters,
ORDERED_SET_G, more than one set can be instantiated:

generic
package ORDERED_SET_G **is**
          ――same specifications for N, INSERT, SMALLEST and EMPTY
          ――as given in ORDERED_SET
end ORDERED_SET_G;

More than one set is created by simply instantiating ORDERED_SET_G the
desired number of times as shown below:

package SET_1 **is new** ORDERED_SET_G;
package SET_2 **is new** ORDERED_SET_G;

The set operations are referred to by qualifying the operations with the name
of the instantiated package. For example, the functions named EMPTY
associated with the packages SET_1 and SET_2 are referred to as

SET_1.EMPTY

and

SET_2.EMPTY

Many instances of an object implemented by a package can be declared either by implementing the package as a generic package without parameters or by using limited private types. How do these two approaches differ? Analyzing the differences between these two approaches is left as an exercise for the reader. *Hint*: Analyze the visibility rules and how the operations provided by the two implementations are referenced.

6. Matching Rules for Generic Formal Parameters [12.3.1]

The following rules must be obeyed in matching generic formal parameters with the corresponding actual parameters when instantiating a generic subprogram or package:

1. *Ordinary Parameters*—The type of the generic actual parameter must match the type of the generic formal parameter and satisfy any associated constraints.

2. *Formal Private Types*—A formal private type can be matched by any actual type subject to the following conditions. If the formal private type

   a. is a limited private type then it can be matched by any type including a task type.

   b. is not a limited private type then it can be matched by any actual type for which the assignment, equality and inequality operations are available.

   c. has discriminants then these must match the discriminants of the actual type.

3. *Formal Scalar Types*—A formal scalar type specified as

   a. (< >)   matches any discrete type

   b. **range** < > matches any integer type

   c. **digits** < > matches any floating point type

   d. **delta** < > matches any fixed point type

4. *Formal Array Types*—The actual parameter type must have the same number of indices as the generic formal type. Then, after substituting any generic types in the formal array type by the corresponding actual type, the array types must have the same component and index types (in the same order), and the same constraints. If either the generic formal array type or the corresponding actual parameter is unconstrained then the other must also be unconstrained.

5. *Formal Access Types*—If the object type in the generic formal access type is generic, then it is first replaced by the corresponding actual type. After the substitution has been done, the generic formal access type and the actual access type must have the same object type.

6. *Formal Subprograms*—If there are any generic types in the formal generic subprogram they are first replaced by the corresponding actual types. After the substitution has been performed, the generic formal subprogram and the actual subprogram must be such that the corresponding parameters have the same type, the same mode and the same constraints. If the formal subprogram is a function, then the generic formal and actual result types and the constraints on them must also be the same.

An operator can be passed as a generic actual parameter for a generic formal function subprogram parameter. Similarly, a function can be passed as a generic actual parameter for a generic formal parameter that is an operator.

An entry can be passed as a generic actual parameter for a generic formal procedure subprogram parameter.

7. Examples

The first example is a generic package that can be used to instantiate stacks of any size and element type. This example is followed by a generic sort procedure, which can be used to sort arrays of any element type, such as employee records, provided the comparison operator is defined for the type. Subprograms cannot be passed as ordinary parameters in Ada (as is possible in many languages, e.g., Pascal and Algol 60). The generic facilities can be used to accomplish passing of subprograms as parameters as is illustrated by the generic integration procedure. The next example is a generic package that can be used to create sets with different element types. The last two examples illustrate how the generic facilities can be used to implement classes of operations, such as general array operations and the MAPLIST function of Lisp.

7.1 Stacks

The problem is to implement a generic stack package that can be used to instantiate stacks of different sizes and element types. The specification of such a package, STACK_G, given earlier, is reproduced here:

```
generic
   SIZE: POSITIVE;
   type ELEM is private;
package STACK_G is
   procedure PUSH(E: in ELEM);
   procedure POP(E: out ELEM);
   STACK_OVERFLOW, STACK_UNDERFLOW: exception;
end STACK_G;
```

The body of generic package STACK_G is

```
package body STACK_G is
   SPACE: array(1..SIZE) of ELEM;
         --SIZE and ELEM are the generic formal parameters
   INDEX: INTEGER range 0..SIZE := 0;

   procedure PUSH(E: in ELEM) is
   begin
      if INDEX = SIZE then
         raise STACK_OVERFLOW;
      end if;
      INDEX := INDEX + 1;
      SPACE(INDEX) := E;
   end PUSH;

   procedure POP(E: out ELEM) is
   begin
      if INDEX = 0 then
         raise STACK_UNDERFLOW;
      end if;
      E := SPACE(INDEX);
      INDEX := INDEX - 1;
   end POP;
end STACK_G;
```

Any exceptions raised by calls to PUSH and POP are propagated to the caller. Looking at just the body of STACK_G (and ignoring the comments), it is not possible to say whether STACK_G is the body of an ordinary or generic package.

7.2 Generic Insertion Sort

The insertion sort procedure given in Chapter 1 is now modified to make it generic. The specification of the generic version, INSERTION_SORT_G, is

```
generic
   type ELEM is private;
   type VECTOR is array(INTEGER range < >) of ELEM;
   with function ">"(A, B: in ELEM) return BOOLEAN is < >;
            ——if the comparison operator > for elements of type ELEM
            ——is not supplied when instantiating then such an operator
            ——must be present in the context of the instantiation
procedure INSERTION_SORT_G(A: in out VECTOR);
```

Generic procedure INSERTION_SORT_G can be used to instantiate procedures that sort arrays with integer subscripts only. This restriction can be removed by making the index type of the array to be sorted a generic parameter as shown by the specification of the generic procedure GENERAL_INSERTION_SORT_G:

```
generic
   type ELEM is private;
   type INDEX is (< >);     ——any discrete type
   type VECTOR is array(INDEX) of ELEM;
   with function ">"(A, B: in ELEM) return BOOLEAN is < >;
procedure GENERAL_INSERTION_SORT_G(A: in out VECTOR);
```

Although the information supplied by the third generic parameter can be derived from the first two parameters, the treatment of types requires the presence of the third parameter.

The body of INSERTION_SORT_G is

```
procedure INSERTION_SORT_G(A: in out VECTOR) is

   I, J: A'RANGE;
   T: ELEM;
            --type of temporary variable T is the generic
            --formal type ELEM
   L: INTEGER := A'FIRST;
   U: INTEGER := A'LAST;

begin
   I := L;
   while I /= U loop
      T := A(I+1);
      J := I+1;
      while J /= L and then A(J-1) > T loop
         A(J) := A(J-1);
         J := J-1;
      end loop;
      A(J) := T;
      I := I+1;
   end loop;
end INSERTION_SORT_G;
```

Suppose the following declarations are in effect when instantiating INSERTION_SORT_G:

```
type BOOLEAN_ARRAY is array(INTEGER range <>)
                                    of BOOLEAN;

type EMPLOYEE is
   record
      NAME: STRING(1..40);
      ID: INTEGER;
   end RECORD;

type EMPLOYEE_ARRAY is array(INTEGER range <>)
                                    of EMPLOYEE;

function ">"(A, B: in EMPLOYEE) return BOOLEAN is
begin
   return A.ID > B.ID;
end ">";
```

Sorting routines for arrays with elements of type BOOLEAN and EMPLOYEE are instantiated as

```
procedure BOOLEAN_SORT is
    new INSERTION_SORT_G(ELEM => BOOLEAN,
            VECTOR => BOOLEAN_ARRAY, ">" => ">");
        --the generic formal parameter representing the greater
        --than operation has the same name as the generic actual
        --parameter, that is, the symbol >
```

```
procedure EMPLOYEE_SORT is
    new INSERTION_SORT_G(ELEM => EMPLOYEE,
            VECTOR => EMPLOYEE_ARRAY, ">" => ">");
```

If the comparison operator had not been given in the instantiation BOOLEAN_SORT

```
procedure BOOLEAN_SORT is
    new INSERTION_SORT_G(ELEM => BOOLEAN,
                VECTOR => BOOLEAN_ARRAY);
```

then by default a comparison operator from the context of the instantiation would have been used if one existed. Otherwise, the instantiation would have resulted in a compile time error.

In the above instantiation of EMPLOYEE_SORT named parameter notation was used. Positional parameter notation could also have been used. For example,

```
procedure EMPLOYEE_SORT is
    new INSERTION_SORT_G(EMPLOYEE,
                EMPLOYEE_ARRAY, ">");
```

A function with an identifier for its name, instead of an operator symbol, and with two formal parameters can also be supplied as a generic actual parameter for a generic formal parameter that is an operator. For example, function GREATER_THAN, declared as

```
function GREATER_THAN(A, B: EMPLOYEE) return BOOLEAN is
begin
    return A.ID > B.ID;
end GREATER_THAN;
```

is used as the generic actual parameter in the instantiation EMPLOYEE_SORT2

```
procedure EMPLOYEE_SORT2 is
    new INSERTION_SORT_G(EMPLOYEE,
            EMPLOYEE_ARRAY, GREATER_THAN);
```

The types of the formal parameters and result type of the operator ">" in the generic procedure INSERTION_SORT_G must, of course, match those of the function GREATER_THAN.

The generic procedure INSERTION_SORT_G sorts according to the generic operator ">" which normally stands for greater than. If x and y are elements of the array to be sorted and x > y is TRUE then x will appear after y in the sorted array. Thus the array will be sorted in increasing order. Supplying the operator "<" when instantiating INSERTION_SORT_G will produce an instantiation that will sort the array in decreasing order. For example, the instantiation DECREASING_BOOLEAN_SORT will sort the elements of a BOOLEAN array in decreasing order:

> **procedure** DECREASING_BOOLEAN_SORT **is**
>   **new** INSERTION_SORT_G(BOOLEAN,
>   BOOLEAN_ARRAY, "<");

7.3 Integration via the Trapezoidal Rule

Write a generic function INTEGRATE_G that finds the definite integral of a function f: real → real between the limits a and b

$$I = \int_{i=a}^{i=b} f(x)$$

using the trapezoidal rule. It should be possible to instantiate the generic function INTEGRATE_G for different functions f.

The trapezoidal rule approximates the integral of a function between the two limits a and b by the area of the trapezoid with base b−a and heights f(a) and f(b).

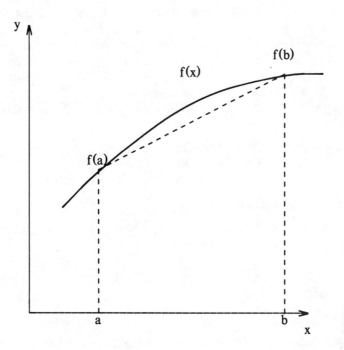

Approximating the integral of function f using one interval

This approximation can be improved by dividing a and b into two equal subintervals, taking the area of the two resulting trapezoids and adding them up. Each of these subintervals can be further divided into two more equal subintervals and the process repeated.

The approximate integral I_n of a function f between the limits a and b using n subintervals

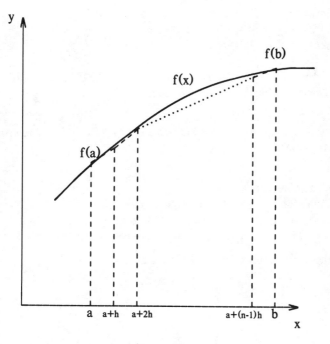

Approximating the integral of function f using on intervals

is given by the equation

$$I_n = h(\frac{f(a)}{2}+f(a+h)+f(a+2h)+ \cdots +f(a+(n-1)h)+\frac{f(b)}{2})$$

where h, the width of the interval, is given by

$$h = \frac{(b-a)}{n}$$

The subdividing process is repeated until two successive approximations of the integral of the function f as calculated by the trapezoidal rule differ in absolute value by less than EPS (EPS > 0), the desired stopping tolerance.

The trapezoidal integration algorithm can be described abstractly as

```
NEW_APPROX := 0;
FINISHED := FALSE;
while not FINISHED loop
    PREVIOUS_APPROX := NEW_APPROX;
    Calculate NEW_APPROX
    FINISHED :=
        abs (NEW_APPROX - PREVIOUS_APPROX) < EPS;
    Divide each subinterval into two equal subintervals
end loop;
```

The specification of generic function INTEGRATE_G implementing the trapezoidal integration algorithm is

```
generic
    type REAL is digits < >;
    with function F(X: in REAL) return REAL;
        --the function F must be supplied when instantiating
    function INTEGRATE_G(A, B, EPS: in REAL) return REAL;
```

The body of the generic function INTEGRATE_G is

```
    function INTEGRATE_G(A, B, EPS: in REAL) return REAL is
       NEW_APPROX: REAL := 0.0;    --random initial value
       PREVIOUS_APPROX: REAL;
       FINISHED: BOOLEAN := FALSE; --not finished to start with
       N: INTEGER;    --number of intervals
       H: REAL;        --interval size
       SUM: REAL;     --temporary variable
    begin
       N := INTEGER(10.0 * (B - A)) + 1;
            --N should be such that the interval size is relatively
            --small; conversion of a real value to an integer
            --involves rounding

       H := (B - A)/REAL(N);      --initial interval size
       while not FINISHED loop
         PREVIOUS_APPROX := NEW_APPROX;
         --calculate NEW_APPROX
            SUM := F(A)/2.0;
            for I in 1..N-1 loop
               SUM := SUM + F(A + REAL(I) * H);
            end loop;
            SUM := SUM + F(B)/2.0;
            NEW_APPROX := SUM * H;
         FINISHED :=
            abs (NEW_APPROX - PREVIOUS_APPROX) < EPS;
         N := N * 2;
                    --number of intervals for next approximation
         H := H / 2.0;
                    --size of interval for next approximation
       end loop;
       return NEW_APPROX;
    end INTEGRATE_G;
```

INTEGRATE_G does not work correctly if the first approximation of the integral of F is within EPS of 0.0, the random initial value assigned to NEW_APPROX. This problem can be solved by forcing the computation of at least two approximations or by initializing NEW_APPROX to an approximation of the integral instead of an arbitrary value:

```
    NEW_APPROX: REAL := (F(A) + F(B))/2.0;
        --the area under the curve approximated as one big
        --trapezoid, i.e., N=1
```

7.4 Sets

In this example, sets are implemented using a generic package SET_G. Each instantiation of SET_G creates a new set. Operations are provided to add and remove an element, take the union or difference of two sets, determine if a set is empty and get a null (empty set). Type SET is designated as a private type so that sets can be assigned to objects of type SET and be compared for equality or inequality.

The specification of package SET_G is

```
generic
    type ELEM is (<>);       --any discrete type
package SET_G is

    type SET is private;

    procedure ADD(S: in out SET; E: in ELEM);
    procedure REMOVE(S: in out SET; E: in ELEM);
    function EMPTY(S: in SET) return BOOLEAN;
    function "+"(X, Y: in SET) return SET;    --set union
    function "-"(X, Y: in SET) return SET;
            --set difference; returns a set that contains all
            --the elements of X except those also present in Y
    function NULL_SET return SET;

private
    type SET_ARRAY is array(ELEM) of BOOLEAN;
    type SET is
      record
          A: SET_ARRAY := (ELEM => FALSE);
      end record;
            --sets will be given the null (empty) set value when
            --created. Only a record type can have a default
            --initial value associated with it; this value applies
            --to all objects of that type. This reason is why
            --the BOOLEAN array A implementing the set has been
            --enclosed in a record. The default initial value can
            --be overridden by an explicit initialization

    end SET_G;
```

The implementation of SET_G is straightforward:

```
package body SET_G is

   procedure ADD(S: in out SET; E: in ELEM) is
   begin
      S.A(E) := TRUE;
   end ADD;

   procedure REMOVE(S: in out SET; E: in ELEM) is
   begin
      S.A(E) := FALSE;
   end REMOVE;

   function EMPTY(S: in SET) return BOOLEAN is
   begin
      for I in ELEM loop
         if S.A(I) then
            return FALSE;
         end if;
      end loop;
      return TRUE;
   end EMPTY;

   function "+"(X, Y: in SET) return SET is
      RESULT: SET;
            --initial value of RESULT is the empty set
   begin
      for I in ELEM loop
         RESULT.A(I) := X.A(I) or Y.A(I);
      end loop;
      return RESULT;
   end "+";

   function "-"(X, Y: in SET) return SET is
      RESULT: SET;
   begin
      for I in ELEM loop
         RESULT.A(I) := X.A(I) and not Y.A(I);
      end loop;
      return RESULT;
   end "-";
```

```
function NULL_SET return SET is
   RESULT: SET;
begin
   return RESULT;    --is null on declaration
end NULL_SET;
```

```
end SET_G;
```

Some examples of the use of package SET_G are

```
package INT_SET is new SET_G(SMALL_INT);
package CHAR_SET is new SET_G(CHARACTER);
```

```
A, B: INT_SET.SET;
X, Y: CHAR_SET.SET;
```

Implementing sets by using a boolean value for each element to indicate its presence or absence results in fast set operations. However, such an implementation does not make very efficient use of storage, especially if the number of elements in a set at any given time is small compared to the maximum number of possible elements that can be in the set. How can sets be implemented so that storage is used efficiently? Investigation of this problem is left to the reader. *Hint*: Implement the set as a list. Compare this implementation with the boolean array implementation with respect to the execution speed of the operations and the storage used for the set elements. What is the impact of ordering the elements of the list? Is there some other more complicated data structure that results in faster operations than those got by using lists but requires less space than boolean arrays?

7.5 General Operations on Arrays

The generic facilities in Ada can be used to define classes of operations. Examples of these operations are given for one-dimensional and two-dimensional arrays:

7.5.1 One-Dimensional Arrays: This example illustrates that several operations on a one-dimensional array, such as computing the maximum of all the elements and the product of all the elements, can be abstracted and written as one generic function VECTOR_OPERATION. This example also illustrates the versatility and the power of the generic facilities in Ada.

Assuming that VECTOR_OPERATION is instantiated as the function THETA_VECTOR for the operator θ, THETA_VECTOR(A) computes the value

$$a_1 \theta a_2 \theta \cdots \theta a_n$$

where a_i are the elements of the array A.[46]

VECTOR_OPERATION has the specification

```
generic
   type ELEM is private;
   type INDEX is (<>);
               --all operations of a discrete type are available
   type VECTOR is array(INDEX range <>) of ELEM;
               --array operations such as indexing and slicing
               --are available
   with function F(A, B: in ELEM) return ELEM;
function VECTOR_OPERATION(A: in VECTOR) return ELEM;
```

The body of VECTOR_OPERATION is

```
function VECTOR_OPERATION(A: in VECTOR) return ELEM is
   RESULT: ELEM;    --A should not be a null array
begin
   RESULT := A(A'FIRST);
   for I in INDEX'SUCC(A'FIRST) .. A'LAST loop
      RESULT := F(RESULT, A(I));
   end loop;
end VECTOR_OPERATION;
```

By instantiating VECTOR_OPERATION with different values of the generic formal parameters, different operations on arrays can be derived. For example,

---

46. VECTOR_OPERATION provides a facility similar to the *reduction* operator in APL.

```
function MAX_FLOAT_VECTOR is
    new VECTOR_OPERATION(ELEM => FLOAT,
        INDEX => INTEGER,
        VECTOR => FLOAT_ARRAY, F => MAX_FLOAT);

function MIN_FLOAT_VECTOR is
    new VECTOR_OPERATION(ELEM => FLOAT,
        INDEX => INTEGER,
        VECTOR => FLOAT_ARRAY, F => MIN_FLOAT);

function SUM_FLOAT_VECTOR is
    new VECTOR_OPERATION(ELEM => FLOAT,
        INDEX => INTEGER,
        VECTOR => FLOAT_ARRAY, F => "+");

function PROD_FLOAT_VECTOR is
    new VECTOR_OPERATION(ELEM => FLOAT,
        INDEX => INTEGER,
        VECTOR => FLOAT_ARRAY, F => "*");

function OR_BOOLEAN_VECTOR is
    new VECTOR_OPERATION(ELEM => BOOLEAN,
        INDEX => INTEGER,
        VECTOR => BOOLEAN_ARRAY, F => "or");

function AND_BOOLEAN_VECTOR is
    new VECTOR_OPERATION(ELEM => BOOLEAN,
        INDEX => INTEGER,
        VECTOR => BOOLEAN_ARRAY, F => "and");
```

FLOAT_ARRAY and BOOLEAN_ARRAY are unconstrained arrays with elements of type FLOAT and BOOLEAN, respectively, and both having indices of type INTEGER. Similar operations can be defined for other unconstrained arrays.

7.5.2 Two-Dimensional Arrays—Generalized Matrix Product: The product of two matrices A (size m × n) and B (size n × p) is given by the matrix C (size m × p) defined as

$$C_{i,j} = \sum_{k=L}^{k=U} A_{i,k} * B_{k,j}$$

$$= A_{i,L} * B_{L,j} + A_{i,L+1} * B_{L+1,j} + \cdots + A_{i,U} * B_{U,j}$$

where L and U are the lower and upper bounds of the second dimension of A and the first dimension of B (U−L+1 = n), respectively.

Procedure MAT_MULT, given in Chapter 1, computed the above product for matrices with floating point elements and indices of type INTEGER only. From this procedure, the element type, the index type, and the operations * and + are abstracted to get a generic procedure that computes the generalized matrix product. Generalized matrix multiplication is implemented by the generic procedure GEN_MATRIX_PRODUCT whose specification is

```
generic
    type ELEM is private;
    type INDEX is (<>);
    type MATRIX is array(INDEX range <>, INDEX range <>)
                                        of ELEM;
    with function "+"(A, B: in ELEM) return ELEM is <>;
    with function "*"(A, B: in ELEM) return ELEM is <>;
procedure GEN_MATRIX_PRODUCT(A, B: in MATRIX;
                                        C: out MATRIX);
```

The body of GEN_MATRIX_PRODUCT is

procedure GEN_MATRIX_PRODUCT(A, B: **in** MATRIX;
                                                      C: **out** MATRIX) **is**
——the array bounds of A, B and C must be appropriate.
——If desired, a check could be prior to computing the
——matrix product

   L: INDEX := A'FIRST(2);   ——index of first column of A
begin
  for I **in** C'RANGE(1) **loop**
    for J **in** C'RANGE(2) **loop**

       ——initialize C(I, J) to the product of the first pair of
       ——elements; cannot initialize it to 0.0, because ELEM type
       ——is generic and the type of the generic actual parameter
       ——corresponding to it is not known. For example, it could
       ——be INTEGER, REAL or BOOLEAN

      C(I, J) := A(I, L) * B(L, J);

      for K **in** INDEX'SUCC(L) .. A'LAST(2) **loop**
        C(I, J) := C(I, J) + A(I, K) * B(K, J);
      end loop;

    end loop;
  end loop;
end GEN_MATRIX_PRODUCT;

The generic procedure GEN_MATRIX_PRODUCT is now instantiated to produce some interesting operations. All the matrices used in the instantiation must have unconstrained index types. The declarations of the matrix types used are not given, but their declarations are clearly suggested by their names.

      procedure FLOAT_MATRIX_PROD **is**
           new GEN_MATRIX_PRODUCT(FLOAT,
                         INTEGER, FLOAT_MATRIX);
        --the operations * and + for floating
        --point will be picked up from the environment

      procedure CONNECTED_2 **is**
           new GEN_MATRIX_PRODUCT(BOOLEAN, INTEGER,
                 BOOLEAN_MATRIX, "or", "and");
        --if the element POINTS(I, J) has the value TRUE
        --when point I is directly connected to J and FALSE
        --otherwise, then the procedure call
        --CONNECTED_2(POINTS, POINTS, RESULT) will
        --update matrix RESULT so that RESULT(I, J)
        --will be TRUE if one can get from I to J
        --directly or via one intermediate point at
        --most (path of length 2).

      procedure SHORTEST_DISTANCE_2 **is**
           new GEN_MATRIX_PRODUCT(FLOAT, INTEGER,
                 FLOAT_MATRIX, MIN, "+");
        --if the element (I, J) of matrix D contains the
        --distance of a point I from a point J then the
        --procedure call SHORTEST_DISTANCE_2(D, D, RESULT)
        --will produce a matrix RESULT such that an element
        --I, J of RESULT will contain the shortest distance
        --from I to J via at most one intermediate point
        --(path of length 2).

As an exercise for the reader, the problem of writing a generic function that traverses a tree in some order is suggested. Among other things, it should take a function F as an actual parameter. Instantiations of this generic function with appropriate functions can be used to produce functions to count the number of nodes in a tree, determine the depth of a tree, determine the width of the tree and so on.

7.6 MAPLIST

Suppose that functions on values of type T are to be extended to operate on lists of elements of type T. The extended functions take as actual parameters a value of type LIST, which is a list of elements of type T, and produce a result of type LIST. The generic function used in producing these extended functions is similar to function MAPLIST in Lisp. MAPLIST takes as actual parameters a function F and a list L. It applies the function F to all the elements of the list L, returning a list of the resulting values, i.e.,

$$MAPLIST(F, L) = (F(L_1), F(L_2), ..., F(L_N))$$

where L is the list $(L_1, L_2, ..., L_N)$.

An ordinary function cannot be written for MAPLIST, because subprograms cannot be passed as parameters in Ada. However, a generic function MAPLIST can be written that must be instantiated for every combination of the function F and the list type L. The difference between the Lisp version and ours is that, in the case of the Lisp MAPLIST, function F need not be known until run time, whereas in our case it must be known at compile time and is specified when instantiating our MAPLIST. This restriction is not really a problem, since functions cannot be manipulated or created at run time in Ada as is possible in Lisp. Moreover, in Lisp all lists are of one type, whereas in Ada lists can be of different types (e.g., those with different element types), as a consequence of which MAPLIST will be have to be instantiated for each type of list to be passed as a parameter.

MAPLIST has the specification

```
generic
     type LIST is private;
     type ELEM is private;

     with function F(E: in ELEM) return ELEM;
          --this is the function that is being extended

     --the following operations for values of the type LIST must
     --be supplied or be available in the context of the instantiation
     --since they are necessary for extending the function F

          with function HEAD(L: in LIST) return ELEM is <>;
               --first element of the list L
          with procedure ADD_LAST(L: in out LIST; X: in ELEM) is <>;
          with function TAIL(L: in LIST) return LIST is <>;
               --the list that is the same as L
               --but minus the first element
          with function EMPTY(L: in LIST) return BOOLEAN is <>;
          with function CREATE return LIST is <>;
               --an empty list
     function MAPLIST(L: in LIST) return LIST;
```

The body of MAPLIST is

```
function MAPLIST(L: in LIST) return LIST is
   A, RESULT: LIST;
begin
   A := L;
   RESULT := CREATE;    --the empty list
   while not EMPTY(A) loop
      ADD_LAST(RESULT, F(HEAD(A)));
      A := TAIL(A);
   end loop;
   return RESULT;
end MAPLIST;
```

The generic function MAPLIST may be instantiated for a list of integers and the function SQUARE as

```
function SQUARE_INTEGER_LIST is
            new MAPLIST(INTEGER_LIST, INTEGER, SQUARE);
```

Of course, the function SQUARE should take an INTEGER parameter and return an INTEGER value, and the appropriate functions for lists of type INTEGER_LIST should be available in the environment of the instantiation, since they have not been explicitly specified.

Chapter 7: **Program Structure and Separate Compilation** [10]

1. Introduction

Large programs are different from small programs, because they are software systems consisting of many components or modules (themselves small programs) and are usually written by different people. A programming language should support both *programming-in-the-small* (as is done by most existing languages such as Pascal and PL/I) and *programming-in-the-large*. Programming-in-the-large is supported by providing facilities for writing modules, information hiding, controlling visibility of objects and specifying dependencies between the modules [DER76].

Ada provides several facilities that support the construction and management of large software projects. It supports both programming-in-the-small and programming-in-the-large. In Ada, for example, program components (such as declarations and bodies of subprograms and packages, and task bodies) can be compiled *separately* and programs can be developed either *bottom up* or *top down*.

1.1 Separate Compilation

The ability to independently compile components of a program is important for constructing large programs and creating libraries of precompiled programs.[47] However, in *independent compilation* no checking is performed to determine whether the program component being compiled is consistent with the program components that have been already compiled. For example, the types of actual parameters in a call to an independently compiled subprogram are not checked to determine whether they match the types of corresponding formal parameters.

The notion of independent compilation was rejected in languages such as Pascal and Algol 68 on the grounds that the lack of type checking during independent compilation would defeat their strong typing mechanisms. Compilation of the whole program, which is safer than independent compilation, was suggested as a better alternative. However, this alternative is not very attractive in terms of cost and time, especially in the development of large programs. The whole

---

47. Independent compilation is one of the reasons for the success of FORTRAN.

program must be recompiled whenever any change, however small, is made. Components of programs cannot be compiled on their own, thus preventing the development of a large program by developing its components, compiling them and testing them, and putting them together at the end to get the final program. Another major disadvantage with this approach is that precompiled libraries of routines cannot be provided.[48]

Independent compilation is a practical necessity, but the lack of consistency checking is a serious problem. The solution adopted in Ada, called *separate compilation*, incorporates consistency checking into independent compilation. A record is kept of the properties of every program component that has been compiled. Whenever a new component of a program is compiled, the record is used to ensure that the new component is consistent with the program components that have been compiled previously.

1.2 Compilation and Library Units [10.1]

An Ada program can be compiled in one compilation by submitting all its text together to the compiler or alternatively, in several compilations by compiling its components separately. *Compilation units* are components of programs, preceded by contextual information, that can be compiled separately. Compilation units have the form

> context library_unit | context secondary_unit

where a *library_unit* is a

> subprogram_declaration
> | package_declaration
> | generic_declaration
> | generic_instantiation
> | subprogram_body

a *secondary_unit* is a

> library_unit_body | subunit

and a *library_unit_body* is a

---

48. The lack of a facility to compile components of a program independently or separately is another one of Pascal's weak points. It is a serious impediment to the usability of Pascal and has led to implementations providing their own nonstandard versions of independent compilation.

subprogram_body | package_body

A *subunit* is the body of a subprogram, a package or a task declared in the outermost part of another compilation unit, with a *body stub* given for it there. A body stub specifies that the corresponding body will be compiled later and that the environment present at the body stub will be used in the compilation.

All library units of a program must have unique names (except, of course, the corresponding declarations and bodies of subprograms or packages). Compiling a subprogram or package declaration establishes it as a library unit.

The *context* portion of a compilation unit consists of *with* clauses that specify the library units upon which the program component being compiled depends, that is, the library units used by the program component. These library units are directly visible inside the program component. The context may also contain *use* clauses which make the components of the specified library units directly visible inside the program component.

1.3 Order of Compilation [10.3]

Compilation units can be compiled in any order subject to the following restrictions, which are imposed to allow checking of consistency between the units and code generation:

1. The specification of a subprogram or package must be compiled before its body (the specification of a nongeneric subprogram can be omitted—the subprogram body may act as its own declaration).

2. A compilation unit, C, can be compiled only after all the compilation units (at least their declarations) used by it have been compiled. These compilation units are specified in the *with* clauses in the context portion of C.

3. A subunit cannot be compiled before the compilation unit containing its body stub.

1.4 Recompilation

The whole program does not have to be recompiled when a compilation unit is modified and recompiled. Recompilation of a

1. compilation unit that consists of a declaration requires the recompilation of all the compilation units that use (i.e., depend upon) this compilation unit.

2. compilation unit that consists of a package body or a subprogram body requires recompilation of only the subunits declared within it. Other compilation units that use the modified compilation unit do not have to be recompiled, since they do not depend upon the internals of a package or subprogram body (the internals being hidden from the user).

3.   subunit does not require the recompilation of any other subunit.

2. Program Development [10.1.1, 10.2]

Discovering the structure of a nontrivial problem and then designing the program to reflect this structure is a hard task. Designing programs so that they reflect the problem structure, i.e., *structured programming*, leads to programs that are readable, understandable, provable and modifiable [DAH72]. Most programming languages discourage the accurate recording of this structure by not providing any recording facilities. Ada, however, provides some recording facilities that support the (partial) preservation of this structure. These facilities support both bottom up and top down development of programs.

Bottom up program development is the construction of a program by first building and testing its components. Such an approach is appropriate for making good use of software tools [KER76] and program libraries available at an implementation. The *with* clause supports the construction of a program using components available as *library units*.

Top down program development is the same as program development by stepwise refinement. By providing facilities in a programming language to support stepwise refinement, the language allows the preservation of the some of the structure of the program development process. Ada supports top down programming in a limited way through the use of body stubs. The bodies of subprograms, packages and tasks in the outermost level of a compilation unit may be compiled separately as subunits by giving body stubs for them. Body stubs have the form

>   subprogram_specification **is separate**;
>
> | **package body** identifier **is separate**;
>
> | **task body** identifier **is separate**;

Bodies corresponding to the stubs are compiled as *subunits*, which have the form

>   **separate**(parent_unit_name) body

Each body being compiled in a subunit must be preceded by the name of the *parent* compilation unit *parent_unit_name* in which its body stub was given. If the parent is a subunit itself then the name must include the name of its parent and so on. The name must be given in full as a selected component starting with the first ancestor that is not a subunit.

Everything visible at a body stub is visible in the corresponding subunit along with any additional context that is specified in the subunit.

2.1 Development of Large Programs

Large programs are generally developed by a combination of top down and bottom up development. The top down approach allows the programmer to start with an overview of the problem while the bottom up approach allows the programmer to try and use the tools (programs) already available in libraries on the system. Also, programs are often developed using primarily a top down approach, but with code written and tested using a bottom up approach.

3. Examples

Two example programs are given—one illustrating facilities in Ada that support the bottom up program development and the other illustrating facilities supporting top down development. Throughout the book, examples have been developed using top down program development but the program development structure is not explicitly reflected by the final versions of the programs. In the second example given here, some of the development structure is recorded in the final version of the program, using the facilities provided by Ada.

The first program computes some statistics about a list of numbers. This program makes use of several programs that were developed earlier. The second program is a package that keeps track of planes in a radar surveillance system. Several body stubs are given in the package and the corresponding bodies are developed later. This program also illustrates dynamic task creation (using access types), unchecked storage deallocation, mutual exclusion, and the interaction between exceptions and tasks.

3.1 Bottom Up Program Development

As an illustration of the bottom up approach, a program that reads in a list of at most 500 integers and computes their mean, median and mode (the most frequently occurring value) is developed.

The generic subprograms INSERTION_SORT_G, VECTOR_OPERATION are available as library units (see sections 7.2 and 7.5.1 of Chapter 6 on Generic Facilities) along with a generic version of subprogram MODE, whose specification is

```
generic
    type ELEM is private;
    type VECTOR is array(INTEGER range <>) of ELEM;
procedure MODE_G(A: VECTOR; MV: ELEM; MF: out INTEGER);
```

Procedure STATISTICS, which computes the required statistics and does its own input and output, uses instantiations of these generic procedures:

```
with INSERTION_SORT_G, VECTOR_OPERATION, MODE_G;
with TEXT_IO; use TEXT_IO;
procedure STATISTICS is
    package IO_INTEGER is new INTEGER_IO(NUM =>INTEGER);
    use IO_INTEGER;

    type INT_ARRAY is array(INTEGER range <>) of INTEGER;
    A: INT_ARRAY(1..500);
    MV, MF: INTEGER;       --mode value and frequency
    N: INTEGER := 0;       --number of values read in

    procedure SORT is
            new INSERTION_SORT_G(ELEM => INTEGER,
                    VECTOR => INT_ARRAY);
    function SUM is
            new VECTOR_OPERATION(ELEM => INTEGER,
                    INDEX => INTEGER,
                    VECTOR => INT_ARRAY, F => "+");
    procedure MODE is
            new MODE_G(ELEM => INTEGER,
                    VECTOR => INT_ARRAY);

begin
    --read in the values
        while not END_OF_FILE(STANDARD_INPUT) loop
            N := N + 1;
            GET(A(N));
        end loop;

    if N /= 0 then
        SORT(A(1..N));
                --note that in a slice, copies of the array elements
                --are not made; it is the array elements that are
                --passed as parameters; only the elements of A in
                --the slice A(1..N) will be sorted.

        PUT("Number of values read = "); PUT(N); NEW_LINE;
        PUT("Mean is "); PUT(SUM(A(1..N))/N); NEW_LINE;
        PUT("Median is "); PUT(A((N+1)/2)); NEW_LINE;

        MODE(A(1..N), MF, MV);

        PUT("Mode value and frequency are ");
        PUT(MV); PUT("  "); PUT(MF);
```

```
    else
        PUT("No Data => No Results");
    end if;
    NEW_LINE;
end STATISTICS;
```

3.2 Top Down Program Development

The problem is to write a package PLANE_TRACKER which is part of a complex real-time radar surveillance system that keeps track of plane positions.[49] This package should be able to handle up to 512 planes at a time. Subprograms are to be provided so that plane positions and velocity (three-dimensional vector of speed with direction) can be updated and queried. More than one task, from the rest of the radar surveillance system, will interact with this package. While waiting for external updates of plane positions and their velocities, the package should update the position of each plane on its own using the plane's old coordinates and velocity.

Every time a new plane is detected by radar the package PLANE_TRACKER is instructed to initiate tracking of the plane. Package PLANE_TRACKER is also informed when a plane is no longer detectable by radar, so that the tracking of the plane may be discontinued. PLANE_TRACKER should tell its users by means of exceptions when it cannot handle any more planes or when a plane is referenced that it is not tracking.

3.2.1 The Solution: The top down program construction facilities provided by Ada are used in developing this program. In addition to separate compilation, the program illustrates, dynamic task creation, storage deallocation, serializing concurrent executions of an operation to make them mutually exclusive, and raising and propagation of exceptions during task communication.

Although more than one task can try to query a plane position simultaneously, the solution presented allows only one task to do this at a time. The primary task communication facility in Ada is the rendezvous mechanism, which allows only one pair of tasks, at a time, to communicate with each other. To allow concurrent queries of the plane position, from several tasks, the data associated with a plane, instead of being part of the task tracking the plane, can be kept outside it, with the task acting as a manager, giving permission to tasks desiring to access this data and keeping track of the tasks accessing the data. More than one task can now be given permission to query this data. Of course, only one task at a time will be allowed to update the data.

---

49. This problem is adapted from DOD79b.

Every time a new plane is to be tracked, a new task is dynamically allocated and initialized with the observed coordinates and velocity. Storage to track 512 planes simultaneously is reserved (i.e., enough to allocate one tracking task for each plane). Requests to track more than 512 planes result in the exception STORAGE_ERROR being raised. This exception is handled within package PLANE_TRACKER and the exception TOO_MANY_PLANES raised and propagated to the user.

Queries and updates of a plane's position are directed to the task tracking the plane in question. At intervals of approximately one second, this task, on its own, updates the location of the plane based on its old location, its velocity and elapsed time. The tracking task is terminated when tracking the plane is no longer necessary. Exception TASKING_ERROR is raised when an attempt is made to query or update information of a plane that is no longer being tracked or on a plane that was never tracked. This exception is handled within package PLANE_TRACKER and the exception ILLEGAL_PLANE is propagated to the user.

An external identification for each plane being tracked is provided to the users. The access value indicating the storage area where the task is allocated is used as the internal identification of the plane. This value is not used as the external identification, because of the following problem. Suppose it is no longer necessary to track plane A and the task tracking it is deallocated. The storage freed may now be allocated to a new task assigned to track a new plane B. References to plane A, which are now illegal, now become references to plane B, and this cannot be checked. To avoid this problem, external names or external identification values are chosen from a large set of values such that the values are repeated only after long intervals. This solution allows the detection of illegal references. The mapping between the external and internal names will be provided by package ACTIVE_PLANES (which also provides the external names).

The specification of PLANE_TRACKER is submitted as a compilation unit to the Ada compiler, so that other parts of the radar surveillance program can be compiled without the body of PLANE_TRACKER. The specification of PLANE_TRACKER is

```
with CALENDAR;
package PLANE_TRACKER is

    type MILES is new FLOAT;

    type PLANE_INFO is
        record
            X, Y, Z: MILES;
            VX, VY, VZ: MILES;
                --velocity also has type MILES for convenience; really
                --it should be some type MILES_PER_HOUR
            T: CALENDAR.TIME;
        end record;

    type PLANE_ID is limited private;

    procedure CREATE_PLANE(I: PLANE_INFO;
                                  ID: out PLANE_ID);
    procedure REMOVE_PLANE(ID: in out PLANE_ID);
    procedure UPDATE_PLANE(ID: PLANE_ID; I: PLANE_INFO);
    function READ_PLANE(ID: PLANE_ID) return PLANE_INFO;
            --read the latest position of the plane ID

    ILLEGAL_PLANE, TOO_MANY_PLANES: exception;
            --ILLEGAL_PLANE is raised when a reference is made to a
            --plane that never existed or is no longer being tracked;
            --TOO_MANY_PLANES is raised when a request is made to
            --handle the 513th plane

private

    type PLANE_ID is new INTEGER;

end PLANE_TRACKER;
```

The body of PLANE_TRACKER is compiled by itself. Several body stubs are used in it to specify the subunits that will be submitted for compilation later on. The body of PLANE_TRACKER is

```
with UNCHECKED_DEALLOCATION;
        --to deallocate storage occupied by the tasks that are no
        --longer needed and have terminated
package body PLANE_TRACKER is

    MAX_PLANES : constant := 512;
            --maximum number of planes at any instant

    task type TRACKER is
      --each instance keeps track of one plane
        entry INITIALIZE(I: PLANE_INFO);
        entry DIE;
        entry UPDATE(I: PLANE_INFO);
        entry READ(I: out PLANE_INFO);
    end TRACKER;

    type PLANE is access TRACKER;

    package ACTIVE_PLANES is
            --Keep track of all the active planes and provides
            --a mapping between the internal and external names
            --i.e., between PLANE and PLANE_ID.
            --Planes are added and removed one at a time.
            --Mutual exclusion is obtained by using tasks
        procedure ADD(P: PLANE; ID: out PLANE_ID);
            --Add a plane to the set of active planes.
            --Only MAX_PLANES planes can be handled.
            --Returns an external id for the plane (values
            --will repeat very infrequently)

        procedure DELETE(ID: PLANE_ID);
        function INTERNAL_NAME(ID: PLANE_ID) return PLANE;
            --raises exception ILLEGAL_PLANE when ID does
            --not correspond to an active plane
    end ACTIVE_PLANES;

    use ACTIVE_PLANES;
    for PLANE'STORAGE'SIZE
            use MAX_PLANES*TRACKER'STORAGE_SIZE;
            --reserve space for MAX_PLANES; this reservation
            --of space is discussed in the next chapter


    task body TRACKER is separate;
```

```
package body ACTIVE_PLANES is separate;
procedure CREATE_PLANE(I: PLANE_INFO; ID: out PLANE_ID)
                                            is separate;
procedure REMOVE_PLANE(ID: in out PLANE_ID) is separate;


procedure UPDATE_PLANE(ID: PLANE_ID; I: PLANE_INFO) is
begin
   INTERNAL_NAME(ID).UPDATE(I);
exception
   when TASKING_ERROR => raise ILLEGAL_PLANE;
end UPDATE_PLANE;

function READ_PLANE(ID: PLANE_ID) return PLANE_INFO is
   I: PLANE_INFO;
begin
   INTERNAL_NAME(ID).READ(I);
   return I;
exception
   when TASKING_ERROR => raise ILLEGAL_PLANE;
end READ_PLANE;

end PLANE_TRACKER;
```

The procedure initiating the tracking of a plane, CREATE_PLANE, is now compiled separately as

```
separate(PLANE_TRACKER)
        --makes available the environment present at
        --the body stub for CREATE_PLANE
procedure CREATE_PLANE(I: PLANE_INFO;
                            ID: out PLANE_ID) is
   P: PLANE;
begin
   P := new TRACKER;
   ADD(P, ID);
        --add plane P to the set of active planes and
        --return its external ID
   P.INITIALIZE(I);
exception
   when TASKING_ERROR => raise ILLEGAL_PLANE;
   when STORAGE_ERROR => raise TOO_MANY_PLANES;
end CREATE_PLANE;
```

A problem occurs if execution of the allocation operation is not mutually exclusive [BRI73] (Ada does not say anything about this), since multiple tasks calling CREATE_PLANE and executing *new* at the same time may end up with identical values for supposedly different dynamic objects. The solution is to force the allocation of the new tracking tasks to be done in a sequential manner. Sequential allocation is accomplished by putting the task allocation in a task ALLOCATOR with allocation requested by an entry call. Multiple entry calls are queued and accepted serially, one at a time. Two modifications are made to the package PLANE_TRACKER:

1. Task ALLOCATOR is declared in the body of PLANE_TRACKER:

```
task ALLOCATOR is
    entry NEW_PLANE(P: out PLANE);
end ALLOCATOR;

task body ALLOCATOR is
begin
    loop
        begin    --begin a block
            accept NEW_PLANE(P: out PLANE) do
                P := new TRACKER;
            end NEW_PLANE;
                --only one entry call is accepted at a time thus
                --effectively making the allocate operation atomic
        exception
            when STORAGE_ERROR => null;
        end;
    end loop;
end ALLOCATOR;
```

Note that the *accept* statement has been put in a block. When an exception occurs in an *accept* statement it is also propagated to the rendezvousing task. If the exception were not handled locally in the block, the task would terminate as a result of the exception is being raised. ALLOCATOR should, of course, not terminate when a request is made to handle the 513th plane.

2. The call to the allocator in CREATE_PLANE is replaced by the entry call[50]

---

50. During the ANSI standardization process, one modification proposed for Ada would have required the propagation of TASKING_ERROR to the calling task, instead of the exception actually raised, if an exception occurred during rendezvous. This modification was eventually *not* incorporated into Ada.

```
        ALLOCATOR.NEW_PLANE(P);
```

The procedure to end tracking a plane, REMOVE_PLANE, is compiled as

```
    separate(PLANE_TRACKER)
    procedure REMOVE_PLANE(ID: in out PLANE_ID) is
      procedure FREE is
              new UNCHECKED_DEALLOCATION(TRACKER, PLANE);
      P: PLANE;
    begin
      P := INTERNAL_NAME(ID);
      P.DIE;
      DELETE(ID);
              --delete plane from the set of active planes
      FREE(P);
              --deallocate the task after plane is deleted
    exception
      when TASKING_ERROR => raise ILLEGAL_PLANE;
    end REMOVE_PLANE;
```

The body of task type TRACKER, which was represented by a body stub in
the compilation unit PLANE_TRACKER, is now submitted to the compiler.
It contains the body stub of procedure UPDATE_POSITION:

Had Ada been modified as suggested above, ALLOCATOR would have had to be called
differently. Incorporation of this modification would result in exception TASKING_ERROR
being propagated to the calling task, instead of the exception STORAGE_ERROR. This
change would require that TASKING_ERROR be handled locally, right at the entry call, so
that it could be determined when a call to ALLOCATOR results in TASKING_ERROR being
propagated back. Exception TOO_MANY_PLANES would then be raised and propagated to
the task requesting tracking of a new plane. Raising exception TOO_MANY_PLANES in the
calling task can be accomplished by surrounding the call to the entry NEW_PLANE in a block:

```
    begin
      ALLOCATOR.NEW_PLANE(P);
    exception
      when TASKING_ERROR => raise TOO_MANY_PLANES;
    end;
```

```
separate(PLANE_TRACKER)
task body TRACKER is
  DATA: PLANE_INFO;
  procedure UPDATE_POSITION is separate;
            --update the coordinates of the plane position
            --based on its velocity, old coordinates and time
            --elapsed since the last update
begin
  accept INITIALIZE(I: PLANE_INFO) do
    DATA := I;
  end INITIALIZE;
  loop
    select
      accept DIE; exit;
    or when DIE'COUNT = 0 =>
        accept UPDATE(I: PLANE_INFO) do
            DATA := I;
        end UPDATE;
    or when DIE'COUNT = 0 and UPDATE'COUNT = 0 =>
      accept READ(I: out PLANE_INFO) do
        I := DATA;
      end READ;
    or delay 1.0;
      UPDATE_POSITION;
    end select;
  end loop;
end TRACKER;
```

The body of procedure UPDATE_POSITION is now given:

```
    use CALENDAR;
    separate(PLANE_TRACKER.TRACKER)
            --selected component notation used to specify the
            --unit containing the body stub
    procedure UPDATE_POSITION is
        NEW_TIME: TIME := CLOCK;
        DELTA_TIME: DURATION := NEW_TIME - DATA.T;
        -- * is defined to multiply velocity and time to give distance
            function "*"(DT: DURATION; V: MILES) return MILES is
            begin
                return MILES(DT) * V;
            end "*";
    begin
        DATA.X := DATA.X + DELTA_TIME * DATA.VX;
        DATA.Y := DATA.Y + DELTA_TIME * DATA.VY;
        DATA.Z := DATA.Z + DELTA_TIME * DATA.VZ;
        DATA.T := NEW_TIME;
    end UPDATE_POSITION;
```

The implementation of ACTIVE_PLANES is left to the reader.

Chapter 8: **Representation Clauses and** [13]
Implementation Dependent Features

1. Introduction

The primary benefit of using a suitable high level language lies in the possibility of defining abstract algorithms in a precise manner that is reasonably independent of the underlying machine characteristics [WIR77a] and independent of the representation of the data types used by an implementation. However, access to the characteristics of the underlying machine and the data type representations used is essential for writing systems programs such as device drivers, process control systems, interrupt handlers, storage allocators and other programs where efficiency is critical, i.e., where every available bit of storage and execution cycle must be used effectively. For example, in a typewriter keyboard driver program, it is necessary to access the keyboard hardware buffer and associate actions with its interrupt vector.

Consequently, a systems programming language should have facilities for dealing with objects at two levels:

1. The abstract level, where only the logical properties are important.

2. The physical level, which is concerned with the details of the machine and the representation.

Facilities for operating at these two levels should be kept separate and be clearly identifiable, because otherwise

1. programs will be harder to understand, since the logical properties of programs will be intermingled with the physical details.

2. changes in data type representations will require modifications to much of the program, instead of just small and isolated portions.

3. it will be hard to move programs from one machine to another, since the physical details, which need to be modified, will not be clearly discernible or separate from the rest of the program.

4. access to the physical level, which is both low level and dangerous, will probably violate the discipline being enforced by the high level language, such as strong typing, to provide error checking. Consequently, it is imperative that facilities allowing access to the physical level be kept separate from the rest of the program and a warning sign be posted.

Ada provides facilities for specifying the logical and physical properties of objects, and these have been kept separate and distinct from each other. The logical properties of objects in a program are specified by their declarations. The program relies on these properties to accomplish its objective. The physical details of these objects and interface of the program with the external environment may be specified explicitly by the programmer using the separate facilities provided especially for this purpose. If the physical details are not specified explicitly by the user then appropriate physical details are supplied by the Ada compiler. Ada allows the specification of physical details such as data type representations, interface with hardware interrupts, machine code insertion, allocation of objects at specific addresses in memory, deallocation of storage and breach of strong typing—all necessary for systems programming.

Most of these facilities should be used only when necessary and with the utmost caution, especially by the novice programmer, since their usage subverts the error checking built into the language.

Ada's facilities for interfacing with the hardware are called *representation clauses* of which there are two kinds—*type representation* clauses and *address* clauses.

2. Type Representation Clauses [13.1-13.4]

Data type representations will normally be selected by the compiler, since in most cases the programmer will be content with the default data type implementations. In the infrequent cases when the programmer is not satisfied with the data type representations selected by the compiler, the programmer has the following options:

1. The programmer can guide the compiler in selecting an appropriate representation by using predefined pragmas. For example, the pragma PACK can be used to indicate to the compiler that storage used in implementing the specified record or array type should be kept to a minimum.

2. The programmer can use a *type representation clause* to specify the actual mapping between a data type and features of the underlying machine by specifying the representation to be used, e.g., the amount of storage to be used, the internal representation of an enumeration type and the layout of a record type.

These pragmas and the representation clauses may be given in a declarative part or in the specification of a task or package. However, the pragmas must precede the representation clauses.

There are three kinds of type representation clauses—*length*, *enumeration representation* and *record representation*.

2.1 Length Clause [13.2]

The amount of storage to be associated with an entity is specified by means of a length clause. It has the form

    for attribute **use** amount;

where *amount* is an integer expression specifying the maximum amount of storage to be associated with the entity specified in the *attribute*. The term *storage unit* will be used to refer to the basic unit of storage allocation for the Ada implementation, e.g, byte or word. The attributes that can be specified are

Object Size	The *size* attribute of a type T (T'SIZE) is used to specify the maximum amount of storage (in bits) to be allocated for objects of type T. The number of bits specified should not be less than the minimum number of bits required to implement an object of type T. If a length clause is not specified, the compiler may allocate some convenient amount of storage. For example, objects of an integer type having the values from 0 to 3 may be allocated one whole byte or one whole word of storage so that the objects can be manipulated easily even though two bits would be sufficient.
Collection Size	The *collection size* attribute of an access type T (T'STORAGE_SIZE) is used to specify the total amount of storage (in storage units) to be reserved for the collection of objects associated with access type T. This attribute allows a programmer to put an upper bound on the number of objects designated by the access type T that can be created (or are allocated at any instant; this assumes that storage occupied by discarded objects is automatically reclaimed by the system or has been explicitly freed by the programmer).
Task Storage	The maximum amount of storage (in storage units) to be allocated for the activation of a task T or for activation of tasks of type T is specified by means of the *task storage* attribute (T'STORAGE_SIZE). The storage specified is the storage that will be used for the data area of T and not for the code generated for T.

Small

Specification of the maximum storage that a task can use prevents the task from using more than its share of storage.

The value of *small* that is to be used for implementing a fixed point type T is specified by using the attribute T'SMALL.

Exception STORAGE_ERROR may be raised if the space reserved by a length clause is exceeded.

2.2 Enumeration Representation Clause [13.3]

The internal representation used for an enumeration type can be specified by giving the internal codes (which must be integers) for the literals of the enumeration type. Such a specification may be necessary when interfacing with external files and devices. As an example, consider a program that uses the enumeration type DAY declared as

type DAY **is** (MON, TUE, WED, THU, FRI, SAT, SUN);

Values of type DAY are to be read in from a external binary file,[51] on which these values are represented by the integers 1 to 7 on the file. These integer values may not correspond to the internal representation used for DAY by an Ada compiler. For example, the internal representation used by an Ada compiler for type DAY may be the integers 0 to 6. This problem is easily solved by instructing the compiler that the integer values 1 to 7 are to be used for DAY. The compiler is instructed as follows:

for DAY **use** (MON **=>** 1, TUE **=>** 2, WED **=>** 3,
            THU **=>** 4, FRI **=>** 5, SAT **=>** 6, SUN **=>** 7);

Another example is a program that generates object code for some computer [DOD79b] and in which the operation codes are defined to be values of enumeration type OP_CODE, which is declared as

type OP_CODE **is** (ADD, SUB, MUL, DIV, MOVE, JMP);

---

51. Values on a binary file are the internal representations of the values of the objects written to the file. All files, except text files, are binary files. This form of a file is more efficient for input and output when compared to text files, since the values on these files being internal representations of the objects, obviate the conversion that would have been required to output these values in a human readable form. A similar conversion is also avoided when reading these values.

It is necessary to map the symbolic operation codes represented by the enumeration literals into the actual operation codes of the computer. The actual operation codes corresponding to the operations ADD, SUB, MUL, DIV, MOVE and JMP for the computer in question are 1, 2, 5, 6, 10 and 12 respectively. The desired mapping is specified by the following representation of the enumeration type OP_CODE:

```
for OP_CODE use (ADD => 1, SUB => 2, MUL => 5,
                 DIV => 6, MOVE => 10, JMP => 12);
```

The internal representation of an enumeration type does not have to consist of contiguous values.

2.3 Record Representation Clause [13.4]

The alignment of a record, and the order, position and size of its components can be specified by means of the *record representation clause*. The allocation of each record can be forced to a starting address that is a multiple of a specified value by using the *alignment clause*. The location of each record component is specified as an offset from the beginning of the first storage unit (numbered zero) allocated to the record. The ordering of the bits, i.e., left to right or right to left, is machine dependent. The number of bits occupied by a component is specified by identifying the first and last bits. The number of bits in a storage unit of a machine is given by the implementation dependent constant SYSTEM.STORAGE_UNIT.

As an example, consider the representation of program status words in an IBM 360-like computer [DOD83]. The program status word occupies two words (each word consists of four bytes) and is used to keep the status of the program with which it is associated. The program status word must be allocated at a double word boundary (i.e., starting at an even word address).

Objects representing program status words are declared to have type PROGRAM_STATUS_WORD, which is declared below, along with some related declarations:

```
WORD: constant := 4;    --4 bytes per word

type STATE is (A, M, W, P);
type MODE is (FIX, DEC, EXP, SIGNIF);
type BYTE_MASK is array(0..7) of BOOLEAN;
type STATE_MASK is array(STATE) of BOOLEAN;
type MODE_MASK is array(MODE) of BOOLEAN;
```

```
type PROGRAM_STATUS_WORD is
  record
      SYSTEM_MASK: BYTE_MASK;
      PROTECTION_KEY: INTEGER range 0..3;
      MACHINE_STATE: STATE_MASK;
      INTERRUPT_CAUSE: INTERRUPTION_CODE;
      ILC: INTEGER range 0..3;
      CC: INTEGER range 0..3;
      PROGRAM_MASK: MODE_MASK;
      INST_ADDRESS: ADDRESS;
  end record;
```

Objects of type PROGRAM_STATUS_WORD are mapped to the underlying machine according to the following record representation and length clauses:

```
for PROGRAM_STATUS_WORD use
  record at mod 8;    --align at even (8 byte) addresses
      SYSTEM_MASK at 0*WORD range 0..7;
                  --allocate the first 8 bits of the first word
                  --for the component SYSTEM_MASK
            --bits 8 and 9 not used
      PROTECTION_KEY at 0*WORD range 10..11;
      MACHINE_STATE at 0*WORD range 12..15;
      INTERRUPT_CAUSE at 0*WORD range 16..31;
      ILC at 1*WORD range 0..1;
                  --allocate the first 2 bits of the second word
                  --for the component ILC
      CC at 1*WORD range 2..3;
      PROGRAM_MASK at 1*WORD range 4..7;
      INST_ADDRESS at 1*WORD range 8..31;
  end record;

for PROGRAM_STATUS_WORD'SIZE use 2 * SYSTEM.STORAGE_UNIT;
      --allocate exactly two words for each program status word
```

3. Address Clause [13.5]

An *address clause* is used to

1. specify the starting address of an object in memory. With this mechanism, program objects can be associated with hardware objects such as device registers and hardware buffers.

2. specify that a subprogram, package or task is to be allocated starting at a specific memory location. Address specification is useful, since some machines and operating systems require that certain programs must be

allocated in specific parts of the memory. For example, if code is being generated for a machine with no memory management, then the locations where the code is to placed in the physical memory must be indicated to the compiler.

3. associate a hardware interrupt with an entry (cannot be an entry family). The occurrence of an interrupt causes a call to the associated entry to be issued. The priority of such calls is higher than that of calls issued by any user-defined tasks.

The address clause has the form

for name **use at** address;

where *name* is the program entity that is being associated with the memory location *address*. Some examples are

for HARDWARE_BUFFER **use at** 8#177562#;
    −−the hardware buffer of a device at location
    −−8#177562# can now be accessed via the program
    −−variable HARDWARE_BUFFER

for PUT **use at** 8#60#;
    −−interrupt at location 8#60# is associated with
    −−the entry PUT. This specification results in
    −−the entry call PUT being issued whenever the
    −−interrupt occurs

4. Change of Representation [13.6]

Ada allows only one representation to be specified for a data type. However, multiple representations may be desirable under certain circumstances, such as

1. enumeration type representations on different external media correspond to different internal representations.

2. one internal representation each may be used for compact storage and fast access.

It should also be possible to convert back and forth between the different representations.[52]

---

52. In Pascal [JEN74], the user can instruct the compiler to store an array in a packed form to economize on storage. However, accessing individual components of the packed arrays is costly and the programmer is advised to unpack the array before accessing it and to pack it afterward. For this purpose, Pascal provides the standard procedures *pack* and *unpack*.

Multiple representations for a type T are implemented by deriving new types from T and associating an internal representation with T and each of the types derived from it. A value is assigned to an object of the type with the desired internal representation. Representation changes are carried out by means of explicit type conversions.

As an example, suppose there are a large number of records of type DESCRIPTOR. To save storage, they are to be stored in a packed or compact form, but before being accessed they should be converted to the unpacked form for fast access.[53] A type PACKED_DESCRIPTOR is derived from DESCRIPTOR and a compact representation specified for it.

```
type DESCRIPTOR is
    record
        --components of descriptor
    end record;
```

```
type PACKED_DESCRIPTOR is new DESCRIPTOR;
```

```
type PACKED_DESCRIPTOR is
    record
        --compact representation to be used for the components
    end record;
```

DESCRIPTOR and PACKED_DESCRIPTOR have the same logical characteristics, although they have different physical representations. The representation of DESCRIPTOR was implicitly supplied by the compiler, while the representation for PACKED_DESCRIPTOR was explicitly supplied by the user. Changes in representation are accomplished by means of explicit type conversions. For example, the following statements first unpack an object P of type PACKED_DESCRIPTOR to an object D of type DESCRIPTOR and then pack D back into P.

```
D := DESCRIPTOR(P);              --unpack
P := PACKED_DESCRIPTOR(D);       --pack
```

---

53. Accessing record components stored in a packed form is slow, since several components may be packed into one storage unit (i.e., machine word). For example, updating a value that does not occupy an addressable storage unit may require that this value be extracted from the storage unit containing it, put by itself into a storage unit, the extracted value updated and, finally, this updated value put back into the packed form.

5. Implementation Dependent Configuration Features and Constants [13.7]

Ada allows the programmer to specify configuration dependent features in a program to help the Ada compiler exploit these features when generating code and yet not violate the restrictions imposed by them. Configuration dependent features such as

1. the computer make and model number,

2. the operating system,

, the amount of memory available and

4. special hardware options.

can be specified. These features are specified by means of implementation dependent pragmas. Some examples are

```
pragma SYSTEM_NAME(UNIX);
pragma STORAGE_UNIT(32);
pragma MEMORY_SIZE(262144);
pragma MACHINE_NAME(VAX11_780);
```

Ada also allows the programmer to access implementation dependent constants known to the compiler by means of constants provided in the package SYSTEM (declared in the predefined package STANDARD). Some of the constants available in the package SYSTEM are

ADDRESS	the type of addresses provided in address clauses; it is also the type of the value returned by the attribute ADDRESS (X´ADDRESS is the starting address of object, program unit, label or entry X)
SYSTEM_NAME	the system name
STORAGE_UNIT	the number of bits per storage unit
MEMORY_SIZE	the total number of available storage units in memory
MIN_INT	the smallest integer supported by the implementation
MAX_INT	the largest integer supported by the implementation.
TICK	the basic clock period, in seconds

An example of the need to access these constants is a user-defined low level input/output routine that invokes different routines depending upon the operating system. This need is illustrated by the following program fragment:

```
case SYSTEM.SYSTEM_NAME is
  when UNIX =>
    code with appropriate calls to UNIX routines
  when MULTICS =>
    code with appropriate calls to MULTICS routines
  when VS_370 =>
    code with appropriate calls to VS_370 routines
end case;
```

The above *case* statement may as an optimization be conditionally compiled (i.e., evaluated at compile time), but this is left to the Ada compiler.

6. Machine Code Insertion [13.8]

Ada provides a facility to insert machine code instructions directly within a program. This facility can cause many problems and errors and should be used rarely. Some situations where it may be desirable to insert machine code in program are

- executing special machine dependent instructions,

- accessing registers which cannot be addressed like memory locations,

- fine tuning a program for very critical efficiency reasons and

- performing hardware functions.[54]

7. Interface to Other Languages [13.9]

One of the problems involved in changing from one language to another is what to do with all the existing software. The cost of rewriting the software in the new language may be prohibitive enough to prevent the switch over to the new language and thus force the continued use of the outdated programming language, despite the fact that it is technically inferior to a new programming language. Ada alleviates the need for rewriting software to some degree by providing a pragma that allows Ada programs to interface with subprograms written in another language. This pragma has the form

pragma INTERFACE(language_name, subprogram_name);

---

54. For example, the UNIX™ operating system kernel consists of about 10,000 lines of code written in the systems programming language C and about 1000 lines of assembly code. 800 lines of this assembly code could have been written in C, but were not for efficiency reasons, and the remaining *had to be written* in assembly language to perform hardware functions that are not possible in C [THO78].

The following example [DOD83] illustrates how two subprograms SQRT and EXP written in FORTRAN can be accessed from Ada programs:

```
package FORT_LIB is
    --the Ada specifications of SQRT and EXP
        function SQRT(X: FLOAT) return FLOAT;
        function EXP(X: FLOAT) return FLOAT;
private
    --these subprograms are implemented in FORTRAN
        pragma INTERFACE(FORTRAN, SQRT);
        pragma INTERFACE(FORTRAN, EXP);
end FORT_LIB;
```

8. Unchecked Storage Deallocation [13.10, 13.10.1]

Ada provides a generic subprogram UNCHECKED_DEALLOCATION for explicitly deallocating or reclaiming storage that has been allocated to access variables. Explicit deallocation of dynamic objects may be necessary if an Ada implementation does not provide a garbage collector and/or explicit memory management is explicitly desired. It is the programmer's responsibility to ensure that only storage that is no longer needed is deallocated.

The generic subprogram UNCHECKED_DEALLOCATION has the specification

```
generic
    type OBJECT is limited private;
    type NAME is access OBJECT;
procedure UNCHECKED_DEALLOCATION(X: in out NAME);
```

Suppose that two access variables X and Y designate the same object and FREE is an appropriate instantiation of the generic procedure UNCHECKED_DEALLOCATION. Then accessing this object using the access variable Y after the statement

```
FREE(X);
```

has been executed is an error, since the space previously occupied by this object has been deallocated and contains a value of some unknown type. It is the programmer's responsibility to ensure that such situations will not occur.

9. Unchecked Type Conversions [13.10, 13.10.2]

Representation viewing, which is called unchecked conversion in Ada, can be achieved by using the generic subprogram UNCHECKED_CONVERSION. Representation viewing allows any bit pattern in storage to be viewed as a value of any desired type. It is the programmer's responsibility to ensure that the bit pattern viewed as a value of some desired type constitutes a meaningful value of that type. Such unchecked conversions may be needed for user-defined storage allocation and deallocation procedures; integers representing memory addresses must be converted to access values of the appropriate type and vice versa.[55]

The specification of the generic subprogram UNCHECKED_CONVERSION is

> **generic**
> **type** SOURCE **is limited private;**
> **type** TARGET **is limited private;**
> **function** UNCHECKED_CONVERSION(S: SOURCE) **return** TARGET;

10. Examples

The use of representation specifications is illustrated by two examples. The first example is a program that reads characters from the typewriter keyboard and outputs them via the typewriter printer. It illustrates the association of program variables with hardware buffers and entries with hardware interrupts. The second program illustrates how a user-defined storage allocator can be written easily in Ada—a program that is hard or impossible to write in strongly typed languages, such as Pascal, that do not provide facilities for bypassing the strong typing mechanism.

10.1 Typewriter Input and Output

The problem is to write a package TYPEWRITER for a PDP/11 computer that provides the user (most likely a systems programmer) with procedures to read a character from the keyboard and to write a character via the typewriter printer.[56] The relevant hardware specifications of the typewriter are

---

55. Another example of the use of unchecked conversion is the implementation of records with only variants in FORTRAN (actually FORTRAN does not even have records). To define a stack whose elements can be either integers or reals, an array of integers is declared. Elements of this array are viewed directly as integers or viewed indirectly as reals by means of the EQUIVALENCE statement. This approach is error prone, since integers can be mistakenly viewed as reals and vice versa, but the programmer has no choice, since FORTRAN does not have records with variants or an equivalent facility.

56. This problem is adaptation of the example in WIR77a.

Keyboard hardware buffer address	8#177562#
Keyboard interrupt address	8#60#
Printer hardware buffer address	8#177566#
Printer interrupt address	8#64#
Interrupt priority	4

The keyboard interrupt occurs after the hardware buffer has been filled with a new character.[57] The printer interrupt occurs after the character put into the hardware buffer has been printed.

One driver task will be defined for the typewriter keyboard and one for the printer. The keyboard driver will have an internal buffer of 64 characters and will be willing to accept characters from the keyboard as long as the buffer is not full. It is from this buffer that the user can read characters using the procedure READ_CHAR. The printer driver has a similar structure.

The specification of the package TYPEWRITER is

```
package TYPEWRITER is
    procedure READ_CHAR(C: out CHARACTER);
    procedure WRITE_CHAR(C: in CHARACTER);
end TYPEWRITER;
```

and its body is

---

57. The character in the hardware buffer should be retrieved before the next character arrives, since otherwise the first one will be lost. We will assume that the task reading characters from the hardware buffer will be able to respond with the required speed to avoid the loss of any characters. It is a consequence of the priority rules that an accept statement executed in response to an interrupt has a higher precedence over those that are to be executed in response to normal entry calls.

```
package body TYPEWRITER is

    task KEYBOARD is
      pragma PRIORITY(4);
           --must have at least the priority of the interrupt
      entry GET(C: out CHARACTER);
      entry PUT;
      for PUT use at 8#60#;
    end KEYBOARD;

    task PRINTER is
      pragma PRIORITY(4);
           --must have at least the priority of the interrupt
      entry GET;
      entry PUT(C: in CHARACTER);
      for GET use at 8#64#;
    end PRINTER;

    procedure READ_CHAR(C: out CHARACTER) is
    begin
        KEYBOARD.GET(C);
    end READ_CHAR;

    procedure WRITE_CHAR(C: in CHARACTER) is
    begin
        PRINTER.PUT(C);
    end WRITE_CHAR;

    task body KEYBOARD is separate;
    task body PRINTER is separate;

  end TYPEWRITER;
```

The bodies of the two tasks KEYBOARD and PRINTER, whose stubs were
given in the package TYPEWRITER, are

```
    separate(TYPEWRITER)
    task body KEYBOARD is
       MAX: constant := 64;    --internal buffer size
       A: array(1..MAX) of CHARACTER;    --internal buffer
       INB, OUTB: INTEGER := 1;    --buffer pointers
       N: INTEGER := 0;    --buffer count

       HARDWARE_BUFFER: CHARACTER;
       for HARDWARE_BUFFER use at 8#177562#;
    begin
       loop
          select
             when N > 0 =>
                accept GET(C: out CHARACTER) do
                   C := A(OUTB);
                end GET;
                OUTB := OUTB mod MAX + 1;
                N := N - 1;
          or
             when N < MAX =>
                accept PUT do
                   A(INB) := HARDWARE_BUFFER;
                end PUT;
                INB := INB mod MAX + 1;
                N := N + 1;
          end select;
       end loop;
    end KEYBOARD;


and
```

```
separate(TYPEWRITER)
task body PRINTER is
   MAX: constant := 64;    --internal buffer size
   A: array(1..MAX) of CHARACTER;    --internal buffer
   INB, OUTB: INTEGER := 1;    --buffer pointers
   N: INTEGER := 0;    --buffer count

   HARDWARE_BUFFER: CHARACTER;
   for HARDWARE_BUFFER use at 8#177566#;
   HARDWARE_BUFFER_EMPTY: BOOLEAN := TRUE;
begin
   loop
      select
         accept GET;    --character printed
         if N > 0 then
            HARDWARE_BUFFER := A(OUTB);
            OUTB := OUTB mod MAX + 1;
            N := N - 1;
         else
            HARDWARE_BUFFER_EMPTY := TRUE;
         end if;
      or
         when N < MAX =>
            accept PUT(C: in CHARACTER) do
               A(INB) := C;
            end PUT;
            INB := INB mod MAX + 1;
            N := N + 1;
            if HARDWARE_BUFFER_EMPTY then
               HARDWARE_BUFFER := A(OUTB);
               OUTB := OUTB mod MAX + 1;
               N := N - 1;
               HARDWARE_BUFFER_EMPTY := FALSE;
            end if;
      end select;
   end loop;
end PRINTER;
```

Tasks declared in the package TYPEWRITER, once activated, can only be terminated by aborting them.

10.2 Storage Allocator

The problem is to write a general purpose storage allocator ALLOCATE similar to the allocator *new* provided in Ada. It is assumed that the implementation dependent package SYSTEM (declared in the predefined package STANDARD) contains the procedure MORE_MEMORY that allocates raw (untyped) memory.[58] Procedure MORE_MEMORY has the specifications

```
procedure MORE_MEMORY(N: in INTEGER;
                      ADDR: out INTEGER);
```

where N is the number of bits to be allocated, and ADDR is the address of the first storage unit (bytes or words) of the storage allocated. An integer number of storage units, containing at least N bits, will be allocated.

ADDR is of type INTEGER and this must be converted to the access type for which storage is being allocated so as to conform to the strong typing rules of Ada. This conversion will be done using the generic function UNCHECKED_CONVERSION.

ALLOCATE will be declared as a generic procedure with generic formal parameters—the access type PT and the type of objects T designated by variables of type PT. The specification of ALLOCATE is

```
with UNCHECKED_CONVERSION;
generic
    type T is limited private;
    type PT is private;    --designates objects of type T
procedure ALLOCATE(X: out PT);
```

The body of ALLOCATE is

---

58. Writing ALLOCATE depends upon the facilities provided by the Ada implementation for Ada programs to interface with the underlying machine. For example, instead of the procedure MORE_MEMORY, the package SYSTEM may provide constants defining the lower and upper bounds for memory that can be used for user-defined storage allocation. In this case, a procedure similar to MORE_MEMORY must be written by the user.

```
procedure ALLOCATE(X: out PT) is
    A: INTEGER;    --will contain the integer version of the address
    function CONVERT is
            new UNCHECKED_CONVERSION(INTEGER, PT);
    use SYSTEM;
begin
    MORE_MEMORY(T'SIZE, A);
    X := CONVERT(A);
end ALLOCATE;
```

Appendix: Stepwise Refinement [GEH81][59]

1. Some Requirements for a Good Programming Methodology

A programming methodology should

1. help the programmer master the complexity of the problem being solved and give some guidelines on how to formulate the problem solution.

2. require the programmer to keep a written record of the program design process. This design can then be read by others and the decisions made appreciated and constructively criticized.

3. result in programs that are understandable.

4. lead to programs whose correctness can be verified by means of proofs. Since proofs are difficult, the methodology should allow for a systematic approach to program testing.

5. be generally applicable and not restricted to one class of problems.

6. allow for the production of efficient programs.

7. allow for the production of programs that can be modified in a systematic fashion.

2. Stepwise Refinement

Stepwise refinement is a top down design approach to program development (first advocated by Wirth [WIR71]) that meets the above criteria. Wirth really gave a systematic formulation and description to what many programmers were previously doing intuitively. Stepwise refinement is considered by many computer scientists to be the most important new programming formalization of the 1970s [BRO75]. This approach is applicable not only to program design, but also to the design of complex systems.

In a top down approach, the problem to be solved is decomposed or refined into subproblems, which are then solved. The decomposition or refinement should be such that

---

59. © 1981 American Telephone and Telegraph Company. Excerpted with permission.

289

1. the subproblems are solvable,

2. a subproblem should be solvable with as little impact on the other subproblems as possible,

3. the solution of each subproblem should involve less effort than the original problem,

4. once the subproblems are solved, the solution of the problem should not require much additional effort.

This process is repeated on the subproblems; of course, if the solution of a problem is obvious or trivial then there is no need to go through with the decomposition process.

If P_0 is the initial problem formulation/solution, then the final problem formulation/solution P_n (an executable program) is arrived at after a series of gradual "refinement" steps.

$$P_0 => P_1 => P_2 => \cdots => P_n$$

The refinement P_{i+1} of P_i is produced by supplying more details for the problem formulation/solution P_i. The refinements $P_0,...,P_n$ represent different levels of abstraction. P_0 may be said to give the most abstract view of the problem solution P_n while P_n represents a detailed version of the solution for P_0.

Each refinement P_i consists of a sequence of instructions and data description P_{ij}

$$P_{i1}$$
.
.
.
$$P_{in_i}$$

In each refinement step more details on how each P_i is to be implemented are provided. The refinement process stops when all the instructions can be either executed directly on a computer or easily translated into instructions executable by a computer.

3. Suggestions for Refinement

Stepwise refinement is an iterative process. If a refinement solution does not turn out to be appropriate, then the refinement process is repeated using the additional knowledge derived from the previous attempt. For large or complex problems, several iterations may be required before a programmer is satisfied with the correctness, elegance and efficiency of the solution. Some suggestions for developing a program by stepwise refinement are

1. The program should be developed in a gradual sequence of small steps. In each step, one or more instructions of the current refinement are refined. The refinement process terminates when the instructions have been expressed in the desired programming language or when they can be mechanically translated to the programming language.

2. Refinements should reflect the instructions they represent in detailed form.

3. Abstract instructions may be invented as desired. However, they must eventually be translatable to an executable form.

4. Information about the problem and its domain should be used in the formulation of abstract instructions.

5. Notation natural to the problem domain should be used.

6. Every refinement represents some implicit design decision. The programmer should be aware of this and should have considered alternative solutions. A written record of the major decisions made should be kept along with the refinements.

7. Recursion should be used when appropriate. Even if the language does not support recursion, recursive solutions should still be considered and, if selected, systematically converted to nonrecursive solutions.

8. Data types should be refined just as the instructions are refined. The programmer should recognize abstract data types and separate their refinements from the rest of the program, i.e., do not refine the data type operations in line—use procedure calls.

9. Data representation should be postponed as long as possible. This minimizes modifications to the design when an alternative representation is used instead of the original one.

10. If an instruction appears more than once, then the programmer ought to consider making it a procedure call. The instruction is then refined only once. Procedure calls should also be used when they clarify program structure.

11. The programmer should try to use loop invariants when developing program segments containing loops. Loop invariants give a good idea of the instructions that will constitute the body of the loop and also of the terminating condition for the loop.

Annotated Bibliography

AHO75   Aho, A. V., J. E. Hopcroft and J. D. Ullman. *The Design and Analysis of Computer Algorithms*. Addison-Wesley Publishing Company, 1975.

BAC82   Bach, I. On the Type Concept of Ada. *Ada Letters*, vII, no. 3, November-December 1982. Points out some dangers of Ada's derived type mechanism and some drawbacks of private types.

BAR80   Barnes, J. P. G. An Overview of Ada. *Software—Practice and Experience*, v10, pp. 851-887, 1980. Describes the development of Ada. Presents an informal description of the language. Points out the differences between the pre-ANSI and preliminary versions of Ada.

BAR82   Barnes, J. P. G. *Programming in Ada*. Addison-Wesley Publishing Co., 1982. Contains a fairly complete description of pre-ANSI Ada.

BLA80   Black, A. P. Exception Handling and Data Abstractions. Research Report RC 8059, IBM, T. J. Watson Research Center, Yorktown Heights, N. Y. 10598. Presents a simple treatment of exceptions in the context of formal (algebraic) specifications of abstract data types.

BRI73   Brinch Hansen, P. Concurrent Programming Concepts. *Computing Surveys*, v6, no. 4, December 1973. Discusses the advantages of high level features for concurrency in programming languages so that concurrent programs can be more readily understood and so that assertions in a program can be stated and checked automatically. Features from event queues and semaphores to critical regions and monitors are discussed. Contains many examples.

BRI77   Brinch Hansen, P. *The Architecture of Concurrent Programs*. Prentice-Hall, 1977. Contains a discussion of how to construct concurrent programs systematically using monitors. The development of an operating system called Solo is described. The programming language Concurrent Pascal is used.

293

BRI78   Brinch Hansen, P. Distributed Processes: A Concurrent
             Programming Concept. *CACM*, v21, no. 11, November
             1978. Brinch Hansen proposes that processes communicate and
             synchronize by means of procedure calls and guarded regions.

BRO75   Brooks, F. P. *The Mythical Man Month*. Addison-
             Wesley, Reading, Massachusetts, 1975. The book contains
             essays on software engineering, which I found to be enjoyable
             reading. In these essays the author discusses the management of
             large software projects based on his experiences in managing the
             development of IBM System/360 and its operating system
             OS/360.

BRO76   Bron, C., M. M. Fokkinga and A. C. M. De Haas. A
             Proposal for Dealing with Abnormal Termination of
             Programs. Mem. Nr. 150, November 1976, Twente
             University of Technology, The Netherlands.

BRO81   Brown, W. S. A Simple but Realistic Model of Floating
             Point Computation. *ACM Transactions on Mathematical
             Software*, v7, no. 4, pp. 445-480, December 1981. The
             semantics of real arithmetic is based on a model of real (actually
             floating point) arithmetic developed by Stan Brown and described
             in this paper. According to Stan Brown, the model of floating
             point computation is intended as a basis for developing efficient
             portable software. The model can be expressed in terms of four
             environmental parameters. Using appropriate values for these
             parameters, a program can be tailored to its host computer.

BRO82   Brosgol, B. Summary of Ada Language Changes. *Ada
             Letters*, v1, no.3, March-April 1982. As a result of the
             ANSI Canvass Approval process for Ada, a procedure required
             for approving Ada as an ANSI standard, revisions to Ada
             [DOD80b] have been recommended. These revisions consist of
             many small and localized modifications.

COM81   Special issue on Ada of the IEEE *Computer*, June 1981.
             Contains introductory articles on Ada, the Ada Environment, an
             Ada Language System, Ada for the Intel 432 Microcomputer and
             the Ada Compiler Validation Capability.

CON73   Conway, R. and D. Gries. *An Introduction to
             Programming*. Winthrop, 1973. Introductory book on PL/I
             and PL/C. Emphasis is on the development of correct and
             understandable programs. Programs are developed and explained
             using stepwise refinement (called *top down program
             development*).

COX80   Cox, M. G. and S. J. Hammarling. Evaluation of the Language Ada for use in Numerical Computations. Report DNACS 30/80, National Physical Laboratory, Teddington, Middlesex, U.K., July 1980. Discusses the suitability of the preliminary version of Ada for numerical computations. Plus points of preliminary Ada (that apply to the pre-ANSI version of Ada—array slicing, array assignment, strong typing, range constraints and exceptions. Minus points—storage order of arrays is unspecified (they would like the order to be specified so that this information can be used to improve program efficiency), restrictions on parameters to prevent aliasing.

DAH72   Dahl, O. J., E. W. Dijkstra and C. A. R. Hoare. *Structured Programming*. Academic Press, 1972. A classic book on the disciplined and methodological approach to programming that has come to be known as *structured programming*.

The book contains three articles. In the first article, "Notes on Structured Programming", Dijkstra outlines the methods and discipline used by him in programming. Abstraction is a very powerful tool in mastering complexity and should be used in the design of programs. Programs are developed using *invariants* and stepwise refinement using the three types of decomposition—*concatenation*, *selection* and *repetition*.

Hoare, in the second article titled "Notes on Data Structuring", applies the above principles to the design of data structures. The abstract versions of the program should rely only on the logical properties of the abstract versions of the data structures and not on details of the implementations of the abstract data structures. Implementation details of the abstract data structures should be postponed as long as possible, preferably until the writing of code, since this helps make a program independent of its implementation.

In the final article, "Hierarchical Program Structures", Hoare and Dahl talk about the connection between the design of data structures and the design of programs. The *class* concept of Simula 67 and coroutines are advocated as important program development ideas.

DAH74   Dahlquist, G., Å. Björck and N. Anderson. *Numerical Methods*. Prentice-Hall, 1974.

DAV81   Davis, J. S. Ada—A Suitable Replacement for COBOL. Technical Report, Army Institute for Research in

Management Information and Computer Science, Georgia Institute of Technology, Atlanta, Georgia 30332. The authors are of the opinion that Ada is superior to COBOL in facilitating good software development and maintenance practices. Ada does not provide built-in features for data formating and input/output. Ada may reduce total life cycle cost, but conversion from COBOL to Ada is not recommended for the near future.

DEN75   Dennis, Jack B. An Example of Programming with Abstract Data Types. *Sigplan Notices*, v10, July 1975.

DER76   DeRemer, F. and H. H. Kron. Programming-in-the-large Versus Programming-in-the-small. *IEEE Transactions on Software Engineering*, vSE-2, pp. 80-86, June 1976. Existing programming languages do not support the development of large programs. Large programs are systems that are composed of modules or small programs which are usually written by different people. A language for programming-in-the-large should support the definition of modules, support information hiding and allow the specification of the dependencies between the modules. The ideas presented in this paper are the forerunners of the concept of packages in Ada

DIJ68a   Dijkstra, E. W. Cooperating Sequential Processes. In *Programming Languages* edited by F. Genuys, Academic Press, 1968. The concepts of concurrent statements, semaphores and critical regions are introduced and mutual exclusion is discussed.

DIJ68b   Dijkstra, E. W. Goto Statement Considered Harmful. *CACM*, v11, pp. 147-148, March 1968. Dijkstra argues that the good programming constructs are those that allow the understanding of a program in time proportional to its length. In trying to understand a program containing *goto*s used in an undisciplined manner, the reader of the program is forced to repeatedly jump from one part of a program to another; the reader must follow the execution path of the program to understand the program. This slows program understanding. Constructs such as the *if-then-else* statement and the *while* loop do not cause such slowdowns.

DIJ76   Dijkstra, E. W. *A Discipline of Programming*. Prentice-Hall, 1976. A classic book in which Dijkstra explains a programming methodology based on the idea of statements being considered as predicate or specification transformers. Programs are constructed side by side with proofs of their correctness.

DIJ82   Dijkstra, E. W. *Selected Writings on Computing: A Personal Perspective*. Springer-Verlag, 1982.

DOD79a   *Preliminary Ada Reference Manual. Sigplan Notices*, v14, no. 6, part A, June 1979. The suitability of Ada was tested by using this definition to write many large and complex programs. Based on the experience gained by this testing and evaluation, the definition of Ada was modified resulting in its pre-ANSI form [DOD80b].

DOD79b   *Rationale for the Design of the Ada Programming Language. Sigplan Notices*, v14, no. 6, part B, June 1979. A comprehensive document that provides justification for the design of the preliminary version of Ada. This document is a must for all those interested in language design and those who want to know more about Ada.

DOD80a   *Requirements for Ada Programming Support Environments (Stoneman)*. United States Department of Defense, February 1980. In addition to specifying the requirements for an Ada Programming Support Environment (ASPE), it provides criteria for assessment and evaluation for ASPE designs and offers guidance for ASPE designers and implementors.

DOD80b   *Reference Manual for the Ada Programming Language*. United States Department of Defense, July 1980. Also published by Springer-Verlag, 1981. This document is the official document defining pre-ANSI Ada. Differences between this version of Ada (as defined here) and the preliminary version of Ada [DOD79b] are informally summarized by Barnes [BAR80] and informally detailed by Winkler [WIN81].

DOD82   *Reference Manual for the Ada Programming Language*. United States Department of Defense, 1982. In July 1982, the United States Department of Defense released for editorial review a revised *Reference Manual for the Ada Programming Language*. The revised manual incorporates changes to Ada made in the process of getting it adopted as an ANSI standard. This book reflects these changes to Ada. Adoption of Ada as an ANSI standard is expected by the end of 1982. Although some editorial changes to the *Reference Manual for the Ada Programming Language* are likely, no further changes to Ada itself are expected. In any case, if there are any changes to Ada, they are likely to be esoteric in nature, addressing pathological issues, and will, in all probability, have no impact on the material presented in this book.

(Ada was adopted as an ANSI standard in February 1983.)

DOD83   *Reference Manual for the Ada Programming Language.* United States Department of Defense, January 1983. ANSI standard Ada.

ECO81   Esperanto for Computers. Science brief in *The Economist*, September 12, 1981. Overview of developments leading to the design of Ada. Also contains a discussion of the programming languages that have preceded Ada and of Ada's chances of success.

FEU82   Feuer, A. and N. Gehani. A Comparison of the Programming Languages C and Pascal. *ACM Computing Surveys*, v14, no. 1, March 1982. The definition of *strong typing* in this paper is due to Narain Gehani and Charles Wetherell.

FIS78   Fisher, D. A. DoD's Common Programming Language Effort. *Computer*, pp. 24-23, March 1978. Describes the background, scope and goals of the project that lead to the design of Ada. Contains brief synopsis of the various versions of the requirements—Strawman, Woodenman, Tinman and Ironman. Discusses the philosophy underlying the technical requirements.

GAN77   Gannon, J. D. An Experimental Evaluation of Data Type Conventions. *CACM*, v20, no. 8, August 1977. Experimental evidence that strong typing in programming languages leads to increased program reliability and clarity. Fewer debugging runs are required than in the case of programming languages that are not strongly typed.

GEH77   Gehani, N. H. Units of Measure as a Data Attribute. *Computer Languages*, v2, pp. 93-111, 1977. Proposes the incorporation of units of measure in a programming language in a manner analogous to the specification of the types of objects. Specification of units allows the automatic detection of a class of errors not normally detectable in existing programming languages. It also results in better error correction, better program documentation and automatic conversion between different but equivalent set of units.

GEH80   Gehani, N. H. Generic Procedures: An Implementation and an Undecidability Result. *Computer Languages*, v5, pp. 155-161, December 1980. Points out the advantages of

generic procedures and proposes a simple but powerful notation
for incorporating generic procedures in a language along with an
efficient implementation technique.

GEH81   Gehani, N. H. Program Development by Stepwise
Refinement and Related Topics. *BSTJ*, v60, no. 3, March
1981. Takes another look at stepwise refinement in the context
of recent developments in programming languages and
programming methodology such as abstract data types, formal
specifications, and multiversion programs. Offers explicit
suggestions for the refinement process.

GEH82a   Gehani, N. H. Concurrency in Ada and Multicomputers.
Computer Languages, v7, no. 1, 1982. Points out the
problems that will arise in implementing Ada on a network of
computers with no shared memory. The problems result from the
fact that tasks can share data using global variables and pointers.

GEH82b   Gehani, N. H. Databases and Units of Measure. *IEEE
Transactions on Software Engineering*, vSE-8, no. 6, pp.
605-611, November 1982. A serious impediment to the
integrated use of databases across international boundaries,
scientific disciplines and application areas is the use of different
units of measure, e.g., dollars and rupees for currency, and miles
and kilometers for distance. This impediment is eliminated by
extending data definition languages to allow the units of measure
to be specified. Conversions are performed automatically along
with the detection of inconsistent usage.

GEHA82c Gehani, N. H. Ada's Derived Types and Units of
Measure. Submitted for publication. Types in programming
languages cannot model many properties of real world objects
and quantities. Consequently errors resulting from the
inconsistent usage of program objects representing real world
quantities cannot be detected automatically. Two solutions to
tackle this problem—*derived* types in Ada and *units of
measure*—are compared and analyzed. The conclusion is that the
units of measure approach is better than the derived types
approach, since it ensures that objects are used consistently with
respect to their units, detects more errors, does not prevent
meaningful uses of objects, is convenient and elegant.

GOO75   Goodenough, J. Exception Handling: Issues and a
Proposed Notation. *CACM*, v18, no. 12, pp. 683-696,
December 1976. Detailed discussion on how exception handling
should be incorporated into programming languages.

GOO80   Goodenough, J. et al. Ada Compiler Validation
           Implementors' Guide. Softech, 460 Totten Pond Road,
           Waltham, MA 02154. Attempts to find all the holes, even the
           minute ones, in Ada. This guide is especially important for the
           implementor. Testing suggestions for the implementor are also
           provided.

GRI71   Gries, D. *Compiler Construction for Digital Computers.*
           Wiley, New York, 1971. Classic book, slightly outdated but
           still worth reading, on the practical aspects of compiler
           construction.

GRI75   Gries, D. Recursion as a Programming Tool. Technical
           Report TR75-234, Department of Computer Science,
           Cornell University, Ithaca, N. Y. 14853, April 1975.

GRI76   Gries, D. An Illustration of Current Ideas on the
           Derivation of Correctness Proofs and Correct Programs.
           IEEE Transactions on Software Engineering v2, no. 4, pp.
           238-243, 1976. Explains how to develop correct programs. A
           non-trivial example (a line justifier) is developed hand in hand
           with its correctness proof.

GRI77   Gries, D. and N. Gehani. Some Ideas on Data Types in
           High Level Languages. *CACM* v20, no. 6, June 1977.
           Also presented at the *ACM Conference on Data* in Salt
           Lake City, Utah, March 1976.

GRI79   Gries, D. **cand** and **cor** before **and then or else** in Ada.
           Technical Report TR79-402, Department of Computer
           Science, Cornell University, Ithaca, N. Y. 14853, 1979.
           Criticizes the semantics of the **and then** and **or else** operators in
           the preliminary version of Ada. The semantics have since been
           corrected.

GRI81   Gries, D. *The Science of Programming.* Springer-Verlag,
           1981. Teaches the development of correct programs in
           conjunction with their correctness proofs. The program
           development approach used is based on Dijkstra's predicate
           transformers [DIJ76].

HAL80   Halloran, R. Pentagon Pins its Hopes on Ada; Just ask
           any Computer. *The New York Times*, p18E, November
           30, 1980.

HAM82   Hammarling, S. J. and B. A. Wichmann. Numerical
           Packages in Ada. In *The Relationship between Numerical
           Computation and Programming Languages* edited by J. K.

Reid, pp. 225-344, North-Holland Publishing Company, 1982. Although Ada was not designed for numerical computation, it meets most of the needs of numerical computation. This paper discusses the suitability of Ada in implementing numerical packages and libraries.

HIB81   Hibbard, P., A. Higen, J. Rosenberg, M. Shaw and M. Sherman. *Studies in Ada Style.* Springer-Verlag, 1981. Contains a reprint of an article by M. Shaw on the impact of ideas on abstraction in modern programming languages. This article is followed by a set of five Ada program written by the other four authors. The style of the solutions, represented by the Ada programs, is said to be influenced by the facilities in Ada.

HOA62   Hoare, C. A. R. Quicksort. *Computer Journal*, v5, no. 1, 1962.

HOA74   Hoare, C. A. R. Monitors: An Operating System Concept. *CACM*, v17, no. 10, October 1974. The monitor is proposed as a method of structuring an operating system. Contains several excellent illustrative examples.

HOA78   Hoare, C. A. R. Communicating Sequential Processes. *CACM*, v21, no. 8, pp. 666-677, August 1978. Ada's tasks are based on Hoare's proposal that parallel processes should communicate using input and output commands. Combined with Dijkstra's guarded commands, this idea becomes very powerful and versatile. Structuring programs as a composition of communicating sequential processes is advocated by Hoare as fundamental. Contains many excellent examples.

HOA81   Hoare, C. A. R. The Emperor's Old Clothes. *The 1980 ACM Turing Award Lecture, CACM* v24, no. 2, pp. 75-83, February 1981. The author recounts his experiences in the design, implementation and standardization of programming languages and issues a warning for the future. He urges that Ada, which is a large and complex language containing unnecessary and dangerous features (e.g., exception handling), not be used for applications where reliability is critical, e.g., nuclear reactors and cruise missiles. Hoare takes this view, because he believes that it will be hard to implement a reliable compiler for Ada and write reliable programs in Ada.

HON79   Set of Sample Problems for the DoD High Order Language Program. Honeywell, Inc., Systems and Research Center, 2600 Ridgway Parkway, Minneapolis, MN 55412. Solutions to some programming problems in the language GREEN (the name initially given to the preliminary version of Ada).

HOR79   Horning, J. J. Effects of Programming Languages on Reliability. In *Computing Systems Reliability* edited by T. Anderson and B. Randell, Cambridge University Press, 1979. The first part of the paper is a comprehensive survey of programming language features (e.g., types and the treatment of types) that aid in the development of correct programs. Acknowledging the fact that faults and exceptional situations are inevitable in real programs, the author discusses language features (e.g., exception handling) for writing fault tolerant programs in the second part. The final part of the paper is a discussion of language features that encourage program correctness proofs.

HUS80   Huskey, V. R. and H. D. Huskey. Lady Lovelace and Charles Babbage. *Annals of the History of Computing*, v2, no. 4, pp. 299-329. This paper reports the correspondence between them.

IBM70   PL/I (F) Language Reference Manual, Form GC28-8201, IBM Corporation, 1970.

ICH80   Ichbiah, J. View-graphs for Jean Ichbiah's Presentation. In *Proceedings of the Ada Debut*, Defense Advanced Research Projects Agency, Arlington, VA 22209, September 1980. Contains a set of view-graphs that give an overview of Ada.

ISO81   Second Draft Proposal of the ISO Pascal Standard (January 1981). *Pascal News*, no.20.

JEN74   Jensen, K. and N. Wirth. *The Pascal User Manual and Report*. Springer Verlag, 1974. The user manual includes details of the implementation of Pascal on the CDC 6000 by Wirth. The report contains the definition of Pascal and is considered to be the de facto Pascal standard. It is small (about 75 pages) and, perhaps, because of this smallness there are some ambiguities and several details missing.

KER76   Kernighan, B. W. and P. J. Plauger. *Software Tools*. Addison-Wesley Publishing Co., 1976. The book explains how to write good programs that make good tools. These tools are intended for use in the construction of other programs. Real nontrivial examples are given.

KER81   Kernighan, B. W. and P. J. Plauger. *Software Tools in Pascal*. Addison-Wesley Publishing Co., 1981. See KER76.

KID81   Kidman, B. P. The Type Concept in Ada. *Australian Computer Science Communication*, v3, no. 1a, pp. . 74-84, May 1981. Examination of the treatment of types in Ada. The author considers this part of the design of Ada as being successful.

KNU73   Knuth, D. E. *Sorting and Searching*. Addison-Wesley, Publishing Co., 1973.

KNU74   Knuth, D. E. Structured Programming with **goto** Statements. *Computing Surveys*, v6, no. 4, pp. 261-301, December 1974.

LAM83   Lamb, D. A. and P. N. Hilfinger. Simulation of Procedure Variables Using Ada Tasks. *IEEE Transactions on Software Engineering*, vSE-9, no. 1, pp. 13-15, January 1983. Ada does not allow the declaration of objects of type procedure (similar to the declaration of objects of types integer, real, array, task and so on). Tasks, which are similar to procedures, syntactically more than semantically, are used to simulate procedure variables.

LEB82   LeBlanc, R. J. and J. J. Goda. Ada and Software Development Support: A New Concept in Language Design. *Computer*, pp. 75-81, May 1982. Ada has excellent facilities for the development of large scale software. Much of Ada's complexity is due to these features. Ada is unfairly criticized as being complex in comparison with languages, such as Pascal, which have no facilities for large scale software development.

LED81   Ledgard, H. *ADA: An Introduction*. Springer-Verlag, 1981. A brief introduction to a subset of pre-ANSI Ada. Also contains the full pre-ANSI Ada Reference Manual [DOD80b].

LED82   Ledgard, H. and A. Singer. Scaling Down Ada (or Towards a Standard Ada Subset). *CACM*, v25, no. 2, pp. 121-125, February 1982. Authors make suggestions for trimming and streamlining Ada with the intention of reducing its size and complexity which, they claim, is the most significant technical obstacle to its success.

LEV77   Levin, R. Programming Structures for Exception Condition Handling. Ph. D. Thesis, Computer Science Department, Carnegie Mellon University, 1977.

Programming methodologies have failed to address a crucial aspect of program construction—exceptions. Surveys exception handling facilities in languages that preceded Ada, e.g., PL/I and Bliss. Proposes an exception handling mechanism for programming languages that has been designed taking into account issues of verifiability, uniformity, adequacy and practicality.

LIS74   Liskov, B. H. and S. N. Zilles. Programming with Abstract Data Types. *Sigplan Notices*, v9, no. 4, April 1974.

LIS76   Liskov, B. H. Discussion in the *Design and Implementation of Programming Languages* edited by J. H. Williams and D. A. Fisher, p25, Springer-Verlag, 1976.

LIS77   Liskov, B. H. et al. Abstraction Mechanisms in CLU. *CACM*, v20, pp. 564-576, August 1977.

LUC80   Luckham, D. C. and W. Polak. Ada Exception Handling: An Axiomatic Approach. *ACM Transactions on Programming Languages and Systems*, v2, no. 2, April 1980. The exception handling of preliminary Ada is considered.

MCC79   McCorduck, P. *Machines Who Think*. W. H. Freeman and Company, 1979. A personal inquiry into the history and prospects of artificial intelligence.

MCG82   McGettrick, A. D. *Program Verification Using Ada*. Cambridge University Press, 1982.

MOO77   Moore, L. D. *Ada: Countess of Lovelace—Byron's Legitimate Daughter*. John Murray, 1977. The first full biography of Ada. I found it somewhat boring. The article titled *Lady Lovelace and Charles Babbage* [HUS80] is much shorter and more interesting.

MOR73   Morris, J. H., Jr. Types are not Sets. *ACM Symposium on Principles of Programming Languages*. Boston, MA, 1973. Introduces the notion that types are sets of values plus a set of operations.

MOR81   Morris, A. H., Jr. Can Ada Replace FORTRAN for Numerical Computation? *Sigplan Notices*, v16, no. 12, pp. 10-13, December 1981. Unconvincing arguments for concluding that Ada is not suitable as a replacement for FORTRAN.

NIS81   Nissen, J. C. D., P. Wallis, B. A. Wichmann and others.
         Ada Europe Guidelines for the Portability of Ada
         Programs. Technical Report, National Physical
         Laboratory, Teddington, Middlesex, TW11 0LW, UK.
         Guide to aid programmers in designing and coding portable
         programs.

PAR72   Parnas, D. On the Criteria to be used in Decomposing
         Systems into Modules. *CACM*, v15, pp. 1053-1058,
         December 1972. The advantages of composing a system from
         modules are widely recognized. Suggests rules for decomposing a
         system into modules by comparing two decompositions of a
         software system—one composed of modules representing
         execution steps and the other representing logical functions. The
         second formulation uses the *principle of information hiding*, i.e.,
         only information relevant to the user of the module should be
         available to the user and all other information should be hidden.
         The second formulation is easier to modify and understand than
         the first one.

PRA75   Pratt, T. W. *Programming Languages: Design and
         Implementation.* Prentice-Hall, 1975.

PYL81   Pyle, I. C. *The Ada Programming Language.* Prentice-
         Hall International, 1981. This book is a fairly comprehensive
         introduction to Ada. It contains brief, but not exhaustive, notes
         for FORTRAN and Pascal programmers interested in Ada.

ROB81   Roberts, E. S., E. M. Clarke, A. Evans, Jr. and C. R.
         Morgan. Task Mangement in Ada: A Critical Evaluation
         for Real-Time Multiprocessors. *Software—Practice &
         Experience*, v11, no. 10, October 1981. Preliminary Ada is
         used in the discussion.

SCH80   Schwartz, R. L. and P. M. Melliar-Smith. On the
         Suitability of Ada for Artificial Intelligence Applications.
         SRI International, 333 Ravenswood Avenue, Menlo Park,
         California 94205, July 1980. The preliminary version of Ada
         is considered to analyze its suitability for programming artificial
         intelligence (AI) applications. Although a useful proportion of
         AI programs can be written in Ada, the authors do not feel that
         preliminary Ada is suitable as a general research programming
         language for AI.

SKE82   Skelly, P. G. The ACM Position on the Standardization of
         the Ada Language. *CACM*, v25, no. 2, pp. 118-120,
         February 1982. Adoption of Ada as an ANSI standard involves

a *canvass process*. 96 organizations responded to the canvass, out of which 66 favored the adoption of Ada as an ANSI standard, 23 objected and 7 abstained. ACM objected to the standardization of Ada based on its present specification [DOD80b]. This report contains the reasons for the objection and the DoD's response. The ACM objection was based on a membership response—72 no votes, 39 yes votes and 4 abstentions.

SYM80   *Proceedings of the ACM-SIGPLAN Symposium on the Ada Programming Language*, Boston, Massachusetts, December 1980. Contains technical papers discussing experiences in using Ada, writing Ada compilers, issues in implementing different aspects of Ada and so on.

THO78   Thompson, K. UNIX Implementation. *BSTJ*, v57, no. 6, part 2, pp. 1931-1946, July-August 1978.

WAS80   Wasserman, A. I. *Tutorial: Programming Language Design*. IEEE Computer Society, 1980 Contains reprints of articles on various aspects of programming language design— design philosophy, control structures, data types, the designs of Pascal and Ada, exception handling and programming language design experience. In particular, it contains the document describing the final requirements (called *Steelman*) which formed the basis for the design of Ada.

WEG80   Wegner, P. *Programming with Ada: An Introduction by Means of Graduated Examples*. Prentice-Hall, 1980. Introduction to the preliminary version of Ada.

WEG81   Wegner, P. A Self-Assessment Procedure Dealing with the Programming Language Ada. *CACM*, v24, no. 10, pp. 647-677, October 1981. A set of short mechanisms to help readers assess and develop their knowledge of Ada.

WEG83   Wegner, P. On the Unification of Data and Program Abstraction in Ada. Conference Record of the *Tenth Annual ACM Symposium on Principles of Programming Languages*, pp. 256-264, Austin, Texas, January 1983. Ada provides two equivalent mechanisms for hiding data representations called *data abstraction* and *program abstraction* and related to the type and generic mechanisms, respectively. Data abstraction is used to provide the user with a private type and operations on objects of this type. Program abstraction (instantiation of a generic package) provides a user with operations on an object hidden from the user. Providing two different abstraction mechanisms increases Ada's complexity. Unification of these two abstraction mechanisms is proposed. Author claims that it is not too early to start thinking of redesigning Ada with the view of producing a successor to Ada.

WEL77   Welsh, J., M. J. Sneeringer and C. A. R. Hoare. Ambiguities and Insecurities in Pascal. *Software — Practice and Experience*, v7, no. 6, pp. 685-696, November 1977. Contains a discussion of the issue of type equivalence. Type equivalence is classified into two categories—name and structural.

WEL81   Welsh, J. and A. Lister. A Comparative Study of Task Communication in Ada. *Software—Practice and Experience*, v11, pp. 257-290, 1981. Compares the mechanism for process communication in Ada with those in Hoare's communicating sequential processes and Brinch Hansen's distributed processes.

WET81   Wetherell, C. S. Problems with the Ada Reference Grammar. *Sigplan Notices*, v16, no. 9, pp. 90-104, September 1981. The Ada Grammar in the Ada Reference Manual is not quite complete and is not suitable for use in the automatic generation of parsers. A revised grammar is presented.

WET83   Wetherell, C. S. Private Communication. February 28 and March 18, 1983.

WIC81   Wichmann, B. A. Tutorial Material on the Real Data-Types in Ada. Technical Report, National Physical Laboratory, Teddington, Middlesex, TW11 0LW, UK. Introduces the novel features of Ada in the area of numerics to programmers familiar with numeric computations but not with Ada.

WIN81   Winkler, J. F. H. Differences between Preliminary Ada and Final Ada. *Sigplan Notices*, v16, no. 8, pp. 69-81, August 1981. Listing of the main differences between the preliminary version of Ada [DOD79a] and the pre-ANSI version of Ada [DOD80b].

WIR71   Wirth, N. Program Development by Stepwise Refinement. *CACM*, v14, no. 4, 1971. Classic paper on stepwise refinement. F. P. Brooks in his book *The Mythical Man—Month* calls stepwise refinement the most important programming formalization of the 1970s.

WIR73   Wirth, N. *Systematic Programming: An Introduction.* Prentice-Hall, 1973.

WIR76   Wirth, N. *Algorithms + Data Structures = Programs.* Prentice-Hall, 1976.

WIR77a   Wirth, N. Modula: A Language for Modular Multiprogramming. *Software—Practice and Experience*, v7, 1977 The high level language Modula is an attempt to break one of the last holds of assembly language programming, viz., machine dependent system programming such as device drivers. Modula is a Pascal descendant. It has facilities for multiprogramming and has been designed specifically for the PDP-11 computers. It introduces the concept of the module (similar to the Ada package) and has the concepts of processes, interface modules and signals.

WIR77b   Wirth, N. The Use of Modula. *Software—Practice and Experience*, v7, 1977.

WIR77c   Wirth, N. Design and Implementation of Modula. *Software—Practice and Experience*, v7, 1977.

WIR80   Wirth, N. Modula-2. Technical Report #36, Institut fur Informatik, ETH, CH-8092 Zurich. Modula-2 is the result of experience gained by Wirth from designing, implementing and using Modula. The concept of processes has been replaced by the lower level notion of coroutines. The advantage of this is that now the programmer can write any desired scheduling algorithm and not be forced to use the one built into the language for the scheduling of processes as in Modula. Modula-2 also supports the notion of programming in the large by providing separate definition and implementation modules. The language is tailored to the PDP-11 series of computers (as was Modula).

WIR82   Wirth, N. *Programming in Modula-2*. Springer-Verlag, 1982.

ZUC81   Zuckerman, S. L. Problems with the Multitasking Facilities in the Ada Programming Language. Technical Note, Defense Communications Engineering Center, Reston, Virginia. Author claims that Ada's unconventional multitasking facilities do not provide capabilities equivalent to multitasking facilities in existing languages.

Index

& operator   26, 4
* operator   27, 28
+ operator   26, 27
− operator   26, 27
/ operator   27
/= operator   26
< operator   26
<= operator   26
<> (box)   14
= operator   26
> operator   26
>= operator   26

A

abnormal task   152
abort statement   152
abs operator   27, 28
abstract data type representations, advantages of hiding   108
abstract data types and packages   108
accept statement   133, 143
access rights of a file   45
access type   21
access, direct and sequential file   45
actual parameter   40
actual parameter, default initial value for an   40
adding operators   26
address clause   276
ADDRESS attribute   279
aggregate, array   16
      completeness of an   16
      qualification by type name of an   17
      record   20
allocator, object   21, 22
      storage   21, 22

and operator   24
and then operator   24
anonymous type   79
array   13
array aggregate   16
array aggregate, N-dimensional   18
array attributes   18
array element   16
array slice   16
array type   13
array type, constrained   13
        unconstrained   13, 14, 15
array, null   14
arrays example, *general operations on*   246
ASCII package   4
assignment statement   28
attribute, ADDRESS   279
        CALLABLE   144
        COUNT   143
        collection size   273
        size   273
        small   274
        task storage   273
attributes   77
attributes of discrete types   10
attributes, array   18
        fixed point   12
        floating point   12
        scalar type   9
        task   153

B

base type   77
basic declaration   98
basic declarative item   98
binary tree, ordered   94
binary tree search example   94
block, localizing an exception using a   51
block statement   32
blocks and scope of declarations   32
BNF notation   5

body stub   257, 258
body, package   100
        task   136, 137
boolean type   10, 24, 82
bottom up program development example   259
box   14
buffered communication between tasks example   158

C

calculator example   1
CALENDAR package   175
call, entry   133
CALLABLE attribute   144
carriage return character   4
case statement   29
catenation   4
character set, basic   3
        expanded   3
        transliteration to the basic   4
character type   10
characters, control   4
        replacements for unavailable   5
        special   3
clause, address   276
        enumeration representation   274
        length   273
        record representation   275
        representation   272
        type representation   272
CLOCK function   175
collection size attribute   273
comments   4
communicating sequential processes   133
communication, task   133
compilation unit   52, 256
compilation unit, context of   257
        parent   258
        independent   255
        order of   257
        separate   255
completion of a task, block, or subprogram   145

concurrency   133
concurrency, desirability of   133
conditional entry call   148
constant   5
constant declarations, examples of   6
constant, number   7
    private type   104
constrained array type   13
constraint compatibility, range   82
constraint, accuracy   11
    fixed point   12
    floating point   83
    index   13
    range   82
CONSTRAINT_ERROR, predefined exception   203
constraints on types   77
context of compilation unit   257
contextual information   2
controls character   4
conversion, implicit   80
    type   78, 80
convert to upper case via tasks example   139
COUNT attribute   143

D

data abstraction   108
data encapsulation and packages   97
deadlock   143
deallocation, object   23
declaration   5, 41
declaration, derived type   78
    entry   143
    exception   203
    multiple object   79
    object   5
    private type   103
    single object   79
    subtype   77
    type   8
declarations, blocks and scope of   32
    examples of constant   6

            examples of variable   7
            order in   35
definition, type   8
delay statement   145
delta of a fixed point real   11
delta   12
dependence on a master, task   145
derived type   78
derived type, declaration   78
derived types, use of   78
digits   83
direct file   45
direct file operations   47
DIRECT_IO, predefined generic package   44
discrete type   9
discrete types, attributes of   10
discriminant, initial value for a   86
discriminants and other record components   87
discriminants, assigning a value to a   87
            record type with   85
disk scheduling example   200
dynamic object   21
dynamic object, creating an unconstrained type   22
            lifetime of a   23
            reference to a   22

E

eight queens example   125
elevator example   182
END_OF_FILE function   47, 48
entity   5
entry   133
entry call   133
entry call, conditional   148
            timed   148
entry calls, queuing   141
entry declaration   143
entry family   144
entry of a terminated task, calling an   143
enumeration literals as parameterless functions   43
enumeration representation clause   274

enumeration type   9
ENUMERATION_IO, generic package   48
errors in representing reals   11
example, *binary tree search*   94
        bottom up program development   259
        buffered communication between tasks   158
        calculator   1
        convert to upper case via tasks   139
        disk scheduling   200
        eight queens   125
        elevator   182
        factorial   213
        FIFO package   116, 212
        general operations on arrays   246
        generic insertion sort   235
        generic set implementation   244
        home fire/energy/security monitoring   217
        Horner's rule   73
        implementation of semaphores in Ada   157
        implementing Modula's ranked signals   166
        implementing signals via Ada tasks   154
        insertion sort   63
        integration via the trapezoidal rule   239
        key manager   107
        last wishes of a subprogram   224
        Lisp function MAPLIST   251
        matrix addition   38
        matrix multiplication   72
        merging sorted files   219
        mode of a sorted array   60
        mortal dining philosophers   177
        no equal subsequence   120
        nuclear reactor   214
        ordered set   99, 100, 104
        parsing   225
        printing a tree   92
        producer and consumer tasks   137
        quicksort   66
        reversing a string   15
        roots of a quadratic equation   207
        set of priority queues   116
        shortest job next scheduler   170
        square root   37
        steady state temperature distribution   53

       storage allocator   286
       swap   37
       symbol table manager   110
       task scheduling   161
       top down program development   261
       Towers of Hanoi   61
       traffic light   171
       typewriter input and output   282
       using variant records   91
exception   201
exception PROGRAM_ERROR, predefined   147
exception declaration   203
exception handler, activation of an   206
       specification of an   204
exception handlers, blocks and scope of   32
exception handling facility, advantages of having an   202
exception propagation   202
exception using a block, localizing an   51
exception, cleaning up after an   219
       handling an   202
       identity of an   203
       raising an   202, 204
       reraising an   205
       retrying an operation raising an   209
       suppressing an   210
exceptions and last wishes of a subprogram   224
exceptions and recursion   213
exceptions and tasks   209
exceptions raised during declaration processing   208
exceptions raised during statement execution   206
exceptions, predefined   203
exit statement   33
exponentiation operator   28
expression   23
expression, qualified   81
       static   23
external file   45

F

factorial example   213
FIFO package example   116, 212

file access rights   45
file management operations   47
file operations, direct   47
    sequential   47
    text   47
file terminator, end of file   48
file type   44
file, direct   45
    external   45
    internal   45
    sequential   45
    standard input   48
    standard output   48
files, using   45
    using text   49
fixed point attributes   12
fixed point constraint, satisfaction of a   12
fixed point real   11
fixed point type   12, 85
FIXED_IO, generic package   48
FLOAT_IO, generic package   48
floating point attributes   12
floating point constraint, satisfaction of a   83
floating point objects, portability of program with   84
floating point real   11
floating point type   12, 83
for loop execution and a null range   31
for loop   30
formal parameter   36
formal parameter, generic   228, 230
formal parameters, matching rules for generic   233
function call   40
function subprogram   34
function subprogram, termination of   34
functions, enumeration literals as parameterless   43

G

garbage collector   23, 115
Gauss-Seidel method   59
general operations on arrays example   246
generic facilities   227

generic facilities, advantages of   227
generic formal parameter   228, 230
generic formal parameters, matching rules for   233
generic insertion sort example   235
generic package   227
generic package or subprogram body   230
generic package or subprogram specification   228
generic package or subprogram, instantiation of   227, 231
generic packages without parameters   232
generic set implementation example   244
generic subprogram   227
generic subprogram name   230
GET, text input procedure   48
goto statement   33
goto statement, unrestricted use of   33

H

home fire/energy/security monitoring example   217
Horner's rule example   73

I

identifiers   3
if statement   29
implementation dependent features   279
implementing signals via Ada tasks example   154
in mode   36
in out mode   36
in parameter   36
in out parameter   36
independent compilation   255
index constraint   13
induction, principle of   62
infinite loop   31
information hiding and packages   97
initial value for an actual parameter, default   40
input   44
input, interactive   50
input, standard   48

insertion sort example   63
instantiation of a generic subprogram or package   227
integer type   10, 82
INTEGER_IO, generic package   48
integers, smallest and largest   10
integration via the trapezoidal rule example   239
interactive input   50
interface to other languages   280
internal file   45
interrupt, hardware   152

J

Jacobi method   54, 59

K

key manager example   107

L

label   33
languages, interface to other   280
last wishes of a subprogram example   224
layout control operations   48
length clause   273
letters, lower case   3
            upper case   3
limited private type   103
limited type   103
limited private attribute   103
line feed character   4
line terminator, end of line   48
Lisp function MAPLIST example   251
literal, character   4
            numeric   3
literals, base of   3
logical operators   24, 26

loop invariant   65
loop name   32
loop parameter, implicit declaration of   31
loop statement   30
loop, *for*   30
        infinite   31
        while   30
loops and the *exit* statement   33
LOW_LEVEL_IO, package   45

M

machine code insertion   280
main program   2, 51, 56, 63, 139
master, task dependence on a   145
matrix multiplication example   72
matrix addition example   38
membership operators   26
merging sorted files example   219
mod operator   27
mode of a sorted array example   60
model numbers   11
Modula's ranked signals implementation example   166
mortal dining philosopher example   177
multiplying operators   27
mutual exclusion   149

N

NATURAL, predefined INTEGER subtype   10, 82
nesting   42
no equal subsequence example   120
not operator   27, 28
nuclear reactor example   214
null array   14
null range   14
null record   19
null statement usage, example of   51
null statement   28
null, access value   21

number constant   7
NUMERIC_ERROR, predefined exception   204

O

object allocation   21
object allocator   22
object creation   5
object creation, dynamic   21
object deallocation   23
object declarations, type definitions in   7
object, definition of an   5
    dynamic   21
    initial value of an   5
    lifetime of a dynamic   23
    reference to a dynamic   22
    static   21
operator overloading   38
operator overloading example   73
operator precedence   24
operator, exponentiation   28
    adding   26
    logical   24, 26
    membership   26
    multiplying   27
    relational   26
    short circuit   24
    unary   27
or else operator   24
or operator   24
ordered set example   99, 100, 104
others   18, 29, 88, 205
out mode   36
out parameter   36
output   44
output, standard   48
overloaded subprograms, ambiguity in calls to   41
overloading example, operator   73
overloading on other subprograms, effect of   41
overloading, convenience of   41
    illustration of visibility rules and   43
    operator   38

subprogram   41

P

package body   100
package specification   97
package with no body, example of   98
package, body of generic   230
        generic   227
        specification of a generic   228
        visible part of   98
packages   97
packages and abstract data types   108
packages and information hiding   97
page terminator, end of page   48
parameter modes   36
parameter, actual   40
        formal   36
        private type   103
parameters, matching of   40
parent type   78
parentheses, use of   23
parsing example   225
POSITIVE, predefined INTEGER subtype   10, 82
pragma   52
precedence, operator   24
printing a tree example   92
priority of a task   153
priority on a rendezvous, influence of   153
priority, order of scheduling tasks with equal   153
private type   98, 103
private type declaration   103
private type objects   103
private type objects, limited   103
private type parameter   103
private attribute   103, 98
procedure call   40
procedure subprogram   34
producer and consumer tasks example   137
program development   258
program development example, bottom up   259
program development example, top down   261

program development, bottom up   258
      top down   258
program, main   2, 51, 56, 63, 139
PROGRAM_ERROR, predefined exception   147, 204
programming-in-the-large   255
programming-in-the-small   255
programs, development of large   259
PUT, text output procedure   48

Q

queues, example of *priority*   116
quicksort example   66

R

raise statement without an exception name   204
raise statement   204
raising an exception   204
range constraint, satisfaction of a   82
range, null   14
real type   9, 11
recompilation   257
record aggregate   20
record component   19
record definition, general form of   88
record discriminant and other record components   90
record representation clause   275
record type   18
record type with discriminants   85
record type, recursion in a   90
record, null   19
      variant   88
records with discriminants, examples of   87
records, use of variant   88, 89
recursion   95
recursion and exceptions   213
recursion in subprograms   34
recursive type definition, example of a   92
refinement, stepwise   53

relational operators   26
rem operator   27
renaming   44
rendezvous   133, 134
rendezvous mechanism and mutual exclusion   149
rendezvous, influence of priority on a   153
representation clause   272
representation viewing   76
representation, change of   277
reserved words   4
return statement   33
roots of a quadratic equation example   207

S

scalar type   9, 82
scheduling of tasks, controlling the   161
scheduling strategy, implementing a general task   163
scheduling shortest job next example   170
scope of entities   42
select statement alternative   146
select statement, open alternative of a   146
        terminate alternative in a   146
select statement   145
selected component notation   19
selective wait   146
semaphore implementation example   157
separate compilation   255
sequential file   45
sequential file operations   47
SEQUENTIAL_IO, predefined generic package   44
set implementation example, *generic*   244
set of priority queues example   116
signals, implemented by Ada tasks   154
size attribute   273
slice, array   16
small attribute   274
sort, example of *generic insertion*   235
sort, insertion   63
sort, quick-   66
special characters   3
specification, package   97

　　　task　　　136
square root example　　　37
statement *block*　　　32
　　　abort　　　152
　　　accept　　　133, 143
　　　assignment　　　28
　　　case　　　29
　　　delay　　　145
　　　exit　　　33
　　　goto　　　33
　　　if　　　29
　　　loop　　　30
　　　null　　　28
　　　raise　　　204
　　　return　　　33
　　　select　　　145
static expression　　　23
static object　　　21
steady state temperature distribution example　　　53
stepwise refinement　　　53, 289
storage allocator example　　　286
storage deallocation, unchecked　　　281
STORAGE_ERROR, predefined exception　　　204
string　　　4
string example, reversing a　　　15
string operators　　　15
string type　　　15
strong typing　　　75
strong typing, bypassing　　　76
　　　definition of　　　75
stub, body　　　257, 258
subprogram　　　34
subprogram body　　　34
subprogram call　　　40
subprogram overloading　　　41
subprogram specification　　　34
subprogram specification, omission of　　　35
subprogram, body of generic　　　230
　　　generic　　　227
　　　specification of a generic　　　228
subprograms as parameters by using generic facilities　　　234
subtype　　　6, 76
subtype declaration　　　77
subtypes, use of　　　76

subunit   257
swap example   37
symbol table manager example   110
systems programming language, desirable facilities for a   271

T

task   133
task activation   145
task attributes   153
task body   136, 137
task communication, example of buffered   158
task completion   145
task dependence on a master   145
task scheduling example   161
task scheduling strategy, implementing a general   163
task specification   136
task storage attribute   273
task termination   145
task type   151
task, abnormal   152
    activation of a task   151
    activation of an allocated task   151
    blocking of calling   144
    explicit termination of a   152
    priority of a   153
    suspension of calling   143
tasking mechanism, asymmetry in   135, 143
TASKING_ERROR, predefined exception   204
tasks and exceptions   209
tasks, array of   151
    communication between   143
    dynamic creation of   151
terminate alternative   146, 147
termination of a task   145
terminator, end of file   48
    end of line   48
    end of page   48
text file operations   47
text files, using   49
TEXT_IO, facilities provided in   48
    predefined generic package   44

timed entry call   148
top down program development example   261
Towers of Hanoi example   61
traffic light example   171
transliteration into the basic character set   4
tree, binary   94
        ordered binary   94
type conversion   78, 80
type conversion, unchecked   281
type declaration   8
type definition   8
type definitions in object declarations   7
type equivalence   79
type name   8
type representation clause   272
type, access   21
        array   13
        base   76, 77
        boolean   10, 24
        boolean   82
        character   10
        definition of a   5
        derived   78
        discrete   9
        enumeration   9
        file   44
        fixed point   12, 85
        floating point   12, 83
        incomplete   90
        initial value for a   19
        integer   10, 82
        parent   78
        private   98, 103
        real   9, 11
        record   18
        recursive access   90
        scalar   9, 82
        string   15
        sub-   76
        task   151
types that can be defined   8
types, mutually dependent   90
typewriter input and output example   282

U

unary operators   27
unchecked storage deallocation   281
unchecked type conversion   281
unconstrained array type   13, 14, 15
unconstrained array type formal parameter example   38
underscore character   3
unit, compilation   34, 256
       program   34
use clause   44, 98

V

variable   5
variable declarations, examples of   7
variant record   88
variant record, null component list in a   88
variant records, use of   88, 89
variant records example, *using*   91
visibility of declarations in a package   99
visibility rules   41, 42
visibility rules and overloading, illustration of   43
visibility, direct   43, 44

W

wait, selective   146
when clause   146
while loop   30
with clause   257

X

xor operator   24